THE UNITED STATES AND CHINA
1906—1913

The United States and China

1906-1913

A Study of Finance and Diplomacy

CHARLES VEVIER

RUTGERS UNIVERSITY PRESS

NEW BRUNSWICK, NEW JERSEY

1955

For My Mother and Father

PREFACE

Edward H. Harriman, Jacob Schiff, William Howard Taft, Philander C. Knox, Francis Huntington Wilson, Willard Straight—the great and the near great—all worked to extend American influence in China in the years 1906 to 1913.

They organized in New York and Washington. They planned in China's frontier outpost in Mukden, Manchuria, and at Bad Gastein, an Austrian spa. Their messages traveled to London, Paris, Berlin, St. Petersburg, Tokyo, and Peking.

From this welter of activity there emerged a series of ambitious projects: the purchase of the Chinese Eastern Railway and the South Manchurian Railroad, the construction of the Chinchow-Aigun Railroad, the creation of the Manchurian Bank, the construction of the Hukuang Railroad, participation in large loans for China. These enterprises were the substance of American policy in China in this period.

This book is a critical account of that policy. It is an attempt to examine a diplomatic formula in action and the difficulties that beset it in execution. This study is based on a re-evaluation of the Straight Papers and the records of the State Department, but it is not a biography of Willard Straight or a diatribe against investment bankers. The approach emphasizes American relations with China as they were affected by the techniques of cooperation between Washington and Wall Street. Insofar as foreign policy is not an abstract entity, an understanding of it requires an exposition of the relationship of individuals, interests, and governments to it. This is best done, not by conveniently freezing the movement of history, but by attempting to maintain pace with it, keeping influential factors in full view. Historical narrative has been employed, therefore, to give this sense of motion to activities carried on in the United States, Europe, and Asia.

Obviously, there are differing means of examining the question, and those who have critically read this manuscript should not be held responsible for its approach, interpretation, or errors. They are guilty only of friendship and interest in the subject. My appreciation is extended to Fred Harvey Harrington of the University of Wisconsin for his encouragement and perceptive direction of this study in another and earlier form. William Appleman Williams of the University of Oregon shared his knowledge of Russian-American relations in the Far East with me and helped clarify points of view. L. Ethan Ellis of Rutgers University read the manuscript and raised valuable questions regarding its organization. George Marvin of Washington, D.C., was most helpful in recalling events in which he participated and the atmosphere surrounding the American drive in China.

The Research Council of Rutgers University gave financial aid for putting the manuscript in final form. Taylor Parks, Historical Officer of the Department of State, together with the staff of the General Records Division of the Department of State in the National Archives and the Manuscript Division of the Library of Congress, extended assistance in my researches. My appreciation has been expressed to those individuals who have permitted me to examine the private manuscript collections indicated in the bibliography.

My greatest debt is to my wife, Marcia Gold Vevier, who innocently fell into the pitfalls of financial diplomacy but rallied to make this book a family affair in the truest sense.

CHARLES VEVIER

Rochester, New York
November, 1954

CONTENTS

THE UNITED STATES AND CHINA
1906—1913

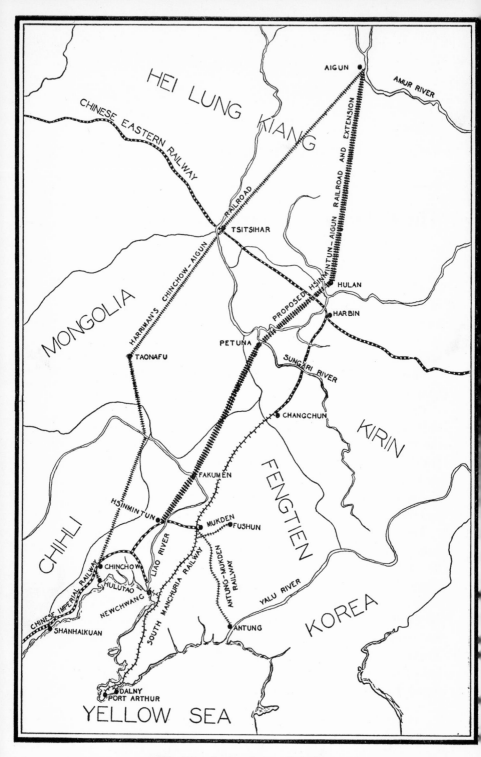

The Manchurian Scene of Action
(From a map drawn by Frederick D. Cloud, June 20, 1909)

CHAPTER ONE

The Rubicon of Imperial Responsibility

The Spanish-American War in 1898 blurred the imprint of the Civil War upon the nation's memory. Young men and new leaders, aware of the significance of history for their own time, set out to fulfill personal ambitions and to make their country a world power. The achievements of the past had been substantial; but more could be done. Or so it seemed.

Before the war with Spain broke out, a set of ideas and attitudes, reworked and reshaped to match desire, affected the thinking of an influential knot of American scholars, politicians, and military men. Some of them expressed their views in positive, optimistic terms; others were pessimistic and less certain. Most of them were American nationalists, and they were worried.

They fretted over the social upheaval that had accompanied the growth of American industrialism, and they wondered if the United States had not arrived at a dead end in history. They believed in force, Anglo-Saxonism, Social Darwinism, and the American economic system; and they were influenced by the behavior of the European powers that were engaged in imperial activity. Admiral Alfred Thayer Mahan, publicist of a modern-day mercantilism, linked sea power with the health of the political state. He urged the United States to enter the scramble for bases and

3

markets in less developed areas in order to assure itself of a position as a world power. History, Mahan asserted, demonstrated the importance of his formula. It just needed doing.

An earlier heritage of belief rooted in the researches of the German universities and associated with a contemporary Anglophilism gave credence to the doctrine of Anglo-Saxon supremacy. The white man's burden grew heavy under the responsibility of bringing his social, political, and religious ideas and institutions to the less fortunate. "We must remember that we are a Christian as well as a commercial nation," proclaimed an enthusiast. "We are a moral as well as a material force. We are a civilizing as well as an exploiting agency." [1]

As the advocates of Anglo-Saxonism prepared to radiate moral light, the Social Darwinists levied their own standards against others less combative. The idea of natural selection heightened the color of white Anglo-Saxons in their own eyes, and the dogma of the survival of the fittest rarely exposed the logical circularity of the view to these earnest believers. The struggle for existence merely pointed out what the successful survivors of the battle for life already knew— that the use of force had much to do with the achievement of victory.

Life was a grim business indeed, and it became more grim as interested parties surveyed history and examined economic statistics at the end of the century. Brooks Adams, a diligent student of history and economics, was persuaded that the United States needed foreign trade markets, while many businessmen feared the "Bogey of the Surplus." An excess of manufactured goods convinced them that the industrial system of the United States faced disaster. Although export figures climbed, they were interpreted to mean that the home market could no longer absorb the output of American factories.[2] The dreaded surplus was true of investment capital as well as manufactured goods. Europe had realized the danger of declining interest rates and turned to foreign investment, explained Charles Conant, an American economist and publicist, in 1898. Despite the fact that the United States still imported capital, interest rates on investment funds at home had been declining for the past five years. "The great civilized peoples have today at their command the means of developing the decadent nations of the world," Conant argued. The conclusion seemed clear—the United States had to extend its investment and production market to foreign areas.[3]

The Spanish-American War, a product of jingoism and deliberately whipped-up hysteria, sharpened the desire and drive for strategic overseas possessions and economic outlets. Senator Henry Cabot Lodge drew up a "large policy," while his good friend, Theodore Roosevelt, the Assistant Secretary of the Navy, made a national hero out of Admiral Dewey. Although the war was fought mainly in Cuba, significant naval action took place in the Pacific. When all was settled, the United States possessed Samoa, Guam, the Philippine Islands, and Puerto Rico. Cuba became an American protectorate. The United States had strengthened itself in the Caribbean, but with the annexation of Hawaii during the hostilities, it also assumed considerable interest in the Pacific. And it was this American thrust toward Asia that fell in with important developments in the Far East.

Late in the 1880's, Japan began a successful penetration of Korea, contesting China's claims for control. The Manchu Empire failed to maintain a hold over the Hermit Kingdom because of its own internal weakness. Corruption and factionalism at the Korean court blended well with Japan's dogged persistence in eyeing Korea for its own imperial purposes. Negotiations between Tokyo and Peking over Korea did not resolve the points of difference, and the Sino-Japanese War broke out in 1894.

Japan's successful performance surprised the world as

well as the Chinese. The Treaty of Shimoneseki, signed on April 17, 1895, forced China to recognize Korea's independence and autonomy, an acknowledgment that permitted Japan to exert primary influence in Seoul. The Chinese, in addition, promised to open a number of their ports to trade, pay an indemnity, and cede Formosa, the Pescadores, and part of Southern Manchuria lying east of the Liao River to Japan.

On the day the treaty was signed, Russia asked France, Germany, and Britain to intercede and force the return of the Liaotung area to China. The Tsar's government had good reason for its action. Led by the Finance Minister, Count Sergius Witte, the Russians planned to construct a railroad across Siberia to Vladivostok, connecting their Pacific possessions with European Russia. Japan's occupation of the Liaotung area was a distinct threat to Russia since Witte also intended to run a line across Manchuria, with a branch going south to connect with a warm water port in Manchuria or Korea. France, Russia's European ally, assented. Germany, in heavy rivalry with Great Britain, feared the creation of an Anglo-French-Russian combination in the Far East that might inspire a similar coalition in Europe, and joined the intercession. Despite Britain's abstention because of a growing pro-Japanese sentiment in London, the other three powers went ahead and forced Japan's withdrawal from the Liaotung Peninsula.

But the Manchu Empire's weakness had been exposed, and China's saviors soon became her raiders, demanding rights and concessions for themselves. In the summer of 1895, the French compelled the Chinese to grant favorable trading, mining, railroad, and boundary privileges in Southwest China. Three years later, France received a lease on the harbor of Kuangchowwan.

Still seeking a warm water port and hoping to carry through the Siberian railroad scheme, Russia exploited the fund of good will with China that it gained from leadership in the intervention against Japan. Making shrewd use of French funds that were available because of the Franco-Russian alliance, the Tsar's diplomats in July, 1895, guaranteed a loan to China for the indemnity payment to Japan. Late in the same year, St. Petersburg founded the Russo-Chinese Bank to finance railroad activity in Manchuria. Once they had established the bank, the Russians asked China for cooperation in permitting construction of the Manchurian branch of the Trans-Siberian Railroad. After considerable delay and negotiation, the two countries agreed in June, 1896, that the Russo-Chinese Bank could construct a line across Northern Manchuria. The agreement also provided for a defensive alliance against possible Japanese attack in Asiatic Russia, China, or Korea. It was Germany's turn next.

In 1897, Germany, ambitious for imperial acclaim and privilege, decided upon Kiao-chow in the Shantung Peninsula as a naval base. The Kaiser was impatient for action, and the murder of two missionaries permitted Germany to claim that it had been insulted. Troops were landed in November, 1897, and by March, 1898, Germany had a lease of Kiao-chow, together with railroad, mining, and preference rights for capital, materials, and personnel to be used by the Chinese administration in Shantung. With one bold step, Berlin had secured a sphere of influence in China.

Once again, the Russians came upon the scene. In June, 1897, China approached St. Petersburg for a loan to repay the last installment of the Japanese indemnity. Witte laid down severe terms, a reflection of the Russian ambitions for railroad and industrial supremacy in Manchuria and Mongolia. The Finance Minister's demands also revealed his desire for a port in the Liaotung area that would be connected with the Manchurian section of the Trans-Siberian Railroad. The Russians, in December, anchored several battleships off

Port Arthur, the strategic base located on the Liaotung Peninsula. By March, 1898, Russia received a lease of Port Arthur and Talienwan.

The Russian stroke stifled the possibility of British intervention which the Chinese had hoped to bring about by negotiating with Great Britain for a loan to pay Japan. Unsuccessful in an attempt to acquire trade rights at Talienwan, and failing to secure German or French support to block Russia, the British solaced themselves by taking Weihaiwei, opposite Port Arthur at the entrance to the Gulf of Pechili. The final partition of China by the powers appeared to be at hand, an eventuality that alerted the United States.

Demetrious Boulger, an ardent imperialist propagandist, touched a sensitive American nerve in 1900. Satisfied with the inevitability of China's dismemberment, he urged the United States to stake out a sphere of influence. In view of the record of the powers in China, the decrepitude of the Chinese Empire, and American possession of the Philippines, Boulger felt that it was time to inform Americans of the facts of international life. Historic American policy was a thing of the past. "A regretful glance backwards is permissible," he sympathized, "but the American people have crossed the Rubicon of imperial responsibility." [4]

The problem appeared simple to Boulger, but it presented great difficulties to John Hay, President McKinley's Secretary of State. Appointed to office in September, 1898, by a Republican administration, Hay faced the opposition of American anti-imperialists, many of whom were Democrats. At the same time, he had to respond to the demands of economic pressure groups that insisted upon a vigorous American policy in China. During his tenure as Ambassador to Great Britain, he had agreed with the necessity for stronger American action in the Far East but was away on vacation when Lord Salisbury approached the United States in March, 1898, for cooperation in maintaining the open door in China.

Occupied with the Cuban crisis, President McKinley turned London's offer aside. Hay reopened the matter with Secretary of State William Day later in June, but Washington rejected it again, and the British moved into Weihaiwei.[5]

Following the panic of 1893 in the United States, American trade with China had increased. The sale of manufactured cotton goods to North China and Manchuria was most important and by 1900 absorbed one half of American exports in this category. Thus, the Russian advance in these areas made American cotton interests apprehensive.

Less significant at the time, but fundamentally vital for the future was the search conducted by Americans for railroad concessions in China. In 1895, the American China Development Company was organized for the purpose of acquiring railway construction rights. Among the stockholders were some of the leading financial and railroad figures in the United States: James Stillman of the National City Bank; Charles Coster, railroad expert of J. P. Morgan and Company; Jacob Schiff, senior partner of Kuhn, Loeb and Company; and Edward H. Harriman, the little Napoleon of American railroad organization and operation. The company also numbered other bankers and representatives of American sugar and steel producers among its stockholders. With this imposing group of men and institutions interested in the possibility of the Chinese railways, the company's financial power far outran the one million dollars that it claimed for its capital value. The manufacturers and exporters of kerosene, flour, and iron and steel products expanded the picture of American economic interests in China. Their sales were not overly large, but they enjoyed the pleasure of expectation by looking forward to large sales in the Chinese market.

In January, 1898, representatives of these interests established the Committee on American Interests in China, later reorganized as the American Asiatic Association. Its frank purpose was to campaign for a change of government policy regarding aid to be given economic interests that sought to multiply the American stake in China. The association concentrated upon achieving freedom of trade in Chinese ports without interference from the powers claiming spheres of interest.

Arguments that stressed Darwinism, Anglo-Saxonism, and navalism created much heat out of meager kindling; but specific interests, pointing to trade figures, Chinese leaseholds, and concession agreements, fanned a greater blaze. The American role in the Philippines and China was part of a single picture. The successful imperialist argument for annexation of the Islands had shaped the thinking of the administration and public opinion. Now American responsibility in the Philippines made intervention in China necessary in order to protect interests in the Far East that were threatened by other powers.

Secretary Hay was influenced by official and unofficial advisers who advocated the preservation of Chinese territorial integrity and equal trade privileges for the powers. Lord Charles Beresford, who made his famous junket to the Far East in 1898 amid a storm of headlines, kept in close touch with Hay, warning him of the possibility of the partition of China and the danger that menaced trade in North China and Manchuria. William Woodville Rockhill, scholar and diplomat, served as Hay's adviser on Far Eastern Affairs and supported China's rights to control its own territory. The Rockhill-Hay connection was rounded out by Alfred Hippisley, an English employee of the Chinese Maritime Customs Service that administered China's treaty ports and supervised the collection of revenue. Hippisley's major allegiance was to the Customs Service, and he wanted to maintain trade in China. Great Britain's foreign policy disturbed him, for he believed that London was willing to back down on the issue of equal treatment of trade in the ports in order to gain Far Eastern allies. Hippisley and Rockhill exchanged views, and when the Englishman played on the Russian threat to American trade in North China and Manchuria, he received a favorable response.

Late in August, 1899, Rockhill sent Hay a draft of the first open door note, based largely on a memorandum submitted by Hippisley. A week later, it was sent to the powers. The contents of the note were quite frank. They recognized the existence of the spheres of influence in China and asked only for equal treatment of all trade in the spheres controlled by the foreign governments. The powers did what they could in a tight situation; they deflected Hay's request with evasive answers and insisted upon exceptions for some of their leased territories. In March, 1899, Hay announced what was obviously not true, that the nations addressed had replied favorably. American public opinion acclaimed the Secretary of State.

The applause for Hay scarcely had died down, when the Boxer Rebellion broke out in 1900. With one eye on the Democratic party's convention and another on the powers, some of which desired to use the outbreak as an excuse for the final partition of China, Hay released to the press his open door circular of July, 1900. More worldly-wise this time, the American Secretary did not request any replies from the powers. The July circular strongly emphasized the autonomy and territorial integrity of China and restated the theme of equal commercial opportunity. The powers, each uncomfortable with the others' presence in China, paid scant attention.[6]

The open door notes had two related aims. Washington strove for the continued functioning of American trade in those parts of China that were under foreign domination, and it attempted to hold China together, fearing outright ownership of the empire by the powers and a consequent restriction of American enterprise. The note of 1899 stressed trade; the circular of 1900 emphasized territorial integrity. From the American point of view, both notes were designed for economic ends and were successful, as A. Whitney Griswold states, in maintaining the expansionist, imperialist pace set by the Philippine conquest. Hay's action recognized the shape of things to come in China. The United States prepared to make fast before its interests were carried away by the tide of international political and economic aggrandizement. Four months after the release of the July circular, Hay attempted to secure a naval base and territorial concessions for the United States at Samsah Bay. It was Japan that reminded the American Secretary of State of the open door notes.

The cold reception accorded Hay in 1900 was due, in large part, to Russia's effort to control Manchuria. Late in the fall of that year, the Russians moved troops into Manchuria ostensibly to protect their Chinese Eastern Railway from the Boxers, and at the same time they opened talks with China with the obvious intention of creating a Russian monopoly in the area. St. Petersburg maintained its pressure on Peking until early in 1902, when the Anglo-Japanese alliance was signed. The United States augmented the resistance of the newly found allies by protesting against Russian schemes in the name of the open door. This combination, not sealed by any pact between the United States and the Anglo-Japanese group, pushed the Russians back and forced them to declare that they would evacuate Manchuria. By this time, Washington was resigned to the loss of China's rights in Manchuria, and Hay struggled for the protection of American interests, regardless of which power exercised political dominion.

Having overreached herself, Russia's policy became confused, as her politicians and diplomats fought for the ear of the Tsar. One group favored peaceful penetration of the Far East, while the other took a more aggressive stand toward the United States in Manchuria and Japan in Korea. The Russians attempted to block an American effort to secure open treaty ports in Manchuria in 1903, placing Hay in an uncomfortable position. Convinced that the country would not go to war to back a vigorous Manchurian policy and yet determined to secure trade rights and protect American interests, Hay needed friends who would not exact the price of a formal alliance for their aid. Happily for him, China finally signed a treaty with Washington, and the Russians went too far with Japan.[7]

Japan opened negotiations with Russia in the summer of 1903, while Hay poked very carefully in the debris of Russia's policy, hoping to get a trade treaty from China. The Korean clique at St. Petersburg that advocated an anti-Japanese course of conduct had gained complete control over Russian Far Eastern policy by this time. Tokyo and St. Petersburg exchanged demands; neither country was satisfied, but the Russians exhibited more patience than Japan. Offended by Russia's performance in Manchuria, Washington assured Tokyo if its benevolent neutrality. Upheld by the American offer of tacit support and the Anglo-Japanese alliance, Japan seized the initiative. In February, 1904, the Japanese attacked the Russian fleet off Port Arthur, and the Russo-Japanese War began. Japan fought for its own imperial scheme in Korea, but insofar as Russia was its enemy, it protected American and British trade rights in Manchuria. For the time being, Japanese force buttressed American diplomacy and received American support in return.

President Roosevelt used Japan to check Russia. The trade treaty negotiations with China in 1903 led him to condemn Russian "mendacity" which prevented the United States from pursuing its "great and growing trade" in Manchuria. In addition to the promise of benevolent neutrality, Roosevelt and Hay aided Japan by scotching a German plan for deneutralizing Manchuria during the war.[8] But the policy of balance required Roosevelt to warn the Japanese diplomats against allowing their country to get a "big head" and embarking on a career of aggression because of victories over Russia. "Such a career would undoubtedly be temporarily very unpleasant to the rest of the world," he admitted, but "it would in the end be still more unpleasant for Japan." [9]

Even before the peace negotiations were set in motion, with Roosevelt as the intermediary, the President felt that Japan ought to have a protectorate over Korea and assume Russia's rights in Port Arthur and the Liaotung leased territory. China, however, must retain complete sovereignty over Manchuria.[10] In stating these terms, Roosevelt underestimated the possible emergence of a strong Japan. By insisting upon China's retention of sovereignty over Manchuria and then countenancing Japan's dominance in the area, Roosevelt, in effect appointed China as caretaker of its own estate, hoping that only respectable poachers would be allowed in through the front gate. On other occasions, the President spoke of creating a balance in Manchuria between Russia and Japan and wanted protection for American trade in North China and Manchuria. He did not succeed for the reason that he wanted too much and gave too little.

NOTES

1. John Barrett, "America's Duty in China," *North American Review,* 171 (August, 1900):146.
2. Charles S. Campbell, Jr., *Special Business Interests and the Open Door Policy* (New Haven, 1951), 1–10.
3. Charles A. Conant, "The Economic Basis of Imperialism," *North American Review,* 167 (September, 1898):326.
4. Demetrious C. Boulger, "America's Share in the Partition of China," *North American Review,* 171 (August, 1900):173.
5. Tyler Dennett, *John Hay* (New York, 1934), 285.
6. Paul A. Varg, *Open Door Diplomat—The Life of W. W. Rockhill* (Urbana, 1952), 26–36; A. Whitney Griswold, *The Far Eastern Policy of the United States* (New York, 1938), 36–87. Both accounts based on the Rockhill Papers. Also Dennett, *Hay,* 285–293.

7. Edward H. Zabriskie, *American–Russian Rivalry in the Far East, 1895–1914* (Philadelphia, 1946), 66–88.

8. Roosevelt to Hay, May 22, and Roosevelt to Albert Shaw, June 22, 1903, in *The Letters of Theodore Roosevelt,* ed. Elting E. Morison (8 vols., Cambridge, 1951), III, 478.

9. Roosevelt to Spring Rice, June 13, 1904, in Morison, *Letters of Roosevelt,* IV, 830.

10. Roosevelt to George Von Lengerke Meyer, February 6, 1905, in Morison, *Letters of Roosevelt,* IV, 1116.

CHAPTER TWO

Harriman and Japan

In the spring of 1905, the Japanese appeared to be the victors in their war with Russia. Indirectly, through France, and later by direct representation to Washington, Tokyo indicated its willingness to discuss peace with Russia if President Roosevelt acted as mediator. An obvious advocate of Japan's cause, the President had backed Japan's demands for a protectorate over Korea even to the extent of resisting the entreaties of the American Minister to Korea, Horace N. Allen, who favored Russia rather than the Island Empire. Allen had labored long to create a strong economic position for the United States in Korea, and he was confident that Russo-American cooperation would be of greater benefit than anything offered by the Japanese. Roosevelt disagreed and replaced Allen as Minister at Seoul.[1]

Washington went further and consented to Japan's acquisition of Russia's leasehold in and around Port Arthur provided that Japan restored Manchuria to China and upheld the open door in the three Eastern Provinces. Tokyo agreed. Anxious for a peace meeting and determined to prevent Russia's complete collapse, Roosevelt acknowledged that Japan had secured control of Port Arthur and Korea and was dominant in Manchuria. That was enough, he thought, for "in China her [Japan's] policy is the policy to which we are already committed." [2] But if Roosevelt easily accepted Japan's supremacy in Manchuria, which, in form at least, guaranteed the open door for American interests, he also wanted to clarify the situation in the Philippine Islands. And he had an experienced assistant for the task.

William Howard Taft had worked hard in his three years as American Governor in the Philippines, and he returned in the summer of 1905. Taft felt a deep sense of responsibility toward the Islands and their people, but after his departure from Manila late in 1903 to replace Elihu Root as Secretary of War in Roosevelt's cabinet, the situation deteriorated. The Filipinos demanded independence, and poor handling of the question by Congress convinced the Secretary that a return trip was necessary. Aware of the need to educate influential Congressmen in Philippine affairs, he took with him eighty people, including members of both houses of Congress with their wives and Alice Roosevelt, the President's daughter, who was on a tour of the Far East.

President Roosevelt took advantage of Taft's mission and instructed him to sound out the Japanese regarding rumors of their ambitions to overrun the Philippine Islands. At Tokyo on July 27, Count Katsura, the Japanese Prime Minister, denied the allegations to Taft. Both men understood the impossibility of a formal alliance between Britain, Japan, and the United States for the maintenance of peace in the Far East. Katsura, however, suggested a "good understanding or an alliance in practice if not in name" among the three powers. Taft reworded Katsura's proposal in order to deprive it of any official sanction. He felt that if peace were threatened, then "appropriate action of the Government of the United States, in conjunction with Japan and Great Britain, for such a purpose could be counted on by them quite as confidently as if the United States were under obligations to take it." As for Korea, Taft assented to Japan's suzerainty over the Hermit Kingdom.[3]

Back at Portsmouth, on September 5, 1905, Russia and

Japan signed a treaty ending the war. Japan gained a protectorate over Korea, the Russian leasehold at Port Arthur and Talien, part of the Chinese Eastern Railway from Changchun to Port Arthur, together with properties and rights that went with it, and the southern half of Sakhalin. Both nations promised to evacuate Manchuria, with the exception of their leaseholds, to restore to Chinese administration those parts of Manchuria under military occupation, and not to "obstruct any general measures common to all countries, which China may take for the development of the commerce and industry of Manchuria." The next day, Roosevelt, who had approved of Taft's talks with Katsura, acknowledged that the Japanese had triumphed.[4] Thus, with this settlement of Korea's future and of America's relation to the Philippines, peace in the Far East was established for the time being. Successful in its purpose, the Taft mission took ship for home and met another group of returning American travelers headed by Edward H. Harriman.

The summer of 1905 was a busy season for American tourists in the Far East. Harriman, feeling the need for Pacific breezes, had assembled an entourage of family, friends, a business associate, and his personal physician to help him enjoy the voyage and the splendors of the Orient. The American railway king did not smile much, Alice Roosevelt observed, and she remembered him as a "small, brown, taciturn man who never seemed to play." [5] She was right; Harriman did not have the time. He was not oppressed by weighty problems of international relations, but as later developments unfolded, his trip had considerable significance for the United States, perhaps more than that of the Taft excursion.

With the assistance of his banking allies, Kuhn, Loeb and Company, Harriman rose to a position of supremacy in the American railroad world through his reorganization of the Union Pacific Railroad in 1897. By 1900, Harriman was chairman of the company's executive board, with all the power of decision and execution in his hands. Once he secured the Union Pacific, Harriman expanded his operations by attempting to buy control of two competing systems, the Southern Pacific and the Northern Pacific Railroads. His activities conformed with the general trend toward American railroad centralization, but they also had great import for the future of American interests in the Far East.

The Union Pacific owned one half of the stock of the Occidental and Oriental Steamship Company, whose ships carried goods from San Francisco to China and Japan. At the same time, the Oregon Railroad and Navigation Company, a Union Pacific subsidiary, owned the Portland and Asiatic Steamship Line with a similar traffic to the Far East. The Southern Pacific Railroad in 1900 bought control of the Pacific Mail Steamship Company, one of the major American lines doing business in Asia; the latter, in the course of its operations, had acquired a smaller shipping line from the Santa Fé Railroad system. When the Southern Pacific bought into the Pacific Mail, Harriman made a personal purchase of enough shares of stock to gain him a position on the shipping company's board of directors. The following year, the Union Pacific Railroad took over the Southern Pacific Railroad and its shipping properties.[6] In the space of four years, Harriman assumed the leadership of a large portion of American shipping enterprise in the Pacific.

Harriman was not the only American railroad operator with an interest in Far Eastern commerce. James J. Hill, builder and operator of the Great Northern Railroad, did much to bring American attention to the possibilities of Pacific trade. Hill, to whom "an empty car was thief," had labored to create a paying freight load for the Great Northern's traffic going east from the Pacific coast. His efforts stimulated an Eastern market for Western lumber that soon outweighed the East-West traffic. In order to redress the balance, Hill sought a new source of westward-moving freight. He enlarged a demand for American flour, manufactured cotton goods, and steel rails in China and Japan and contracted with a Japanese shipping concern for the transportation of American exports from the Seattle terminal of the Great Northern Railroad to the Far East. Hill went into the shipping business himself in 1903 and 1904 and founded the Great Northern Steamship Company as another attempt to capitalize on Asiatic trade.

Harriman and Hill, however, lacked Chicago terminals for their lines, a serious handicap for any Far Eastern undertaking, since Chicago was fast becoming the industrial heart of the nation as it already was the center of farm production. Hill, moreover, sought an entrance into St. Louis in order to bring his road closer to the large cotton industry that furnished a basic commodity in the Asiatic trade. The Burlington Railroad met the needs and desires of both men, and they competed for its purchase, with Hill winning out. Hill's success not only gave him an advantage for Pacific trade, but also, since the Burlington's tracks paralleled those of the Union Pacific, he was in a position to compete with Harriman.[7]

Backed by Kuhn, Loeb and Company, Harriman began to buy stock in the Northern Pacific Railroad, which controlled the Burlington. Harriman's backdoor approach forced J. P. Morgan and Company into the fray because of its interest in the Northern Pacific. Discovery by Hill and Morgan of Harriman's tactics precipitated a bitter war in the stock exchange, causing a minor panic in the market. Both sides ended the costly struggle by creating the Northern Securities Company, a holding company under the leadership of the House of Morgan, which admitted Harriman to a directorship. Unfortunately for the promoters, Theodore Roosevelt began his advertised trust-busting campaign. The government filed suit against the Northern Securities combination, and the Supreme Court ordered its dissolution. The administration's action angered Hill, and he resolved to halt his efforts to extend trade in the Pacific until the government openly aided American commercial interests in that area.[8] Harriman was left alone in the field, and hence was sensitive to the situation created by Japan's victory over Russia.

With the peace of Portsmouth near at hand, the American Minister in Tokyo, Lloyd Griscom, became suspicious of Japan's general intentions in the Far Eastern area. Griscom detected a strong Japanese desire to control shipping in the Pacific, and he warned Harriman of such a contingency. The railway magnate exhibited little concern. He knew of Japan's intentions through an offer made to him for the purchase of the Pacific Mail Steamship Company and had refused to sell. But understanding little of actual conditions governing shipping enterprise in the Far East, he prepared for a trip to Japan and China. "Ostensibly Mr. Harriman was coming on a pleasure trip," Griscom recalled, "but at the same time he had a weather eye cocked for the welfare of the Pacific Mail Steamship Company." [9] Though family, friends, and doctor went along on the Harriman junket in the summer, the presence in the party of R. P. Schwerin, Vice-President of the Pacific Mail, testified to the activity of Harriman's "weather eye." His connections with Kuhn, Loeb and Company, which had rendered Japan vital financial aid during the war, promised to open the doors of official Japan to him, and Washington assisted by ordering its diplomats to render aid "in obtaining commercial information." [10]

Harriman's arrival in Japan assumed the appearance of a triumphal entry. Japanese financiers and statesmen wined and dined the group in an incessant round of parties and entertainments. They even exhibited the last of the shoguns to the Americans as a special privilege. While Japanese officialdom played host, mobs rioted in the streets, expressing their disappointment at the terms of the Portsmouth Treaty that deprived Japan of an indemnity. Harriman, "quite oblivious to the uproar," made the most of his acquaintance with prominent Japanese. His main concern, the protection of his interest in the Pacific Mail Steamship Company, began to shift as he read the Japanese newspapers and came in contact with the state of affairs in Manchuria.[11]

The Russo-Japanese War had exhausted both combatants. Assisted by the house of Kuhn, Loeb and its associates in London and Hamburg, Japan had floated large loans in Europe and the United States. The Portsmouth settlement gave Japan the southern branch of the Russian-built Chinese Eastern Railway from Port Arthur to Changchun. Yet, costly military operations and poor Russian management had weakened the condition of the line, and the Japanese, financially strained, faced the problem of rehabilitation of the property with little financial resources at their command. The Russians were confronted with a similar financial problem. During the Russo-Japanese War, rumors had circulated that they wanted to sell the Chinese Eastern Railway, but the sale had not materialized. Within this context of Russian and Japanese financial insecurity and Japan's newly acquired holdings in Manchuria, Harriman's desire for the furtherance of his interests led to the formulation of a great and ambitious plan.

One night during his stay in Tokyo, after reading maps and newspapers, Harriman turned to Minister Griscom: "Griscom, there's no doubt about it. If I can secure control of the South Manchuria Railroad from Japan, I'll buy the Chinese Eastern from Russia, acquire trackage over the Trans-Siberian to the Baltic, and establish a line of steamers to the United States. Then I can connect with the American transcontinental lines, and join up with the Pacific Mail and the Japanese transpacific steamers. It'll be the most marvelous transportation system in the world. We'll girdle the earth." [12] To carry out this plan, the man with the "genius of a Bismarck, of a Roman Caesar" proposed to ally himself with the competing Japanese shipping interests that had offered to buy control of the Pacific Mail Steamship Company, create new shipping lines, and loop the system neatly together with his American railroads and the Japanese-owned railroad running from Pusan in Korea to Mukden in Manchuria. The "only way to find out what is best to be done is to start doing something," he told Griscom. The American Minister received his instructions. "You know all these Japanese. I want you to help me."

Griscom tempered his enthusiasm for the welfare of American interests abroad with his fear of the attitude of the American government at home. He knew of Harriman's enmity for Roosevelt because of the Northern Securities trouble, and he was forced to weigh American commercial possibilities against his own diplomatic future. "If Mr. Harriman could put through his deal, American trade in Manchuria and Korea would advance by leaps and bounds," he concluded. Griscom promised to help Harriman and then wrote Roosevelt outlining the situation.

Having set down the principles of the grand design, Harriman and his party departed on a jaunt to China and Korea, leaving Griscom behind to open negotiations with Japanese officials. The American Minister met with surprising success. Prime Minister Katsura, "never an easy person to convince," approved of cooperation with Harriman, as did other important officials.

When Harriman returned to Tokyo in mid-October, 1905, he drew up a memorandum with the Japanese on behalf of himself and "associates." The agreement provided for the purchase of Japan's recently won Manchurian railroad with funds furnished by a syndicate headed by Harriman. The Japanese government and the Harriman group would have joint ownership of the road, with permission to work the valuable coal mines that were part of the original railway grant. The same joint representation would apply also to industrial enterprise undertaken in Manchuria. A Japanese-controlled corporation with provisions for equal administration was to be founded. (The Harriman syndicate had to incorporate through a Japanese company.) In case of war with China or Russia, the company agreed to follow the orders of the Japanese government in facilitating the movement of troops. Finally, Henry W. Denison, an American advisor to the Japanese government, would serve as arbitrator between the two groups, while J. Soyeda, President of the Industrial Bank of Japan, was to be the medium of communication.[13]

After signing the agreement, Harriman informed President Roosevelt of his Far Eastern plans. The President turned the letter over to Secretary of State Root and expressed interest in the information he received. "Whenever you can get on here," he replied, "let me know . . . when we can talk at length over those Eastern matters." [14] Confident that something had been done, Harriman then left Japan for the United States. Unfortunately for the success of the scheme, the Japanese delegates, headed by Baron Jutaro Komura, returned from the peace negotiations at Portsmouth and raised objections to the agreement with Harriman. The Japanese thought they could get needed funds for Manchurian railway development in London, and Baron Goto, the future head of the South Manchurian Railroad, opposed any joint control that might weaken Japan's hold in Manchuria.

Komura hurriedly sent for Griscom and told him that the plan would have to be postponed. "We don't know yet what our rights are in Korea and Manchuria," he informed the Minister. Until such rights were clearly defined, he added, the plans for joint ownership and operation of the South Manchurian Railroad would have to be delayed.[15]

Soyeda, the Japanese banker, wired the same news to Harriman. Marquis Katsura, he explained, had learned from Baron Komura of the necessity for the acquiescence of China in the new arrangement for Manchuria. Russia, moreover, had to be consulted with respect to the regulation of the connecting railroad services between the Russian and the Japanese sections of the line from Harbin to Port Arthur. In addition, the railroad's earning capacity and the specific rights and properties belonging to it were uncertain. The Japanese thought it better to hold the Harriman memorandum "in abeyance for the time being." Soyeda promised Harriman that the Japanese government would consult him before making arrangements with other capitalists; but he made it clear that any new international agreement resulting from negotiations with China and Russia would "probably necessitate some essential changes in the proposed arrangement." [16] Rebuffed but not discouraged by Japan's nullification of the agreement, Harriman stepped up his effort to create and control a world-wide transportation system. This time, he worked through the direct intervention of Jacob Schiff, head of Kuhn, Loeb and Company, an organization with financial ties to Tokyo.

Shortly after the outbreak of the Russo-Japanese War, Jacob Schiff strode into the London office of Lord Revelstroke, head of the banking firm of Baring Brothers, and denounced Russia. Lord Revelstroke informed Schiff of Japan's efforts to borrow money in the London market to finance the war and explained the reluctance of English bankers to lend the full ten millions in sterling. Schiff took a considerable share in the loan and participated in four more Japanese loans.[17] The American banker's motives were clear.

Since early 1901, the Russian government had attempted to secure loans in the American financial market, but its mistreatment of its Jewish minority alarmed the banker, who was a leader of American Jewry. Schiff listened to Russian overtures for funds, but he refused to help unless Russia ceased its persecution of the Jews. In the spring of 1904, about the same time that he arranged for American participation in the first Japanese loan, Schiff informed the English banker, Lord Rothschild, that he had personally frustrated St. Petersburg's application for American money.[18]

Later that summer, Eduard Noetzlin, a Paris banker intimately connected with the Russo-Chinese Bank and a close friend of Schiff's, approached him, hoping to get funds in exchange for a relaxation of Russia's anti-Semitic policy. Schiff refused to yield until Russia first took definite steps. A few months later, Russia sent Gregory Wilenkin to deal with Schiff. Wilenkin was an agent of Russia's Finance Ministry, and his family, though Jewish, had received special privileges that saved them from anti-Semitic outrages. Wilenkin was as unsuccessful as Noetzlin in his overtures to Schiff.

While Schiff helped the Japanese and blocked the Russians, the House of Morgan attempted to open the American bond market to the Tsarist government in 1905 and 1906. The Morgan effort centered on the Russian delegation at the Portsmouth peace conference in the fall of 1905. Count Witte, head of the delegation, approached J. P. Morgan and Company for a loan, taking the precaution of making a similar request of Kuhn, Loeb and Company. Schiff refused, but Morgan was amenable, though he demanded severe terms. On October 31, 1905, Russia's Finance Minister Kokovtsov advised Morgan that the terms offered Witte for an independent loan were unsatisfactory.[19]

The next day, Schiff advised Charles Steele, a Morgan partner, that Kuhn, Loeb and Company would "not hesitate to give your firm any support it might wish to have from us in any endeavor to open the American market to Russian loans," provided Russia reversed its policy of Jewish mistreatment.[20] Subsequently, Witte informed Kokovtsov that Morgan, who headed an international banking consortium, wanted a meeting in Paris to discuss loan terms. The outbreak of the Revolution of 1905–1906, however, weakened the consortium's confidence in Russia's stability, and in March, 1906, Morgan wired that conditions were not favorable for a loan.

While the Russians attempted to get funds in the United States, Schiff remained favorable to the Japanese. He adopted an almost paternal air toward the newly arisen world power, and he cautioned Baron Korekiyo Takahashi that many financial difficulties still confronted the Island Empire. As a friend, he "was mindful of the prospective economic development of Japan." This message preceded Harriman's unsuccessful trip to the Far East, and in early February of 1906, Schiff himself went to Japan.

As with Harriman, so with Schiff. The Japanese warmly applauded their American benefactor. He received a medal from the government, saw the sights, and toasted the Emperor. He also gave attention to Japan's future role in the Far East. "There is no doubt," he wrote his good friend, Sir Ernest Cassel, the English banker, "that everything is being done to bring China and her great resources under Japanese influence." Schiff approved of Japan's policy. He understood the importance to Japan of the Anglo-American loans in the spring of 1904 and maintained that Japanese control of Korea was desirable in view of the weakness exhibited by the Koreans in the past. He believed as a matter of hard fact that Japan sought "compensation for the tremendous sacrifices made during the recent war" and warned that those who hoped for the preservation of the open door would be disappointed because of Japan's increasing industrial effort and the advantages this country had in "legitimate competition with her rivals." Manchuria, Korea, and China faced Japanese overlordship, Schiff pointed out, and the United States and Europe stood to benefit from Japan's supremacy.[21]

In spite of his approval of Tokyo's new role in the Far East, the earlier Harriman proposals were not picked up by the Japanese while Schiff visited their country. Unsteady financial conditions hindered possible dealings between Kuhn, Loeb and Company and Japan, and Schiff was reluctant to make heavy financial commitments at the time. The Japanese did need funds to carry out the projected extension of their newly acquired railway properties, and rumors circulated that they promised to borrow money from Schiff; but by the time negotiations began, the panic of 1907 broke out in the United States and the deal fell through. As a gesture of gratitude for earlier American aid, Japan placed heavy orders for railway equipment in the United States.[22]

Japan's determination to exploit its own Manchurian properties postponed the execution of Harriman's plans, but they were revived later by Willard Straight, who met the American magnate in the Far East. A graduate of Cornell, Straight went to China to work for the Chinese Imperial Maritime Customs Service in 1901. Within seven months of his arrival at Nanking, after exhibiting considerable proficiency in his study of Chinese, he was sent to Peking. Straight quickly adapted himself to the life in China, but he was restless in his low paying job and wondered about his future. When the Russo-Japanese War began, he accepted a position as a foreign correspondent, covering the war in Korea and Manchuria. During his stay in Korea, he made the acquaintance of Edwin V. Morgan, and when Morgan was appointed American Minister to Korea to replace the troublesome Horace Allen, Straight accompanied him as his private secretary and Vice-Consul.

A sensitive man in his early twenties, Straight went through a period of introspection and self-analysis in these years, trying to discover a purpose in life and set up some values that he could accept. His father and mother were

educated and religious people, without wealth and dedicated
to the service of others. Somewhat of a schoolroom idealist,
he grappled vainly with a feeling that the Golden Rule was
not what it appeared to be on the surface. One must be
"selfish wisely. In other words be hypocritical," he concluded. Perhaps someone could "explode" his arguments,
but no one did at the time. "Money" was "an exceedingly
interesting topic on which to dwell," he reflected. "I like it
all much better and am crazy to get at it and start up the
ladder, if it is to be climbed at all." Straight detested the prospect of becoming a parasite. "I am not of them," he wrote
in his diary. Although he had considerable ability as an
artist, he was determined not to make it his life's work.
"Imagine going through life as an artist—a little brother to
the rich, dawdling at Newport, trying to catch orders . . .
a hanger-on, a tail of a retinue. It is all wrong."

How then did one make one's way in the world? Straight
echoed the dictum of Theodore Roosevelt, "Strenuosity is
the life of the age after all"; and he prepared to take a personal direction that was not to be an easy one. "It's the same
damnable half and half, artist and schemer, the artist is the
best side, the schemer the worst side in me," he admitted.
Who would win out? "I am afraid that there is too much
ambition in my cosmos to let the schemer be driven out by
the better nature," he observed, "hence much tribulation and
many an unhappy hour, and uneasy time, for I am not true
to myself." [23]

As Straight debated with himself, he exhibited a growing
patriotism that colored much of his later action in China
and Manchuria. In the early years of his residence in the Far
East, the reputation of American officials was not of the
best, and Straight was honestly anguished. "My heart shriv-
elled within me as I heard tale after tale of the roguery of
American officials in the East, of the bribery, of a consul
and a group of missionaries," he wrote. "Such things of

Americans, of the great, the proud home of the Eagle, such rotten corruption by the representatives of one's own native land" discouraged him and made him yearn for a vigorous house cleaning.

The emergence of a powerful Japan stiffened his patriotism and forced his thinking into an extravagant criticism of what he feared was a softness in the national fiber. The American is an individualist who employs patriotism as a "safety valve for superfluous eloquence rather than a religion on whose altar he is willing to lay his life if need be, even without knowing the precise reason for his sacrifice." [24] It was just this spirit, he insisted, that had catapulted Japan to a strong position in Asia.

Straight distrusted the Japanese in these years. Although he held no brief for Russia's performance in Asia, he did not give unqualified approval of Japan merely because Russia had been overbearing in Manchuria. "Somehow I cannot see the use in fooling with these people. They are not of us. Why play with them," he mused. He satirized the Japanese as crude little boys masquerading behind Sunday school educations only to reveal themselves later just as evil as Russia. He feared that Japan would take advantage of "the broad humanity argument" [25] that had been put into its hands because of its fighting role against Russia and use it for its own advantage.

Japan's operations in Korea changed Straight's mistrust to open hostility. In large part, he was concerned over Japan's threat to American economic interests, and he anticipated a policy of exclusion and gradual expulsion of non-Japanese interests from the Hermit Kingdom. American support of Japan was a mistake, and he insisted that Tokyo would never show its gratitude to the United States. "Suck the blood and give naught in return. Such are the Japanese—the world's pets." [26]

In September of 1905, Straight noted breathlessly to a

friend, "Good Lord, we have the Princess Alice Roosevelt and her suite coming, the Harrimans the next week and I don't know who along the same line a little later." The arrival of important visitors usually met with an excited response from the diplomatic and consular representatives of the United States in far-off stations, but the projected visits had greater significance for the Vice-Consul.

The visit was important for Harriman, too. Having placed his transportation proposals before the Japanese, he went to China and stopped off at Seoul for a week on his way back to Japan. Straight had the good fortune of conducting the Harriman party to the port of Pusan and seeing to its comfort in Korea. The railway king noted the "intelligence and knowledge of Eastern affairs" displayed by Straight and, impressed by his "character and force," kept him in mind as a "valuable assistant" for the large enterprise that he planned.[27]

When Japan took over Korea's foreign relations, the State Department closed the American Legation at Seoul, in November, 1905, and Straight followed Minister Edwin V. Morgan to another post in Havana. On his way to Cuba, Straight stopped off in the United States from late January to mid-February, 1906. In that short time he dined several times with the Harrimans and improved the connection he had made in Seoul.

Straight's main interest was in the Far East, and he soon tired of Cuba. In the late spring of 1906, he left Havana and went to Washington seeking a new position in the Consular Service. His search met with success. He had powerful friends at court, among them President Roosevelt's daughter, for whom he had found honeymoon accommodations in Cuba. He also knew Harriman and presently gained admittance to the inner chamber to meet President Roosevelt. These contacts, together with Straight's record and his winning personality, helped bring him an appointment.[28]

In May, 1906, Roosevelt endorsed a letter to Secretary of State Root from Richard Harding Davis recommending Straight for an appointment to a consulate in China. After the possibility of a position at Tsingtao fell through, the State Department sent him to Mukden as Consul General in order to watch postwar developments in Manchuria. The opportunity to go to Manchuria pleased Straight greatly, for he felt that at Mukden "the biggest game in the East, save Peking itself, is being played." [29]

After Straight received the appointment and before he took up his post, he visited Harriman at Arden, New York. The Consul General and the financier discussed Harriman's abortive attempt to buy into the Japanese South Manchurian Railroad. Harriman showed Straight all the correspondence on the matter, including the Japanese rejection of the October 12 agreement. "Mr. Harriman's project had not been definitely turned down," Straight recalled, "but it was obvious no further progress could be expected." Before Straight left Arden, Harriman requested him to observe Manchurian railway developments, since he still was "determined if possible to obtain a foothold in that region to carry out his scheme for an around the world transportation system." [30]

Shortly before sailing, in August, 1906, Straight visited Roosevelt at Oyster Bay. The President insisted that Straight travel to Mukden via Europe and the Trans-Siberian Railroad in order to observe the effects of the Russian Revolution of 1905–1906, along with his task of watching Russia and Japan in Manchuria. Straight arrived in Mukden accompanied by the newly appointed Vice-Consul, Nelson Fairchild, on October 4, 1906, finding the situation "rather complex and confusing—particularly to the newcomer." [31] But his drive and ability, together with a changing situation in Manchuria, soon made him a veteran diplomat whose aim was to further his country's interests along the lines of his own desires and purposes.

NOTES

1. Fred Harvey Harrington, *God, Mammon, and the Japanese: Dr. Horace N. Allen and Korean-American Relations, 1884–1905* (Madison, 1944), 317–318, 328; Straight Diary, March 26, 1904, Straight Papers.

2. Henry Cabot Lodge, *Selections from the Correspondence of Theodore Roosevelt and Henry Cabot Lodge, 1884–1918* (2 vols., New York, 1925), II, 153.

3. Tyler Dennett, *Roosevelt and the Russo-Japanese War* (New York, 1925), 112–114.

4. Dennett, *Roosevelt and the Russo-Japanese War*, 263.

5. Alice Roosevelt Longworth, *Crowded Hours* (New York, 1933), 106.

6. Interstate Commerce Commission Reports, *Decisions of the Interstate Commerce Commission of the United States, November, 1906 to December, 1907* (Washington, 1908), 278–284; John H. Kemble, "The Transpacific Railroads," *Pacific Historical Review*, 18 (August, 1949):336.

7. Joseph G. Pyle, *The Life of James J. Hill* (2 vols., New York, 1917), II, 49–66, 109, 116; George Kennan, *E. H. Harriman* (2 vols., New York, 1922), I, 337–338.

8. James J. Hill, "The Future of Our Oriental Trade," *World's Work*, 10 (August, 1905):6465; Jean J. Jusserand, *What Me Befell* (New York, 1934), 296.

9. Lloyd Griscom, *Diplomatically Speaking* (New York, 1940), 261; Kennan, *Harriman*, II, 404; Cyrus Adler, *Jacob H. Schiff* (2 vols., New York, 1928), I, 246; Willard Straight, "Notes on the Late Mr. E. H. Harriman's Interests in the East," typewritten copy in the Straight Papers.

10. Straight, "Notes on Harriman," Straight Papers; Adee to Rockhill at Peking, September 21, 1905, in Alfred Vagts, *Deutschland und die Vereinigten Staaten in der Weltpolitik* (2 vols., New York, 1933), II, 1237.

11. Griscom to Elihu Root, September 15, 1905, *Dispatches From United States Ministers to Japan, September 5, 1905—February 28, 1906* (microfilm copy); Otto Kahn, "E. H. Harriman," *An Address Delivered Before the Finance Forum in New York on January 25, 1911;* Longworth, *Crowded Hours*, 106.

12. Griscom, *Diplomatically Speaking*, 263; George Marvin, "Willard Straight," *Japan*, 13 (October, 1923):19–45.

13. *Memorandum of a Preliminary Understanding, October 12, 1905, Between His Excellency Count Katsura Taro, the Japanese Government and Mr. E. H. Harriman, Representing Himself and Associates,* enclosed in O'Brien to the Secretary of State, National Archives, Record Group * 59:General Records of the Department of State, Numerical File, 1906–1910, 221/120–121.

14. Roosevelt to Harriman, November 25, 1905, Roosevelt Papers.

15. Griscom, *Diplomatically Speaking*, 263–264.

16. J. Soyeda to Harriman, understood to have been sent October 30, 1905, and Griscom to Harriman, n.d., NA, RG59:221/120–121.

17. Straight, "Notes on Harriman," Straight Papers; Adler, *Schiff*, I,

* Hereafter abbreviated as NA, RG.

215, 219, 225, 229; Baron Kentaro K. Kaneko, "American Millions for Japan's War," *World's Work,* 10 (May, 1905):6124–6126.

18. Cyrus Adler and Aaron M. Margolith, *American Intercession on Behalf of Jews in the Diplomatic Correspondence of the United States, 1840–1938* (New York, 1943), 261–299; Adler, *Schiff,* II, 127.

19. Adler, *Schiff,* I, 12, 78, 194, II, 128; J. J. Korostovetz, *Pre-War Diplomacy* (London, 1920), 70; Baron Roman Rosen, *Forty Years of Diplomacy* (2 vols., New York, 1922), I, 274–277; William A. Williams, *American Russian Relations, 1781–1947* (New York, 1952), 53–54.

20. Adler, *Schiff,* II, 133.

21. Adler, *Schiff,* I, 220, 235; Jacob Schiff, "Japan After the War," *North American Review,* 597 (August, 1906):161–168.

22. Adler, *Schiff,* I, 36; Wright to Root, April 5, 1907, NA, RG59: 221/22–23; Wright to the Secretary of State, February 20, 1907, NA, RG59:221/12–14.

23. Straight Diary, October 28 and January 17, 1902, October 27, 1904, and January 14 and May 20, 1903, Straight Papers.

24. Straight Diary, October 4, 1902, and June 19, 1904, Straight Papers.

25. Straight Diary, September 30 and August 12, 1904, Straight to A. C. Coolidge, January 24, 1905, and Edwin V. Morgan, "Recollections of Willard Straight," April, n.d., 1920, Straight Papers.

26. Straight Diary, March 26 and August 5, 1904, July 3 and 12, 1905, and August 12, 1904, Straight Papers.

27. Straight to Schoelkopf, September 17, 1905, Straight Papers; Kennan, *Harriman,* II, 24–25.

28. Morgan, "Recollections of Willard Straight," Straight Papers.

29. William Loeb to Root, May 12, 1906, Straight to Schoelkopf, May 23, 1906, and Straight to Robert Bacon, July 2, 1906, Straight Papers; Straight to Schoelkopf, June 18, 1906, in Herbert Croly, *Willard Straight* (New York, 1924), 199.

30. Straight, "Notes on Harriman," Straight Papers; Kennan, *Harriman,* II, 25.

31. Straight to Schoelkopf, August 11 and 17, 1906, and Straight Diary, October 4, 1906, Straight Papers; Straight to Rockhill, October 5, 1906, NA, RG84:Peking Legation Archives.

CHAPTER THREE

Straight's Manchurian Reserve

Lloyd Griscom distrusted Japan. He had warned Harriman of Tokyo's desire to dominate shipping in the Pacific and had supported the world-wide transportation scheme, hoping that it would extend American interests in the Far East. Griscom also kept a careful watch on Manchuria and observed Japanese traders entering the region in the wake of their armies, setting up shops, making business contacts, and selling Japanese-made goods. His talks with Baron Komura, the opponent of Harriman's project, revealed only that Japan was willing to make good the bargain it had struck with Roosevelt—the maintenance of the open door in Manchuria and the restoration of the area to China in return for American support against Russia. In true open door style, Komura requested American assistance in persuading China to open more Manchurian cities to trade. But Griscom's uneasiness spread through the American diplomatic and consular corps in the Far East. Washington soon learned, as Schiff had predicted, that Japan intended to expand its influence in China.[1]

At the end of the Russo-Japanese War, Thomas Sammons, the American Consul at Newchwang, reported that although Manchuria imported more goods from the United States than from any other nation, the Japanese had important business advantages. Their military occupation of Southern

35

Manchuria provided their own merchants with a lead in tapping new trade areas; they built up a profitable trade relationship with the Chinese by importing most of the bean cake produced in Manchuria; and they employed their newly won control of the South Manchurian Railroad as a means of excluding other trade interests. "Commercially the future will turn largely on the method of applying the 'open door' policy," Sammons wrote, "although in any event Japan may be looked to as the controlling factor."

Early in 1906, the situation had appeared promising for American commercial interests, which had over 20 per cent of the Manchurian trade, consisting mainly of cotton goods, kerosene oil, flour, lumber, canned goods, cigarettes, and sundries. Barring "any abnormal interference," imports of cotton goods and flour should have increased. But one nagging fact stood out. Although both Japan and the United States were directly involved in Manchurian commerce, the presence of strong Japanese interests raised fears that American commercial activity was endangered.[2]

Upon Griscom's departure from his Tokyo post, the American chargé d'affaires, Francis M. Huntington Wilson, strengthened American suspicions of Japanese aspirations in Manchuria. A zealous advocate of American interests in the Far East, Huntington Wilson wondered whether Japan intended to "work beneath the surface for herself only, and for the Orient against the West." He characterized the Japanese government as one of "Oriental inscrutability" with a "talent for intrigue, shrewd and calculating," and he warned Washington against Japan's "protestations of disinterestedness."[3]

This concern for the open door and the growing apprehension of Japan soon led to a diplomatic exchange between Tokyo and Washington regarding the entrance of American traders into Manchuria. American merchants complained that the Japanese prevented the movement of goods and traders into Manchuria, and Secretary Root ordered a protest sent to the Japanese Foreign Office. Huntington Wilson reported delays in receiving replies from Japanese officials and implied that trade obstructions were not accidental in view of Japan's desire to exploit Manchuria. Root renewed his requests for satisfaction, and Huntington Wilson, aided by the British who also felt the pressure on their trade interests, harried the Japanese Foreign Office.[4]

In April, 1906, the American chargé received encouraging news. The Japanese promised to open the cities of Antung and Mukden to trade if China consented and explained that military considerations had delayed the entrance of traders into the area. Japan's reply left Washington cold. Robert Bacon, Acting Secretary of State, expressed "serious concern" about Tokyo's policy of exclusiveness and remarked on the "importance of the question and the gravity of the situation" if the Japanese discriminated against foreigners, using temporary military conditions as an excuse.[5] And while Huntington Wilson wrangled with the Japanese Foreign Office, economic conditions in Manchuria deteriorated.

A postwar depression hit Manchuria in the late spring and summer of 1906. Sales dropped, and the movement of goods slowed down. The Russian port of Vladivostok and the Japanese-controlled entrepôt of Darien captured an increased share of Manchurian trade while Newchwang, the Manchurian port handling American goods, declined. American merchants grumbled about the shift of the traffic to Darien, asserting that the existence of the Japanese military zone and discriminatory freight rates on the South Manchurian Railroad damaged their trade. An investigating committee of English and American merchants resident in Shanghai admitted that trade disruption was due mainly to the confused situation in the military zone, rather than to railroad rate favoritism; however, the committee criticized the continued circulation of Japanese war currency in Manchuria because it tended to divert business to Japanese interests.

The Manchurian trade situation continued its downward spiral. William Woodville Rockhill, the American Minister at Peking, became irritated at the panic displayed by American trade interests. "I cannot understand the senseless scare about Chinese affairs in the United States," he informed his friend, Alfred Hippisley, and he attributed "all the kicking of American exporters" to the overstocking of inventories in anticipation of the continuance of the war.[6]

Rockhill's depreciation of trade complaints did not halt them. The American Association of China, an organization devoted to the preservation and extension of American trade, sent a committee on a trip through Manchuria. This group censured the deficiencies of China's administration of Manchuria and conceded that charges of Japanese favoritism and exclusiveness, while possibly true, could not be proved definitely. The committee urged Rockhill to press the Chinese to take over control of Manchuria from the Japanese as soon as possible.

Rockhill assured the association that he would continue to insist upon equality of commerce in Manchuria in his representations to China, but he refused to allow the depressed economic situation to become the instrument for an anti-Japanese crusade. He believed that trade competition in Manchuria would be sharp but that Japan's financial requirements at home depended upon foreign aid. For Japan "to repel foreign assistance or put foreign capital under any disadvantage would be simply suicidal," he wrote. The American Minister was certain that Japan would offer opportunity and inducement to the United States and other nations to trade in Manchuria, and he blamed American merchants for their own difficulties, since they did not personally establish direct relations with the Chinese consumer. Rockhill resented the rumors that charged him with opposition to Japan in Manchuria. "The reports published are lies," he wrote. "I have so informed the Japanese Minister." [7]

Huntington Wilson stormed at Japan. He disagreed with Rockhill's thesis that Tokyo favored the open door in Manchuria and pointed out that Japan's program of economic nationalism promoted intolerance of competing economic interests. He recommended the adoption of vigorous measures, suggesting the exertion of American and British financial power against Japan in order to restrain its ambitions in Manchuria. On the other hand, Huntington Wilson accepted Rockhill's view that China should understand Washington's serious objections to Peking's weakness in Manchuria. He proposed that the State Department make an "emphatic" approach to the Chinese, who understood nothing but force. It is "sad," he grieved, that the "reasonableness and fairness of Great Britain and the United States have served to diminish their influence at Peking." [8]

While Americans developed qualms over the Manchurian trade situation, Japan moved to fasten its hold on the Manchurian transportation system. Late in December, 1905, Komura signed the Treaty of Peking with China, validating the terms of the Portsmouth agreement and secretly giving the Japanese additional railway rights in Manchuria. Huntington Wilson informed Root of the secret protocols and in response to the Secretary's request sent a copy to Washington. The hidden arrangements provided that no lines running parallel to the South Manchurian Railroad would be constructed "which might be prejudicial" to the Japanese-owned road—a provision that later formed the basis of Japanese claims to railway supremacy in Manchuria.

It was during the summer of 1906, when Schiff negotiated with Tokyo, that Japan created the South Manchurian Railroad Company for the exploitation of its newly acquired railway and mining properties from Port Arthur to Changchun. The terms of the company's charter plainly provided for Japanese government control of the line with China's cooperation, though in view of the power relationships now established in Manchuria, this was merely a token recognition of Peking's authority. Here too, American diplomats pointed an accusing finger.

Ambassador Luke Wright, in Tokyo, noted Japan's growing control of Manchurian railways, explaining that the Chinese, while nominally interested in the new company, had little to say about its actual formation. The American Consul in Yokohama, Henry B. Miller, reported on Japan's progress toward industrial nationalization. He felt that the formation of the South Manchurian Railroad Company revealed a definite trend that demonstrated Japanese intentions to "master" Oriental trade and commerce. American interests, Miller predicted, might soon encounter the rivalry of the whole Japanese nation for trade supremacy in Manchuria. From Peking came the worried comment of Henry P. Fletcher, American chargé d'affaires. "How China can let slip an opportunity to secure a voice in the management of the railway system of Southern Manchuria," he wrote, "and not see that Japan's hold on that section is thereby vastly strengthened is impossible for me to explain." [9]

In line with the policy of nationalization of industry at home, Tokyo instituted government subsidies and loans to its trading interests in Manchuria. This financial aid resulted in the formation of an export union, under the control of the Mitsui Busan Kaisha, which directed and coordinated Japanese trade in Manchuria; this was another strong threat to foreign mercantile interests. In the midst of Japan's unfolding imperial plans and the deepening of American suspicions, Straight arrived in Mukden to add his voice to the anti-Japanese chorus.

The trip across Russia and Siberia had been interesting. The Tsarist government had survived the Revolution of 1905–1906, and Straight found a certain security in learning that Russia still looked to Asia. He recognized serious tension existing between Russians and Japanese at Harbin, Changchun, and in Southern Manchuria. Many observers expressed considerable regret that the war had ended.

Without the need of prompting from like-minded colleagues, the young Consul General regarded Japan as a threat to the United States. He realized the weak American position in Manchuria but the Chinese appeared to be stiffening against Japanese demands, anticipating the final withdrawal of the troops. European interests, moreover, looked to the United States as "the champion of the principle of equal opportunity," and depended on Washington for leadership against Tokyo.[10]

The fortunes of diplomacy, however, conspired to frustrate Straight from the outset. The role of "champion" of the open door first placed the United States in opposition not to Japan, but to China. Late in 1906, the Manchurian Viceroy closed Mukden to foreign trade and revived an ancient transit tax, "likin," on imported goods. The Viceroy's action placed Straight in a difficult position. The tax raised the price of American manufactured goods and made it difficult to compete with Japan in Manchuria; yet any protest that Straight made stood to benefit the Japanese, who were affected by the tax as were other foreign powers. Rockhill ordered Straight to object to the Manchurian authorities and cooperate with the representatives of the other nations in Manchuria. Straight followed his order. He negotiated with the Manchurian authorities, consoling himself with the thought that the Chinese were not fooled "by this endeavor to let some one else do the blustering, for they well know whose chestnuts are being pulled." [11]

In May, 1907, he succeeded in breaking down Chinese resistance on the likin issue and arranged for the issuance of exemption certificates that permitted the passage of goods, pending a later settlement. Straight's eagerness to adjust the matter rested on the American desire to get trade moving again in Manchuria; once accomplished, Japan and Russia would be forced to renew negotiations with China for the installation of customs houses at the Japanese-controlled port of Darien and on the Russo-Chinese frontier.

The customs house problem loomed large for American interests in Manchuria. In order to offset Japan's advantages, acquired by virtue of its position in Manchuria, more customs houses were required so that trade could resume on the older prewar scale. This demand concealed the American fear of growing Japanese competition at the port of Darien that cut into American trade at Newchwang. Rockhill had insisted that American merchants need not pay duties at Newchwang unless China opened more customs houses. Squeezed on one side by the United States and on the other by Japan and Russia, the Chinese did nothing.

Rockhill assumed that after the military evacuation of Manchuria, China would sign customs house agreements with the two Manchurian powers. But Chinese officials informed him that Japan was deliberately stalling negotiations. The American Minister had resisted the claims of American commercial interests in the summer of 1906, but Straight's news from Mukden and Japan's dilatory policy reversed his opinions. "I concluded," he informed Root, "that I should report to you without further delay the highly unsatisfactory condition of affairs in Manchuria." Early in 1907, he took an acid view of China's opposition to Japan. By May of the same year, he informed Washington that Japan proposed merely to permit China to act as a police force for the maintenance of peace and the preservation of order in Manchuria. He recommended "sympathetic support" of China by the United States.[12]

Unfortunately for Straight's early hopes, the Chinese were forced in the spring of 1907 to make supplementary agreements with Japan that clarified Tokyo's growing strength in

Manchuria. Japan received mining advantages along the Antung-Mukden Railroad that linked Korea with Manchuria; China had to admit Japan to participation in any future railroad construction and financing, as well as agree to the use of Japanese personnel, the deposit of earnings in Japanese banks, and the connection of the lines with the South Manchurian Railroad.

Japan also took advantage of the situation in international politics and buttressed its position in Manchuria. Already tied to Great Britain by the alliance of 1902 and 1905, Tokyo received France's recognition of its paramount position in Manchuria in June, 1907. A few weeks later, in direct contradiction to Straight's initial estimate of relations between the two nations, Tokyo signed a convention with Russia recognizing Manchuria as a sphere of influence for Japan and Mongolia for Russia. When Russia concluded an entente with Great Britain over Persia, Afghanistan, and Tibet in 1907, Japan became a working partner of the Triple Entente, with strong support of its policies and ambitions in Manchuria.

Prior to Japan's exaction of more favorable agreements from China and the discovery of important friends in the Triple Entente, Tokyo had increased its influence in Manchuria. Japanese interlopers brushed aside Chinese attempts to recover property seized during the war. A horde of adventurers remained behind in Manchuria after the military evacuation, causing outbreaks of violence, and Manchurian officials were troubled by Japanese encouragement of the importation of opium, the initiation of organized gambling, and the abuse of trade privileges at Antung.[13]

Determined to put up resistance with the only weapons that they had at hand, the Chinese reorganized their balky and outmoded administration of Manchuria. Under the direction of Yuan Shih Kai, chief of the Foreign Office in Peking, Hsu Shih Chang went to Mukden as Viceroy of the three Manchurian provinces, and Tang Shao-yi was appointed Governor of Fengtien. During the period of the administrative reorganization, China engaged in endless negotiations with the Japanese, hoping to protract the process until concrete plans were formulated to stave off Tokyo's march for control.

Straight was pleased with the new state of affairs. Tang had been educated in the United States and was strongly pro-American. "This consulate ventures to hope," Straight reported to Washington, that the State Department would "welcome . . . and encourage the consolidation of Chinese authority as constituting the strongest guarantee of the equality of opportunity in Manchuria." [14] Paralleling the Chinese move, Straight successfully persuaded the State Department to reorganize the American consular districts in Manchuria. Late in 1907, the jurisdictions and limits of the Manchurian consulates were revised, and Mukden became the directing center of American activity in Manchuria.[15]

In the early days of his stay in Manchuria, Straight had decided that "to keep our hold up here is going to be no summer holiday but I think we can do it if we go about it in the right way." The "right way" did not depend solely on potentially harmful struggles with the Chinese for the abolition of likin or the opening of customs houses. More had to be done in Manchuria, a fact recognized by Root when he pleaded for more funds to buy a suitable building in Mukden for the consulate. Mukden is the "outpost of foreign commerce in Southern Manchuria where the United States has an important trade which it must not lose," Root informed the Secretary of the Treasury.[16]

The work of the Consular Service mainly consisted of furnishing commercial information for the benefit of American economic interests, and Straight immediately plunged into this activity. Until his recall late in 1908, he corresponded with representatives of American manufacturers interested in the possibilities of Manchurian markets. He sent trade notes to the State Department outlining economic opportunities that ranged from the sale of watches to the feasibility of importing American windmills. He wrote to publicists interested in the Asiatic trade, suggesting the establishment of a commercial bureau in the Far East to further American influence, and he suggested the proper approach to be used in magazine articles designed for the "practical man whose awakening interest in things oriental we hope will be demonstrated along commercial and industrial lines." [17]

Behind Straight's efforts to advertise Manchuria was the uncomfortable fact that American trade, while substantial in certain items, remained too small. In the first half of 1907, Straight listed only three Americans actually residing in his district and only three companies with important trade interests in Manchuria. He believed as Rockhill did, that a successful American penetration of Manchuria required the presence of interests directly on the scene. He cautioned a supporter of his program to "put a certain sugar coating in your propaganda," in order to vitiate the views of those who felt that the Japanese had the field completely to themselves. If Americans took the trouble, he insisted, they could overcome Japanese competition, for "they [the Japanese] are not a commercial race." Throughout his stay in Manchuria, he emphasized the need of a correct approach to the market, of overcoming the stronger Japanese lead, and the importance of aggressive action.[18]

Straight sent an assistant to Antung to watch the Japanese at that important commercial center and to survey trade prospects. He suggested that China attempt to force Japan's hand by bringing disputed matters to the World Court at The Hague, and he brought attention to the possibility of a Japanese mining monopoly along the right of way of the Antung-Mukden Railroad provided by the 1907 agreements between Japan and China. None of these steps sufficed to tip the balance, and Straight insisted that Manchuria required "politically disinterested support" [19] and the introduction of foreign capital to offset Japan.

Straight's publicizing of Manchurian business opportunities tied in with his continual hand-wringing over the reluctance of American economic interests to enter the Manchurian field. The Japanese lead could be overtaken, he maintained, but the open door must have more than a diplomatic significance. The urgency of the matter was such, he feared, that "unless public opinion or the advice of friendly powers induces a modification of her Manchurian policy," Japan might increase the pressure on China in 1908. [20] China's efforts to bolster its position in Manchuria thus merged with Straight's alarm for the future safety of American interests.

The need for a stronger American stake in the Far East had prompted Straight to write to Harriman in the early days of his stay in Mukden. He played on the possibilities of Pacific shipping, emphasizing the profitable opportunity awaiting those who carried goods directly to North China from the United States and avoided costly transshipment from Shanghai. Straight also kept in mind Harriman's railway project, and he described the condition of the Russian and Japanese lines in Manchuria, expressing the hope that Harriman would call on him for any assistance. [21]

Several months' residence in Manchuria heightened Straight's enthusiasm, for the Manchurian government welcomed the introduction of American capital. Opportunity beckoned in the "new West," particularly for the man who could meet China's railroad needs. Dissatisfied with Japan's administration of the South Manchurian Railroad, the Chinese made vague plans for a line running north from Hsinmintun to Changchun, the junction point of the Russian-controlled Chinese Eastern Railway and the South Manchurian Railroad. The Hsinmintun-Changchun road was more than an expression of China's dissatisfaction; it was a deliberate challenge to the Japanese railroad monopoly in Southern Manchuria. Confident of Chinese cooperation, Straight proposed to scout around for a parallel route to the South Manchurian Railroad.[22]

Straight discussed the matter with Manchurian officials. Certain of Japan's opposition, the planners sought an alternative route that might invalidate Tokyo's expected protest. They soon found one by changing the northern terminal of the proposed line from Changchun to Tsitsihar in Eastern Mongolia. The new railroad was projected in the expectation that it would transport Chinese immigrants going north to settle lands bordering Russian and Japanese holdings and tap the rich mining districts along the right of way. Additional conferences refined the scheme to a road fifty miles in length, running from Hsinmintun to Fakumen with a future extension to Tsitsihar. Straight frankly admitted that the "new road would compete with the South Manchurian Railroad." [23]

When news of the Manchurian administration's intentions leaked out, representatives of French finance and the British and Chinese Corporation, an English group handling Chinese loans, came to Mukden. The Chinese were placed in a difficult position.[24] There was general internal opposition to the employment of foreign funds for Chinese enterprises, while Japan thrust loan funds at Peking in order to maintain a political influence over China's enterprises. In addition, one group of Chinese viewed the construction of Manchurian railroads as a means of combating Japan's influence. Another group, bitter at the tactics employed by British moneylenders in earlier negotiations for the Shanghai-Nanking Railway and mistrustful of the British government for its alliance with Japan, insisted upon employing native capital.[25] Tang Shao-yi, who handled the arrangements for the Manchurian administration, worked quietly, setting the bait before the representatives of foreign capital.

Spurred on by Tang's invitation and the menace of Japanese competition, Straight continued his talks with Manchurian officials. They soon expanded the Hsinmintun-Fakumen line into a larger plan. Straight and Tang decided to create a Manchurian Bank financed by a loan from American capitalists of $20,000,000. The Chinese imperial government would guarantee the loan and specified Manchurian revenues as security. The bank would act as the fiscal agent of the Manchurian administration, directing railroad development, industrial enterprises, agriculture, and the exploitation of mines and forests. The bank's officers would be Chinese and Americans, and no other foreigners were to be admitted unless the Chinese gave their permission.[26]

Now that the bank became part of the negotiations, the railroad was projected past Tsitsihar, on to Aigun close to the Russo-Chinese border and the tracks of the Trans-Siberian Railroad. While Tang negotiated with Straight, he also talked with Lord ffrench, the representative of Pauling, a British engineering concern, and promised to award the construction contract to ffrench's firm. This step merged the hopes of one definite British interest, one as yet unknown American interest, and those Manchurian officials who opposed Japan. On paper at least, it appeared that Tang had planned well.

Straight had the task of securing American money, and he kept Harriman posted on the tentative scheme, though he indicated that the terms were not too attractive at the moment. In June, 1907, Tang and Viceroy Hsu, "apparently very desirous of being friendly," increased their effort, and by early August, the whole plan had been shaped into a comprehensive operation for the development of Manchuria.[27]

With Tang's assent, Straight informed Harriman of the proposal, buoyantly exulting that the deal was "fraught with

tremendous possibilities." It means "that we play the principal part in the development of Manchuria," as well as en-
hancing American influence in China. A month later,
Straight related the general situation to Assistant Secretary
of State, William Phillips, omitting specific mention of his
letter to Harriman, but pointing out the need for a loan to
China that would enable Peking to reinforce its hold on
Manchuria. He wrote of "Empire shaping," promising that
"once we have established ourselves [in Manchuria] we
would be in a position to work through Tang and Yuan
[Shih Kai], who is now in power at Peking and do a tremendous work in furthering the Chinese Renaissance." [28] Manchuria was no longer an end in itself, for Straight's ardor had
carried him from Mukden to the gates of Peking in one short
move.

The blow fell in October, 1907. Harriman rejected the
proposal because of the financial panic that had broken in
the United States. Straight hurried to Tang with the news
that he had no sponsor, but the Governor promised that
neither the Japanese nor the British would get the loan until
a more definite refusal from other American sources was
forthcoming. In characteristic fashion, Tang, the spinner of
great webs of finance, kept Straight interested with talk of
an even larger plan for Manchuria, involving an international loan. [29]

Despite the setback resulting from Harriman's refusal,
Straight maintained contact with the financier, elaborating
on the Manchurian scheme and explaining the loan as an
entering wedge for business activity in China proper. "Nothing is known about Tang's plans for the organization of a
bank," he wrote, "nor is it known that he and I have had
dealings regarding this matter." [30]

Straight also tried unofficially to exert State Department
influence on Harriman. He notified Phillips of Manchurian
developments and requested him to forward private letters

to the railway magnate. Straight also urged Phillips to see Harriman and possibly round up other Americans who would be interested in case Harriman remained obdurate. "For heaven's sake don't discourage him though," he pleaded, "but get him to send someone out to look it over as I firmly believe it's a good thing and a wonderful opportunity." [31]

Harriman's rejection of the proposition forced the Chinese to deal with the British element that was seeking railroad privileges in Manchuria. Employing the economic whip to lash at the Anglo-Japanese alliance, China hoped that the introduction of English capital would lead to British political support against Japan. As he tried to persuade American capital to enter the field, Straight also cooperated with his British allies on the grounds that Japan was the mutual enemy.

In May, 1907, while Tang and Straight made plans, J. O. P. Bland, a businessman and publicist, left China for England. Long an advocate of a firm British policy in the Far East and a caustic critic of Downing Street's alliance with Japan, he hoped to persuade the London *Times,* the most important organ of British public opinion, that the Anglo-Japanese alliance was damaging to British interests in Manchuria. Late in August, he and Lord ffrench returned to Mukden and stayed with Straight at the American Consulate. Learning of the railroad construction project, ffrench had the route surveyed and agreed with China's estimate that a line from Hsinmintun to Tsitsihar was "rich if not richer than the territory tapped by the parallel Japanese line." ffrench opened negotiations with Tang for the construction contract, but the financing of the line remained the main problem. Reluctantly, the Chinese negotiated with Bland, apparently on the assurance from ffrench and Bland that London's support of Japan would be dropped.[32]

The situation made Straight uncomfortable. He had hoped to use American money to finance the line through the

Manchurian Bank, but Harriman's refusal left him without a concrete interest to offer the Chinese. "I don't think that he [Tang] has exactly played the game," Straight wrote, though he admitted that the Governor's "assurances on this point were always rather vague." Restraining his disappointment, Straight supported the ffrench-Bland effort to build and finance the Hsinmintun-Tsitsihar road.[33]

Encouraged by Tang's promise to "brook no interference" from outside sources, ffrench signed a contract with Tang on November 8, 1907, for the construction of a line from Hsinmintun to Fakumen. The friendly rivals "broke a large bottle on the deal" that would "set the whole crowd by the ears." Then they waited for the "explosion." Two weeks later, after an agonizing evening, for Bland, of small talk, horrible music, and discussion of Manchuria's future, Tang signed an agreement for the financing of the Hsinmintun-Fakumen section of the railroad. Bland raised the question of outside opposition, but the Governor assured him that there was none.[34]

The "explosion" came as expected. Japan protested to Great Britain and warned Peking to consult with Tokyo. The Japanese protest was based on Article 3 of the secret protocols drafted at the time of the Treaty of Peking in December, 1905, specifying that China was not to build any lines that competed with the South Manchurian Railroad. China denied the applicability of the protocols on the grounds that such provisions were merely part of the minutes of the treaty meetings and therefore not binding.

Bland quarreled with Tang and accused the Manchurian administration of falsely stating that no protest had been made by Japan when Tang signed Bland's contract. Tang, who has assumed for political purposes that he and Bland had common enemies in Tokyo, pointed out innocently that since Great Britain and Japan were allies, he had taken for granted that both nations had consulted with each other. The fault lay with relations between the British Legation and Bland, Tang pointed out, and not with Mukden. Bland admitted that London and Tokyo were not in touch on the matter and that the British Minister to China had no idea that Japan would use the supplementary articles of the Treaty of Peking as the basis for protest.

Bland's anger represented less of a legitimate complaint against the Chinese than an admission of a decisive defeat administered by Japan. He had planned, together with Dr. George Morrison, Far Eastern correspondent of the London *Times,* to effect a political and economic reversal of British Far Eastern policy and had lost. They had depended on economic pressure to weaken and perhaps break the Anglo-Japanese alliance. Although the British Minister knew of the negotiations and his support had been counted on, Downing Street bowed to the demands of its ally. Even so, Morrison in London and Bland in China launched a propaganda campaign against the Japanese in the Far East and Europe, pointing out the danger to the open door that resulted from Japan's power in Manchuria. Throughout 1908 they tried to shake the position of the British government but failed.[35]

Straight watched and participated in the whole proceeding. He encouraged Bland to keep up the struggle and urged him to push the Chinese into a stronger resistance against Japanese claims. "For Heaven's sake," he exhorted Bland, "make 'em fight." He did what he could to assist by passing on material regarding the Manchurian railway situation to Rockhill, officials at the State Department, the German Consul at Mukden, and the Newchwang Chamber of Commerce.[36]

Irritated by the defeat which he saw early in 1908, Bland did not respond to his friend's encouraging words. "I fully agree that you have an interest as great as ours, if not greater," he wrote Straight, "and I also fully agree that if

this business goes 'phut' the door will be effectively closed."
But he refused to believe that Britain or the United States
would fight Japan to protect China. If the Chinese insist
"on going to political damnation, we must be prepared for
that event." [37]

Throughout the Hsinmintun-Fakumen negotiations,
Straight kept in touch with the State Department. He accepted Tang's interpretation of the circumstances that led
to the drafting of the secret protocols, believing that there
was no agreement in the supplementary articles to the Treaty
of Peking. It was another Japanese trick. Unfortunately for
Straight's belief in Tang, the Assistant Secretary of State,
Huntington Wilson, called Straight's attention to Article 3
of the secret protocols of the Komura Treaty, which Huntington Wilson, as American chargé in Tokyo, had sent to the
State Department.[38]

The Fakumen railway project never came to fruition
under British auspices. Slowly, pro-Japanese public opinion
pointed out the nature of the propaganda campaign conducted by the British interests, and in time, the British publicists who had attempted to reverse the pro-Japanese stand
of the London *Times* had a change of heart.[39]

The potential threat of the Fakumen line, with the certainty of its extension to Tsitsihar to form an inside short
line of communication in competition with the South Manchurian Railroad, was met vigorously and successfully by
the Japanese. Tokyo had exhibited a strong hand in Manchuria, and Straight, ever more concerned for American
interests, sought new ways to bring American influence to
bear on the Manchurian problem.[40]

NOTES

1. Griscom to Rockhill, July 15 and November 6, 1905, Rockhill Papers;
Griscom to Root, November 10, 1905, NA, Diplomatic Dispatches, Japan.

2. *Monthly Consular and Trade Reports* (Washington, 1880), Nos. 303–308 (December, 1905–May, 1906).

3. F. M. Huntington Wilson to the Secretary of State, Confidential, February 5, 1906, NA, Diplomatic Dispatches, Japan.

4. Root to Huntington Wilson, February 21 and March 24, 1906, Huntington Wilson to Root, March 15 and 28, 1906, *Papers Relating to the Foreign Relations of the United States, 1906–1913* (Washington, 1909–1920), *1906*, 170–171, 174.

5. Huntington Wilson to Root, April 5, 1906, Root to Japanese chargé d'affaires Aoki in Washington, April 13, 1906, and Bacon to Huntington Wilson, April 20, 1906, *Foreign Relations, 1906*, 177, 179, 182, 186.

6. Rockhill to Alfred Hippisley, March 29, 1906, Rockhill Papers.

7. J. F. Seamon, W. A. Rudy, and J. A. Thomas to Gilbert Reid, June 25, 1906, *Foreign Relations, 1906*, 211; *Journal of the American Asiatic Association*, 6 (August, 1906):194; James L. Rodgers to Rockhill, July 7, 1906, *Foreign Relations, 1906*, 209; Rockhill to Reid, July 16, 1906, NA, RG59:551/5; Rockhill to Hippisley, August 4, 1906, Rockhill Papers.

8. Huntington Wilson to Root, April 26, 1906, and Huntington Wilson's memorandum of July, 1906, in A. Vagts, *Deutschland und die Vereinigten Staaten in der Weltpolitik* (2 vols., New York, 1933), II, 1238, 1247–1248; Huntington Wilson to Root, January 12 and February 16 and 19, 1906, and Root to Huntington Wilson, January 21, 1906, NA, RG84: Peking Legation Archives.

9. Wright to Root, August 18, 1906, NA, RG59:221: "Japan and Manchuria," *Journal of the American Asiatic Association*, 6 (August, 1906):200–201; Fletcher to Root, October 6, 1906, NA, RG59:2321.

10. Straight to the Assistant Secretary of State, November 18, 1906, NA, RG84:Peking Legation Archives.

11. Rockhill to Root, January 12, 1907, *Foreign Relations, 1907*, 226; Straight to E. V. Morgan, January 23, 1907, Straight Papers.

12. Rockhill to Root, May 17, 1907, *Foreign Relations, 1907*, 131; Rockhill to Root, May 31, 1907, NA, RG59:7608/3.

13. Straight to the Assistant Secretary of State, February 12, 1907, NA, RG84:Mukden Consular Archives; Straight to the Assistant Secretary of State, May 22, 1907, NA, RG84:Peking Legation Archives.

14. Straight to the Assistant Secretary of State, June 19, 1907, NA, RG59:2321/12.

15. Straight to Huntington Wilson, May 24, 1907, Straight Papers; Straight to Rockhill, May 24, 1907, Rockhill Papers; Rockhill to Root, May 31, 1907, NA, RG59:4699/6.

16. Straight to Frank Fearon, December 28, 1906, NA, RG84: Mukden Consular Archives; Root to the Secretary of the Treasury, January 30, 1907, NA, RG59:3275/9.

17. Libby, McNeil and Libby to Fleming Cheshire (Straight's predecessor at Mukden), September 27, 1906, inquiring about markets for its products. This and similar inquiries are to be found in NA, RG84: Mukden Consular Archives.

18. Straight to Denby, December 3, 1907, Straight Papers.

19. Straight to Phillips, December 18, 1907, Straight Papers.

20. Fletcher to Root, January 17, 1908, NA, RG84: Peking Legation Archives.
21. Straight to Harriman, October 31, 1906, Straight Papers.
22. Straight to Harriman, November 15, 1906, Straight Papers.
23. Straight to Harriman, December 7 and 27, 1906, Straight Papers; Fletcher to Root, October 6, 1906, NA, RG59:2321; Straight to the Assistant Secretary of State, January 30 and February 6, 1907, NA, RG84: Peking Legation Archives; Percy Kent, *Railway Enterprise in China* (London, 1907),74.
24. Maurice Casenave, "Recollections of Willard Straight," Straight Papers; Straight to the Assistant Secretary of State, September 28, 1907, NA, RG59:2321/13–15; Straight to Harriman, October 7, 1907, Straight Papers.
25. Straight to Harriman, March 19, 1907, and Straight to E. V. Morgan, January 2, 1908, Straight Papers.
26. "Memorandum of Preliminary Agreement for the Financing, Organization, and Operation of the Manchurian Government Bank," n.d., typed copy in the Straight Papers.
27. Straight to Harriman, March 19, 1907, and Straight Diary, June 16, July 31, and August 2–6, 1907, Straight Papers.
28. Straight Diary, August 7, 1907, and Straight to Phillips, September 8, 1907, Straight Papers.
29. George Marvin's Diary, October 7, 1907, and Straight Diary, October 7, 1907, Straight Papers.
30. Straight to Harriman, October 17, 1907, Straight Papers.
31. Straight to Phillips, October 10, 1907, Straight Papers.
32. Straight to Huntington Wilson, January 31, 1908, and Straight Diary, September 3, 1907, Straight Papers; Marvin to Bacon, November 7, 1907, Marvin Papers.
33. Straight Diary, November 7, 1907, and George Marvin, "Recollections of Willard Straight," Straight Papers.
34. Marvin Diary, November 8, 1907, and Straight to Schoelkopf, March 22, 1908, Straight Papers.
35. Straight to the Assistant Secretary of State, November 9, 1907, NA, RG59:6625/35; Straight to Phillips, December 18, 1907, Straight Papers; Fletcher to Root, January 29, 1908, NA, RG59:3767/16; Marvin to Bacon, November 7, 1907, Marvin Papers; Grey to MacDonald, February 1 and March 3, 1908, *British Documents on the Origins of the War, 1898–1914,* ed. G. P. Gooch and Harold Temperley (15 vols., London, 1932), VIII, 453–454; ffrench to Straight, February 18, 1908, Straight Papers.
36. Straight to J. O. P. Bland, February 6 and 16, 1908, Bland to Straight, December 27, 1907, and Straight to Huntington Wilson, January 31, 1908, Straight Papers; Straight to the Assistant Secretary of State, March 4 and April 1, 1908, NA, RG59:6625/48–49, 55–56; Straight to ffrench, March 8, 1908, and Straight to Schoelkopf, March 23, 1908, Straight Papers.
37. Bland to Straight, February 1, 1908, Straight Papers.
38. Straight to Huntington Wilson, January 31, 1908, Straight Papers;

Fletcher to Root, January 24, 1908, NA, RG59:5767; Straight to the Assistant Secretary of State, February 12 and January 4, 1908, NA, RG59:6625/40, 41–45; Carr to Straight, February 21, 1908, NA, RG59:6625/40.

39. George Bronson Rea, "The Fakumen Railway Question," *Far Eastern Review,* 5 (May, 1909):419. Rea was strongly pro-Japanese. Also *Far Eastern Review,* 2 (February, 1909):297. O'Brien to Root, January 6, 1909, NA, RG59:7611/7; O'Brien to Knox, June 23, 1909, NA, RG59:5767/46–47; Fletcher to Knox, July 29, 1909, NA, RG59:5315/420; Edward T. Williams, "Recollections of Willard Straight," n.d., Straight Papers.

40. Straight to Phillips, February 28, 1908, Straight Papers.

CHAPTER FOUR

Two Missions to Washington

The rumbles of discontent emanating from Manchuria were muffled in 1907 by the roar of American opposition to Japanese immigration. Racial prejudice, corrupt municipal politics, and a desire for cheap labor—all had played an important part in the history of American-Japanese relations. Straight and his friends complained of the Japanese in Manchuria, while President Roosevelt and Secretary Root grappled with the problem of the Japanese in the United States.

For a naval-minded President the controversy with Japan did have its compensations. It permitted Roosevelt to warn of war, strengthen the navy, and prepare for the defense of America's "Achilles heel," the Philippine Islands. "Thank heaven we have the navy in good shape," he exclaimed.[1] By the summer of 1907, his administration had mapped out plans for the defense of Subig Bay and the transfer of the fleet from the Atlantic to the Pacific Ocean.

Despite these preparations, Roosevelt did not want war. In August, 1907, Root, the President's chief adviser, Taft, Roosevelt's special messenger, and George Meyer, Postmaster General and interested onlooker, met with the President at Oyster Bay to discuss measures for pacifying Tokyo without losing face in Washington. Roosevelt had previously decided to send the fleet on a world cruise to demonstrate

American naval might, and the council decided that Taft, who was to leave shortly for the opening of the Philippine Congress, should visit Tokyo and present Japan with an opportunity to open discussions of the issues affecting both nations. These decisions reflected Root's recommendation that the United States show Japan a "courteous but firm attitude," though he and Taft tended to minimize the importance of the mission. Roosevelt insisted that the Secretary of War make the trip, and once again, the faithful Taft went across the Pacific.[2]

Accustomed by now to the visits of important Americans, the Japanese gave Taft a triumphant welcome. In Tokyo, he learned that Japan had no desire for war and was financially incapable of supporting a struggle against the United States. He confirmed earlier reports of Japan's ambitions in China, the fulfillment of which required most of the Island Empire's available funds. Shaken in the past by the onslaught of the powers, China turned to the United States, Taft wrote, "as the only country that is really unselfish in the matter of obtaining territory and monopolies."[3] It was a significant comment.

Taft's reference to China in his report to Washington was due in large measure to the influence of Thomas F. Millard, Far Eastern representative of the *New York Herald*. A drama critic turned foreign correspondent, outspoken in defense of the United States, and strongly anti-Japanese, Millard warmed Taft's sympathy for China and the situation of American economic interests in the country. He pointed to Manchuria as the Chinese trouble spot, telling Taft "privately" what he had already written. "Business interests in China firmly believe that Japan and Russia intend to retain Manchuria." The empire will be carved up by the other powers, "among which the United States will not be included." The consequences for American trade were obvious, but what was Taft to do? Millard suggested that the

Secretary promise Americans resident in China that "we are in the game in earnest, and to stay the limit, to go ahead with redoubled energy." [4] Impressed by Millard's analysis, Taft followed his informant's advice.

He went before an audience of cheering American merchants in Shanghai and delivered a speech redolent with platitudes but sharpened by a promise. Taft made it quite clear that the American stake in China was large enough to justify the employment of "every legitimate means to protect it against diminution or injury by the political preference of any of its competitors." In the future there need be no complaint of "seeming government indifference" to American trade interests in China. Applause flowed out from the ranks of the American colony to the Secretary of War, who, rumor had it, was to succeed Theodore Roosevelt in the Presidency in 1909.

Following Taft to the platform, Millard drove the point home quickly. He warned against a future shrinkage of the American market and proclaimed that it was the task of "statesmanship" to look ahead and discover new outlets for American products. Of course, government could not create trade where none had existed before, but, he said, it "can always pave the way for trade." Millard candidly admitted that there was no "altruistic motive" underlying American Far Eastern expansion, but neither was there the need to carry out commercial relations in anything but a "spirit of friendly reciprocity." [5] These Shanghai declarations were not official statements of policy, but they heartened Straight in Mukden. Millard had directed Taft's gaze northward from China to Manchuria; Straight looked south from Manchuria to China proper. Viewing Manchuria as both an end and a means, he listened to suggestions from others and developed some ideas of his own.

Two days after Millard had briefed Taft, Straight imparted to Washington his views on the importance of creating an exclusive American interest north of the Great Wall. Manchuria's officials welcomed investment in banks, railways, and mines, and if Americans accepted the invitation, Japan's grip might be loosened and Manchuria saved. Then Straight's imagination soared. From Manchuria "as a starting point," he wrote, "the United States might extend its influence and activity to other portions of the Empire." [6] He had already communicated this broader conception of the American role in China to Phillips and Harriman. It was operative in his thinking, and in Straight's case, his thoughts fired his desire for action.

He listened carefully to Maurice Casenave, a former French diplomatic official in China and now, in 1907, working for the Banque de l'Indo-Chine. Casenave had joined in the northward trek with Bland when he learned that the Manchurian administration sought funds. Cognizant of China's weakness and experienced in Far Eastern diplomacy, he wanted to prevent a loan to China that would be based on either a Japanese guarantee in South Manchuria or a Russian guarantee in North Manchuria. A true open door diplomat-financier, Casenave reasoned that in either event all other foreign financial activity would be smothered. He believed that the sensible alternative would be the flotation of an international loan, issued in the financial markets of Europe and the United States. The fundamental problem was to circumvent the antagonisms created by the European treaty system and change the mental attitude of the governments. In this way all nations could participate in a financial combination and avoid the danger of treading on sensitive Russian and Japanese toes. [7]

Straight was interested in Casenave's ideas, for Casenave and Bland welcomed American cooperation in Manchuria. They deprecated the Franco-Japanese and Anglo-Japanese agreements, claiming that certain French and British moneyed groups no longer desired to bolster Japan's industrial

penetration of Manchuria. Bland had convinced Straight of
this during the Hsinmintun-Fakumen negotiations but failed
to block Tokyo when Downing Street refused to back him.
Casenave's own employer, the Banque de l'Indo-Chine, rejected his proposals. But it was heady talk of big things and
Straight was influenced, despite his realization that much of
the antagonism toward Japan arose from personal and business prejudice. Japan was Straight's *bête-noir,* and later,
when Casenave's internationalism prompted his suggestion
that Japan be included in a Manchurian loan and excluded
from "other things," Straight drew the line. "I heartily dis-
approve," he set down in his diary.[8]

The excitement occasioned by Taft's declaration in Shanghai scarcely had died down when Straight learned that Taft
was on the way to Europe via Vladivostok and the Trans-
Siberian Railroad. Straight was determined to drop the Manchurian problem in the lap of the administration in Washington and to urge that the road to China began in Mukden.
A favorable exchange of correspondence with Taft for a
meeting at Vladivostok encouraged the Consul General to
wire the State Department for permission to go ahead. Washington consented, and after three days of work, Straight and
his staff drew up a memorandum analyzing conditions in
Manchuria.[9]

At Vladivostok and on the train trip to Harbin, Straight
delivered a withering indictment, consisting of twenty-one
separate charges, condemning Japan's policy in Manchuria.
Admittedly, Japan was preferable to Russia as a tenant in
Manchuria, he stated, but Tokyo's tactics virtually shut the
open door. Japan's recent pacts with Russia and France had
frightened China. Peking now saw the empire becoming
another Korea and desperately sought financial aid that
would carry with it a strong measure of diplomatic support
to offset Japan. Here was an opportunity for the United
States, and Straight took his cue from Taft's Shanghai state-

ment. Any "concrete expression of our professed interest would be appreciated," he asserted, and if given to China, American trade and influence in the Pacific "should be vastly augmented."

What form should this "concrete expression" of interest take? Straight's answer might have come from either Bland or Casenave. He recommended a loan to China by Anglo-American bankers or an international loan that included France as well as Great Britain and the United States. In any case, he pointed out, American funds would play a part.[10] Taft displayed no enthusiasm for international loans to China, but Straight had promised Casenave to mention it to the Secretary, and he fulfilled his obligation. But Straight had another idea, one that was more in line with his yearnings for the increase of American influence in Manchuria.

Early in 1907, it became apparent that the American share of the indemnity levied on China as a result of the Boxer Rebellion was excessive. Rockhill, who had served as American Commissioner in the indemnity negotiations, had discussed with John Hay the possibility of using any remitted funds for the education of Chinese students in the United States. After an inquiry, Washington reduced its claim and made plans to remit the excess sum to China.[11] Root picked up Rockhill's education project and instructed him to sound out the Chinese.

The United States, in June, 1907, decided to remit all funds in excess of approximately eleven and a half million dollars. Recalling the avaricious behavior of the powers at the Boxer settlement conferences, Rockhill hoped to use the American remission as a control over China and the powers that claimed indemnity charges. Formulating the intention of the remission as a benevolent act, Rockhill wanted to "exercise a beneficial and restraining influence both on China and the beneficiary power," an interesting illustration of Rockhill's conception of himself as China's mentor.

Washington had other views. William Phillips, Chief of the Division of Far Eastern Affairs, read Rockhill's account of the remission to mean that it "would insure us a preponderating influence in the Empire." Huntington Wilson, seeing the diplomatic possibilities, commented that the remission "should be used to make China do some of the things we want. Otherwise I fear her gratitude will be quite empty." [12] The remission was not intended as an act of charity; diplomacy demanded levers to help manipulate policy.

At his post in Mukden, Straight realized this, too. Through his close relationship with Tang Shao-yi, he kept in touch with the remission negotiations. Tang, responsible to Peking for China's retention of its hegemony in Manchuria, suggested using the remitted funds as security for a Manchurian loan. Intent on facilitating the entrance of American capital into Manchuria, Straight broached the subject to Taft at Vladivostok. After listening to Straight's exposition of Manchurian financial requirements, the Secretary observed that the "first move" for an American loan based on the remission had to come from China.[13]

Straight hurried back to Mukden with the news. Obsessed with his Manchurian plans, the Consul General overrated the impression that he had made on Taft at Vladivostok. He was certain that Taft would advise Roosevelt and Root to "regard Manchuria as a fair field," but he cautioned Tang that the United States did not wish to be accused of dictating the purpose for which the borrowed funds were to be used.[14] Having cleared himself officially in Mukden and Washington of any suspicion of unauthorized interference, he suggested the appointment of an American to supervise the employment of the money and privately asked Phillips for the State Department's serious consideration of the proposition.[15]

Straight's enthusiastic support of the indemnity and loan scheme caused trouble for him with the State Department.

His relations with Rockhill had been strained, and the indemnity question made them worse. When Rockhill went to the United States late in 1907 to confer with Root, Straight hoped that the Minister would not return to China. Rockhill's arrival in Washington coincided with a letter Straight had written to Taft relating his talks with Tang. Taft dutifully forwarded Straight's message to Root, who, together with Rockhill, had "practically agreed on the method" of handling the indemnity remission. On orders from the Secretary of State, the Chief of the Consular Bureau reprimanded Straight and ordered him to keep out of the negotiations. Straight denied that he had overstepped his position, but the reprimand temporarily restrained his activity. He still disagreed fundamentally with Rockhill's approach, asserting that the Chinese "would rather strengthen their country a bit before distributing dynamics and moral philosophy in prize packages." Rockhill, however, had Root's backing, and when Straight heard that Rockhill was returning to China, he was glum over the prospect.[16]

During Rockhill's absence, Tang went to Peking to argue the case for Manchuria with imperial officials and won them over to his scheme. Impressed by this show of Chinese determination, Straight attempted to create a favorable atmosphere at the American Legation by passing word on to chargé Fletcher that Taft had promised "he'd try and do something" if China made the first overture. Thus, when Rockhill returned to Peking in April, 1908, Tang, with the support of the Chinese Foreign Office and Straight's unofficial approval, was ready for him.

The Manchurian Governor accepted Rockhill's education aims but differed with him on the means of financing the program. The Governor wanted an American loan secured by the indemnity remission which would create a Manchurian Bank. The bank's earnings would be used in turn to send Chinese to the United States. Rockhill turned a deaf ear to the idea on the grounds that such a loan was premature and not available in the United States.[17]

Congress authorized the remission of the indemnity in May, 1908. Hoping to circumvent Rockhill's objections, Chinese officials stalled the American Minister. They requested the transmission of official notes to China announcing the indemnity remission; they attempted to water down China's obligation to employ the funds for education of Chinese students in the United States; and they contested the wording of the notes, claiming that it appeared as if the educational mission did not come of China's volition. Experienced in Chinese diplomatic tactics, Rockhill remained adamant and threatened to hold back the remission until China completed payment of this scaled-down amount of the indemnity. Throughout the discussions, the American Minister resisted China's efforts to float an American loan with the remission as security.[18]

As a financial and diplomatic contrivance, the indemnity remission scheme had an essential meaning for the solution of the Manchurian problem in China as defined by Straight and Tang. The latter saw China hemmed in by the series of treaties and agreements among the powers. Straight perceived the same bleak vista, particularly where Japan was concerned; but he had the added problem of installing a substantial economic interest in Manchuria that would conform to his ideal of the American role in China. The indemnity question was a means for reversing the trend of affairs in Manchuria and China; but as an isolated instrument, it was too brittle. More tools were necessary and Straight put them to use.

Straight chafed at the general ignorance of Far Eastern matters exhibited in the channels of public opinion. He insisted that most of the news issued from the Far East was Japanese propaganda, and he sought a way to expose Japanese policy in Manchuria. Straight broached the idea of a subsidized Chinese newspaper to his assistant, George Marvin, in August, 1907. Marvin, a few years older than Straight, had entered the Consular Service earlier in the year. Formerly an instructor of history at Groton, he struck up an acquaintance with President Roosevelt, whose sons he had educated in history and literature. Impressed with Marvin's abilities, Roosevelt suggested that he come to Washington if he felt the need for other activity. Facing the dreary prospect of reading history at Oxford during his sabbatical year but actually desiring some adventure, Marvin accepted the President's invitation. He quickly gained admittance to Bacon's office where the Assistant Secretary had just learned of the accidental death of Straight's assistant, Nelson Fairchild. Bacon offered the job to Marvin, who accepted immediately, and the schoolmaster exchanged history at Oxford for diplomacy at Mukden.[19]

Marvin and Straight talked over the peculiarities of news regarding China. Marvin believed that such information had to be "properly treated" in order to give China a hearing in the press as well as disseminate information "about a part of the world which ought to be full of American possibilities in the future both of trade and influence." [20] At Vladivostok, during his visit with Taft, Straight approached Martin Egan, an old newspaper acquaintance. Egan listened to the proposal for publicizing China's case but rejected Straight's invitation to take the job.

Back in Mukden, Straight explained China's need for publicity to Tang and suggested Marvin as a likely candidate. Tang agreed. Marvin cabled the State Department for permission to resign, "so phrasing the cable as to imply the significance of the move." Root, apparently puzzled, requested an explanation, and Straight sent details of the publicity campaign to the Department. With full knowledge of what was planned, Root agreed to Marvin's resignation, with "good wishes for a prosperous career." This reply convinced Marvin that the State Department approved of "the big plan." [21]

In Washington, Huntington Wilson soon heard of the project that revealed Straight's conception of Manchuria's relationship to China. If Marvin's publicity work successfully presented China's case against Japan and stimulated American investment in Manchuria, Straight felt that Tokyo's hands would be tied. China's distrust of the other powers put the United States in an advantageous position. Marvin's work would demonstrate American friendship for China and give the United States great influence in helping China repurchase all foreign built railroads throughout the empire. Straight conceded that he might be "over-sanguine," but he felt that once the United States was established in Manchuria, American commercial influence would spread in China.

Marvin signed a contract with Tang in January, 1908, and immediately commenced operations. "Bully for him, bully for the White Man's burden," Bland exulted, when he learned of the arrangement.[22] Given access to the files of the American Legation at Peking, the Consulate at Mukden, and the Chinese Foreign Office, Marvin traveled in China, Japan, Korea, and the Philippines, making contacts, handing out information on Japanese activity in Manchuria, and keeping in touch with Straight at Mukden. He succeeded in reaching influential organs of public opinion in the United States, Europe, and the Far East, feeding information to the Associated Press correspondent, Frederick McCormick, the New York and Paris editions of the *Herald* through Millard, the London *Times* through Bland and Morrison; and Casenave saw to it that *Le Temps* in Paris carried the anti-Japanese line. Straight kept the Department informed of Marvin's progress and told friendly foreign diplomats in Mukden about the scheme.[23]

The Japanese knew what Marvin was doing. Washington's approval turned to doubt as the immigration crisis with Tokyo deepened. Huntington Wilson insisted that Marvin move out of the American Consulate in Mukden, and he went to Peking. Rockhill, one step behind Straight, feared that China would reap the benefit from Marvin's former status as an American official, but Straight argued that dissociation strengthened China, provided he kept furnishing material for Marvin's pen. But it was no use.

A minor clash between Straight and Japanese officials in Mukden was written up by Marvin, with material furnished by Straight, to demonstrate Japanese aggressiveness. The incident was magnified by the taut relations between Tokyo and Washington, and Straight backtracked. He scolded Marvin for overplaying his hand and advised him to "state facts, draw conclusions, but never bring in the official sources from which you get your information." [24]

Opposition to the publicity campaign mounted in Washington and at the American Legation in Peking. Rockhill objected to it, and a Japanese protest moved Bacon to request Marvin to halt operations. Marvin complied, and Washington, grateful for his cooperation, offered him a better position in the Diplomatic Service if he cared to return. [25] Marvin preferred to wait for developments in China. Soon Straight and Tang made another move.

Tang had taken on considerable responsibility. The empire's officials slowly fell into line with his appeals for a substantial opposition to Japan in Manchuria and permitted him to seek the indemnity remission as security for a loan. As he haggled with Rockhill, he suggested sending a special envoy to Washington for the overt purpose of expressing China's appreciation for the remission gesture. [26] Actually Tang hoped to secure American diplomatic assistance to ward off Japan. The proposal was related to talks carried on by President Roosevelt and the German Ambassador in

Washington late in 1907 and the early part of 1908. The President feared a probable dismemberment of China by the powers who had negotiated the series of agreements that effectively gave Japan a superior position in the Far East, particularly in Manchuria. Prodded by its fear of diplomatic isolation which had been engineered by the Anglo-French bloc, Germany suggested an American-German-Chinese combination with Russian support. The Chinese had no expectation of a written arrangement, Rockhill reported, but they sought "an exchange of views which would have the most important results in the direction sought." Intent on putting through the indemnity remission, the Minister hoped that "some such assurance would gladly be given the special ambassador." [27]

In July, 1908, the imperial government chose Tang as its special envoy to the United States, and he appointed George Marvin as his representative to clear the way in Washington, make important contacts, and find suitable quarters for the members of the mission. Heedful of Tang's intention to secure a loan for the Manchurian Bank, Rockhill alerted Washington. The American Minister deplored China's loan history, pointing out that the Chinese knew very little of financial matters, overestimated their credit rating, and lived from day to day by virtue of unsafe financial expedients. Money lent to China, he cautioned, required strict foreign control to prevent bankruptcy. The educational plan was "an infinitely more valuable return for the money than the wild cat schemes it would be employed in by the Manchurian Bank." [28]

In Washington, Phillips sided with Rockhill. He wanted to publicize the exchange of notes between the United States and China relating to the establishment of the educational mission in order to head off Tang when he arrived seeking a loan. He also tried to comfort Rockhill. "Everyone is absolutely in sympathy with your idea," Phillips informed the

Minister.[29] The Division of Far Eastern Affairs, however, underrated Straight's determination to move American capital into Manchuria. The disappointment caused by Harriman's rejection of the Manchurian loan of August, 1907, did not balk the Consul General, for he continued to write to the American millionaire.

Straight kept Manchurian affairs fresh in Harriman's mind, pointing out China's clever tactics in bidding for British support through the Hsinmintun-Fakumen railroad attempt. The Chinese did not trust non-American capital in Manchuria, and Straight enticed Harriman with hints that Tang was prepared to offer very attractive conditions. He assured Harriman that Washington did not know all of the angles involved in Tang's planning for a Manchurian Bank. "The general outline of the scheme," he wrote, "has been laid before the Department of State but except in telegraphing and forwarding a letter to you through Phillips, your name has not been mentioned and in this one instance only in the most general way." [30]

Straight elaborated on the potentialities of a Manchurian Bank, which could act as the provincial administration's fiscal agent in charge of lending operations and general development. He coupled railway extension and construction in China proper with the bank's operations in Manchuria, pointing out that the Chinese Board of Communications in Peking expected to issue uniform notes, requiring redemption by the Manchurian Bank, thus giving it a hold on transportation throughout the empire. Harriman would be the agent for fulfilling this great enterprise.

> The prospect of directing the railways of a nation may appeal to you. It would, of course, be impossible to assure you that by undertaking the organization of the Manchurian Bank, you would be certain to be entrusted with the larger enterprise. Yet, although there would be many obstacles to be overcome, I personally believe that such would be the case. . . .
> In submitting the proposal for the Manchurian Bank I have

felt sure that the future of such an institution under American management would be intimately identified with the development, not of Manchuria alone, but of all China. Such, however, are only my personal convictions. I have endeavored, therefore, to lay before you a definite plan, trusting that by suggesting the possibilities thereof you yourself might appreciate their magnitude and care to interest yourself therein.[31]

Straight spilled over with ideas of Manchurian opportunities. He confided to his close friend, Fletcher, that Tang was "very keen" on getting money in the United States and that "although we've just had this turn up in Wall Street there may be something doing." Participation in the Manchurian Bank led directly to activity in Chinese railway centralization, Straight added, for Tang was certain that "the people interested therein might get their fingers into the Board of Communications Bank, and then if the President of the Board was intelligent, with him direct national railway enterprise." [32]

Brought to a high pitch of enthusiasm by the knowledge of what a combination of Tang and Harriman might mean in Manchuria and China proper, Straight's optimism sagged as no answer came from Harriman. Straight judged that the Chinese knew that American friendship was not dependent upon financial interests in the Empire, but he was despondent that no private funds were available to deepen the friendship.

In the interim, after Straight's adventure with the Japanese in Mukden, the State Department had sent him on a trip through Manchuria to check on Russian and Japanese activity and to examine trade prospects. His itinerary included stops at possible railway centers and followed the route planned for the ill-fated Hsinmintun-Fakumen railroad. Tired, discouraged, and believing that Washington would soon move him out of Manchuria, Straight witnessed the situation in Chien-tao, where the Chinese and the Japanese were quarreling over the boundary between Korea and

China. He accused Japan of territorial aggression masked by the pretext of protecting the Koreans. Ignoring the American Legation in Peking, he hurriedly sent a wire to Washington that warned of the imminence of an armed conflict in Chien-tao. The wording of Straight's message made it appear that China requested American intervention. Vexed with the Consul's behavior, the Legation corrected the erroneous impression and then reprimanded him for acting on his own.[33]

Just as Peking began to rebuke Straight, Harriman decided to act. Straight received orders to break his trip and report personally on conditions in his locality. The railroad magnate had asked Root to recall Straight for consultations regarding American investment opportunities in Manchuria. The slump of 1907 had passed, and conditions were improved. "Wall Street," Phillips reported to Rockhill, "is feeling confident again and is looking for the investment of capital in foreign lands. It has turned to Manchuria and wants the latest advice on the situation up there, probably, I assume, in the nature of Railways, or the exploitation of the country through the central Manchurian Bank scheme." [34]

Before his departure, Straight talked matters over with Tang, who soon expected to leave for the United States. Straight induced Tang to make a substantial offer to American financial interests, cautioning him that "our people are first of all business men" who insist that any financial deal "be placed before them in as definite a form as possible." [35] The night before Straight left Mukden, he signed a memorandum with Tang "along the lines of our previous discussion." The agreement provided for a loan of twenty million dollars for the creation of a bank that would be the fiscal agent of the Manchurian administration. The remitted indemnity and a Chinese imperial guarantee secured the loan. Several tentative projects were outlined, among them being the purchase of the Chinese Eastern Railway from Russia and the construction of a railroad from Tsitsihar to Aigun. Straight's hopes for prominent American participation were rewarded with the provision that the Manchurian administration and the American lenders were to administer the enterprise jointly. Shortly afterward, Tang signed an agreement with Lord ffrench for the construction by Pauling of a road from Chinchow to Tsitsihar, thus effectively duplicating the technique he had used earlier in the Hsinmintun-Fakumen railway negotiations.

With the signed document tied around his neck in a wallet, Straight, accompanied by Bland and Marvin, left for the United States via Siberia and Europe. Arriving home in September, 1908, Straight rushed to tell the good news to Huntington Wilson, who was "delighted by this first success and the future possibilities it held." [36] Both men quickly went into action, renting a house for Tang and beginning preparatory talks with American officials. At the Division of Far Eastern Affairs, Straight saw Phillips, whose sympathy with Rockhill's opposition to a loan for a Manchurian Bank had withered in the face of the powerful influence behind Straight. Straight's recall indicated that "American interests in the Far East were going to assume a pretty definite shape," and Phillips sent Straight to see Harriman. Fletcher, home on leave at the time, tried to present Rockhill's position to Bacon, but "Straight and Marvin were running in and out all the time," [37] and had the field to themselves.

Straight did not divulge the Tang memorandum to Harriman until he received State Department clearance. Bacon, who was Acting Secretary in Root's absence, permitted Straight to "show Harriman his document and speak ahead with him or any other businessmen about the advisability of trade relations and proposed schemes. I have told Harriman that I would do all I could to be of assistance to him." [38]

When Phillips left on a trip to Central America, Straight replaced him as Chief of the Division of Far Eastern Affairs, a post from which he directed the strategy and tactics of linking Mukden and Peking to New York and Washington.

Marvin had a difficult time as he made the rounds of Washington officialdom. Rockhill's opposition to Tang placed Root and Roosevelt on their guard. The immigration question had caused the President and the Secretary of State considerable distress. Long and tedious negotiations with the Japanese, together with the stubbornness of the California legislature and the San Francisco School Board, made the President irritable and touchy. He was in no mood to start trouble with Japan over Manchuria. As for China, Roosevelt had flirted late in 1907 with Germany's overtures for a possible working arrangement with China. In March, 1908, the Chinese still deliberated, and Roosevelt made no move, waiting for Peking to exercise the initiative. By April, he showed his impatience at the slow pace of the Chinese, and in June, Washington and Berlin decided not to back Peking.[39] Unaware of these developments, Marvin absorbed the blows intended for Tang as he walked into a nest of opposition.

He presented Tang's case to Acting Secretary of State Bacon, outlining China's difficulties with Japan and pointing up the need for American capital in Manchuria to reinforce the weak Chinese hold on the area. Bacon was exasperated over China's "moluscous inability" to maintain control. The American position in Manchuria was thin, the Acting Secretary complained; for despite the theory of the open door, few Americans took advantage of it. Washington welcomed "a more tangible position," and Bacon promised to "keep an open and hospitable attitude for Mr. Tang," though he warned that any diplomatic alliance was out of the question.[40]

Marvin then walked head-on into President Roosevelt, whose attitude "seemed a little hostile" to the Tang mission. "What is the real purpose of this Embassy you represent?" he asked. Marvin's explanations to the President were not convincing, and Roosevelt turned the matter over to Root with the injunction that "the people would not entertain the thought of a war with Japan over any Manchuria aggression, and that we were in no position to have a bluff called." He had "never bluffed in his life," Roosevelt said, and "didn't believe in bluffing." Marvin's persistence kept him in full pursuit of the administration despite the fact that the President reiterated to him on another occasion the "conservative position regarding the China question." Roosevelt, Root, and Bacon "seemed a little chary of the Embassy undertaking," and they had good reasons for their reluctance.[41]

Japan learned of Tang's mission and warned him against stirring up any trouble in Washington, but he was already en route to the United States. Determined to block a Sino-American agreement, Tokyo revealed a diplomatic weapon that it held in readiness for such an eventuality. In the fall of 1907, the Japanese Ambassador in Washington, Aoki, suggested that the United States and Japan come to agreement on Far Eastern matters. Aoki had emphasized the problems of Pacific shipping, respect for territorial rights, the maintenance of the *status quo* in the Far East, and the preservation of the open door and the territorial integrity of China; but Japan withdrew the overture.

Now confronted by danger, Japan renewed Aoki's earlier offer. Ambassador Takahira approached Root, after seeing President Roosevelt, in late October, 1908, and handed the American Secretary a note similar to the one Aoki had composed a year earlier. The Japanese draft omitted the phrase, "territorial integrity and administrative entity of China," and significantly stressed the maintenance of the *status quo*. In his capacity as Chief of the Division of Far Eastern Affairs, Straight argued against the omission on the grounds that it left China helpless against Japanese aggrandizement. He also pointed out the danger of the *status quo* provision, claiming that it validated the agreements between Japan and the powers that gave the Japanese supremacy in Manchuria. Root, who felt that Japan had more rights and interests to protect in Manchuria than had the United States, agreed with Straight's objections to the extent of persuading Takahira to substitute the phrase "independence and integrity of China." In this way, Root believed he had "negatived the special interest of Japan in China." [42]

Straight protested that the agreement was a "terrible diplomatic blunder to be laid to the door of T. R." In effect, one basic aim of Tang's trip to the United States, that of coming to some diplomatic arrangement with the United States for the protection of China's territorial dependencies, had gone for naught.[43] When Tang arrived in Washington on November 30, 1908, the Root-Takahira agreement was ready for signature.

Unable to change the decision of their superiors, Straight and Huntington Wilson managed to have signature of the agreement deferred until Tang arrived in Washington and was apprised of the situation. But the news rocked Peking. Yuan Shih-Kai, Chief of the Foreign Office, showed "considerable disappointment and some irritation." Influenced by Tang, Yuan had hoped for diplomatic support against Tokyo. To add to his troubles, the Empress Dowager, his principal backer, was dead, and he now faced the enmity of a strong pro-Japanese clique, as well as the new Emperor and the Prince Regent, who both hated him.[44] Yuan asked Rockhill if China's objections would halt the official exchange of notes between the United States and Japan. The American Minister had to admit that Washington had no intention of consulting Peking in a matter dealing largely with China's interest. Ironically, Yuan commented that the preservation of the *status quo* in China would have been more effectively accomplished if the United States had waited for Tang to make his case.

Rockhill floundered in a sea of diplomatic formalism. He

told Yuan that Tang's mission did not alter Root's view of
Japan. Since the stated aim of Tang's mission was only to
thank the President for the remission of the indemnity, no
agreement between China and the United States had been
officially possible. The American Minister admitted that it
was common knowledge that Tang sought some kind of diplomatic arrangement with the United States, but in his re-
buttal, he tried to make capital of the fact that Yuan publicly
had denied such a purpose.

As American representative of the United States in China,
Rockhill was forced to gloss over the fact that the United
States and Japan had made an agreement, largely concerning China, without China's consent and after only brief consultation of China's emissary a few hours before the notes
were signed. Roosevelt's letter to the Kaiser confirmed American reluctance to negotiate with the Chinese. "The Chinese
are so helpless to carry out any fixed policy, whether home
or foreign, that it is difficult to have any but the most cautious
dealings with them." [45] Official Washington had chosen
Tokyo, not Peking.

Peking's failure to get a diplomatic hearing in Washington helped rather than hindered Straight's efforts to obtain
American funds for China. As a government official, Straight
failed to prevent the Root-Takahira agreement with Japan;
but as a government official called home for consultation
with a private economic interest, Straight succeeded in fas-
tening Harriman's influence on American policy in China.

Straight, with Huntington Wilson's assistance, first paid
attention to China's general loan needs in a memorandum
dealing with the confused and deteriorating trade picture in
China. As China's envoy, Tang was charged with the task
of borrowing money to finance a program of financial reform and the abolition of restrictive trade taxation. Straight
thought it "reasonable to suppose" that the Chinese would
float such a loan through American as well as British, French,

and German banks, and Huntington Wilson urged Root to confer with Tang, who was worried about the effects of the Root-Takahira agreement on his plans.[46]

The proposal for a general loan struck a responsive chord in the State Department, for it coincided with the aims of the commercial trade treaty signed by the United States and China in October, 1903, and the Anglo-Chinese Treaty of 1902. Root met with Tang and learned that China wanted to abolish likin (the internal trade tax that had bothered Washington in 1906–07), increase its tariff, revise mining codes, and set up a currency system on a gold basis. Tang placed China's needs at "two or three hundred million," which, if added to the revenue accruing from a higher tariff, would help accomplish the reforms.[47]

Root favored such a loan. Here was a matter that rested on a treaty and which conformed to established American policy in China. The Secretary of State, however, was careful in his instructions to Straight.

> As for the negotiation of a loan, whether in the United States or in Europe, which has been mentioned as a necessary condition precedent to the carrying out of the treaty provisions above referred to, the State Department has no wish or authority to involve the United States in any obligation either legal or moral with reference to such a loan. Keeping in mind and scrupulously regarding this fact I wish you to render to Mr. Tang unofficially all proper assistance by way of facilitating him in meeting such representatives of American finance and commerce as he may wish to meet for the prosecution of his mission. And to any person whom Mr. Tang may desire to have informed of the views of the Department you are at liberty to exhibit this letter.[48]

Root explained his action as a precautionary measure taken against the possibility of adverse criticism. He thought it "better to have Straight acting under express instructions which will furnish a justification for anything that he may do in assisting Mr. Tang," he informed the President, "rather than leave it open for evil minded persons to suspect that there is something surreptitious." Roosevelt gave his approval.[49]

Straight, who had other loan projects in mind, followed orders. He introduced Tang's loan plan to Harriman, "who was keenly interested in the project and was prepared to take up the matter when it assumed more definite form." Having previously received Bacon's permission to show Harriman the Manchurian Bank memorandum, Root's instructions permitted Straight to bring Tang's schemes for Manchuria closer to Harriman and Schiff without risking the charge that he had overstepped his authority. The boundary between official public policy and officially supported private interest was difficult to maintain.

Soon after receiving permission to show Harriman the Tang memorandum, the railway king referred Straight to his banking associates, Kuhn, Loeb and Company. Otto Kahn, Schiff's partner, reacted so favorably to the Manchurian Bank project that Straight cabled Tang "that matters were progressing satisfactorily" and "the loan could be arranged." [50]

Undaunted by the Root-Takahira agreement, Tang had an interview later with Root regarding loan matters. The Secretary of State repeated his and Rockhill's insistence on the establishment of a definite relationship between the released indemnity funds and the educational mission in order that Washington "could help China protect the revenues against the aggression or demands of any other country." With this as an opening, Tang inquired whether China might use the interest of the remitted funds to finance the educational mission, while another portion of the remitted funds could be used for the security of a loan. Root's reply was characteristic. "I said nothing following this explanation," he stated, "either of objection or to approval, but I think it would have been fair for him to infer from my silence and

passing to other subjects that I had no objection to make."
Straight interpreted this to mean that the government approved of a Manchurian loan based on a portion of the remitted funds, thus partly overthrowing Rockhill's objections.[51] The way seemed clear for Kuhn, Loeb and Company
to take up the Manchurian Bank loan, but the National City
Bank of New York raised a momentary threat. A. Wendell
Jackson, a mining promoter with properties in Manchuria,
approached Tang in Tokyo and offered to buy the returned
Boxer indemnity bonds from China. The envoy was not
ready to negotiate at that time and suggested that Jackson
meet him in Washington after he had received the bonds from
the American government. Tang, however, indicated that
he favored Jackson's offer because of Jackson's mining investments in Manchuria.

Jackson went to London, Paris, and New York after his
talk with Tang and formed a banking syndicate, led by the
National City Bank, which proposed to take all the Boxer
bonds if Tang agreed on the proper price and conditions.
The Manchurian Governor carefully told Jackson that he
would ask the advice of the American government "as to
how or with whom he should deal in order to sell his bonds
to an American." At the same time, the State Department
was requested to endorse Jackson's attempt to buy the bonds
on the grounds that Jackson merely sought to benefit the
America position in Manchuria and did not care for personal
profit.

Straight met Jackson in Washington and discussed the
promoter's proposals. Jackson repeated the details concerning the banking syndicate, mentioning that the President of
the National City Bank, Frank Vanderlip, was prepared to
come to Washington at any time to perfect the necessary
arrangements. Straight repeated the story to Tang for confirmation, but the envoy denied giving Jackson such definite
assurance.[52]

After another encounter between Tang and Jackson, the Chinese envoy told Straight that he had refused to answer any questions about the remission and requested Straight to keep Jackson away from him. Straight, who personally had offered the loan to Kuhn, Loeb and Company a month earlier, now told Tang officially that "he [Tang] must of course understand that this government could not in any wise suggest or reccommend to him capitalists who would undertake to float the proposed loan, nor could the Department in any way connect itself or be identified with his financial projects. . . . I [Straight] told him that it would be very unfortunate if it should be imagined in various quarters that this Government as such was assisting him in his financial plan. . . ." Straight then set Jacob Schiff's mind at ease by explaining that Jackson's attempt to intrude in the loan had failed.[53]

In Washington, Straight acted as intermediary between Harriman and Tang. He made sure that Tang understood "clearly the character of his relations" with Harriman and received assurance that China's emissary had not committed himself in any way with anyone else.[54] On December 28, Roosevelt signed the executive order remitting the indemnity. Straight promised to show it to Harriman, and when this had been done, Tang would be free to go to New York and confer with the financier.

The projected conference with Harriman involved more than the financing of the Manchurian Bank, for Straight also had Manchurian railway problems in mind. As early as 1904, Russia found its responsibilities in the Chinese Eastern Railway a heavy burden. Finance Minister Kokovtsov surveyed the status of Russia's economic activity in the Far East and discovered severe weaknesses in the structure of the Russo-Chinese Bank due to the reluctance of Russian capital to invest in the Far East and China's opposition to grant attractive monopolies. Kokovtsov decided that Russian policy must encourage foreign investment and thus fill the vacuum created by the government's withdrawal from direct economic participation in Asiatic enterprise.

Officials of the Chinese Eastern Railway had approached American capitalists in the summer of 1906 regarding sale of the line, but nothing came of this overture. Two years later, Straight learned that Russia had offered to sell the line to China. The Manchurian administration recognized the commercial and political advantage of such a purchase, and Straight, viewing Manchuria through Harriman's eyes, saw the potential value of the Chinese Eastern Railway to Harriman's world-wide transportation system. The Russian road in Manchuria was to connect the Trans-Siberian Railroad and the Japanese-controlled South Manchurian Railroad. China's desire to extend the Imperial Chinese Railroad system north from Hsinmintun to Tsitsihar might help in fulfilling Harriman's dream through some working out of a combination of these lines. Straight extolled the virtues of the country covered by Russia's road and the projected Hsinmintun-Tsitsihar extension. He assured Harriman that any American who financed the purchase of the Chinese Eastern Railway from Russia on behalf of China would have the cooperation of the English interest that had prior rights for financing the Hsinmintun-Tsitsihar line.[55]

Straight's anxiety increased when the Japanese Minister of Communications visited Mukden in an effort to ward off Russia's sale of its property to China in May, 1908. When he returned to the United States, Gregory Wilenkin, St. Petersburg's financial emissary, had suggested that Russia and Japan sell their Manchurian railroad holdings to China with money furnished by an international syndicate headed by Kuhn, Loeb and Company. With the approval of Kokovtsov and Iswolsky, the Russian Minister of Foreign Affairs, Wilenkin presented the proposals to Schiff in the fall of 1908, and both men agreed that the transaction required concurrent action by Russia and Japan. But Schiff moved away from the Russian connection.

Earlier in August he had explained to a Japanese banker that Tokyo's financial difficulties hindered effective operation of the South Manchurian Railroad and asked if Japan wished to sell its line on the basis of the canceled agreement made with Harriman in 1905. Straight wrote a memorandum for Schiff in December, repeating the banker's own analysis of Japan's financial weakness and stressing the importance of persuading Tokyo to sell the South Manchurian Railroad. The sale of the Japanese holding would open the way for a similar move by Russia.[56] Straight's reasoning appealed to Schiff, for it avoided the necessity of dealing with Russia— a prospect that the banker did not relish.

Having briefed Schiff, Straight sought China's agreement, and he consulted Tang in Washington. The envoy was certain that Japan never would dispose of its Manchurian railway, but he "received the proposition favorably," stipulating that the financial interests approaching Russia and Japan should do so not as Peking's agents, but as interested parties offering to negotiate with China.

Once Straight had cleared the ground with Tang, Schiff wrote again to his Japanese friends. "Someone high in the confidence of our own Government," he stated, had suggested that Kuhn, Loeb and Company make a proposition for both railroad lines. He dwelt on the danger to Japan of Russian influence in Manchuria, and he covertly threatened Tokyo with the reminder that "the possibility will always exist that with the South Manchurian Railroad exclusively in Japan's hands, at some time the Chinese Government might be induced to build a parallel line." In view of these facts, Schiff thought it a "desirable thing" for American capital to be made the "stakeholder" of transportation in Northern and Southern Manchuria.[57] A few days after Schiff wrote to the Japanese, events in China abruptly terminated negotiations in Washington and New York.

An unstable internal situation, created in part by the effects of the Root-Takahira agreement, overthrew the Yuan faction in Peking early in January, 1909. Tang was ordered home. Angered by this setback, Straight argued that Japan was in back of the recall. Washington wired Peking for confirmation, for Tang had created a good impression in the American capitol, and his loan talks had been "making satisfactory headway." [58] Lacking authorization to continue talks with American interests, Tang dropped the negotiations, although he did go to New York for conferences with Harriman.[59]

The Chinese envoy journeyed home via Europe, and the State Department kept him in full view. Rockhill and the British Minister had appealed to the Chinese imperial government to spare Yuan, and Straight thought it likely that he would regain his position, "a development which, of course, we all devoutly hope for." [60] Official orders went out to the American ambassadors in London, Paris, and Berlin to keep in touch with Tang, while Straight asked a newspaper friend to watch Tang's movements.

Tang's mission was not a basic failure. Despite the coolness of the Roosevelt administration toward the anti-Japanese policy in Manchuria advocated by Straight, the State Department, through its encouragement of the loan negotiations, created a favorable atmosphere for American economic interests to move into Manchuria and challenge Japan. Straight had achieved his primary purpose of encouraging American capital sufficiently to enter the Manchurian arena. Tang's recall was a temporary defeat, but Straight set about to add further force to the American push in the Far East.

NOTES

1. Roosevelt to Root, July 13, 1907, in Joseph B. Bishop, *Theodore Roosevelt and His Time Shown in His Own Letters* (2 vols., New York, 1920), II, 64.

2. Philip C. Jessup, *Elihu Root* (2 vols., New York, 1935), II, 26; Roosevelt to Taft, August 8, 1907, and Taft to Charles Taft, August 18, 1907, Taft Papers; Henry F. Pringle, *The Life and Times of William Howard Taft* (2 vols., New York, 1939), I, 301.

3. Taft to Root, October 4, 1907, and Taft to Roosevelt, October 5, 1907, Taft Papers.

4. John B. Powell, *My Twenty-Five Years in China* (New York, 1945), 8; Millard to Taft, September 26, 1907, "Memorandum on American Trade and Interest in China," Taft Papers.

5. *Far Eastern Review*, 20 (October, 1907):141–145.

6. Straight to the Assistant Secretary of State, September 28, 1907, NA, RG59:2321/13–15.

7. "Manchurian Loan: Role of Casenave," October 30, 1907, Straight Papers.

8. Straight Diary, October 29, 1907, Straight Papers.

9. Straight to Taft, October 29, 1907, and Taft to Fergusson, October 30, 1907, Taft Papers; Straight to the Assistant Secretary of State, November 4, 1907, Straight to Reeves, October 3, 1907, Marvin's Diary, November 4, 1907, Huntington Wilson to Straight, November 4, 1907, and Straight Diary, November 11 and 12, 1907, Straight Papers.

10. Straight to Taft, n.d., "Memorandum on Manchurian Affairs," NA, RG59:2413/97–99; Straight to the Assistant Secretary of State, November 9, 1907, NA, RG59:2321/16–18; Straight to Denby, December 3, 1907, Straight Papers.

11. Rockhill to Roosevelt, July 12, 1905, Rockhill Papers; Roosevelt to Guild A. Copeland, February 13, 1907, and Root to Copeland, February 16, 1907, NA, RG59:2413/12–14; Root to Asa Morton, April 24, 1907, NA, RG59:2413/40–42.

12. Written comment by Phillips and Huntington Wilson on Rockhill dispatch to Root, August 5, 1907, NA, RG59:2413/79.

13. Straight Diary, November 20, 1907, Straight Papers.

14. Personal interview with George Marvin, Washington, D.C., June 15, 1951, Straight to Reeves, December 4, 1907, Straight Diary, December 2, 1907, Straight to Taft, December 2, 1907, and Straight to Casenave, December 4, 1907, Straight Papers; Straight to the Secretary of State, "Memorandum of an Interview with Their Excellencies the Viceroy and the Governor," November 23, 1907, NA, RG59:4213/92–94.

15. Straight to the Assistant Secretary of State, December 9, 1907, NA, RG59:2415/92–94; Straight to Phillips, December 18, 1907, Straight Papers.

16. Straight to Taft, December 2, 1907, Straight Papers; Taft to Root, January 21, 1908, NA, RG59:2413/97–99; Rockhill Diary, January 25, 1908, Rockhill Papers; Carr to Straight, February 10, 1908, NA, RG59:2413/92–94; Straight to Fletcher, March 17, 1908, Straight Papers.

17. Straight to the Assistant Secretary of State, March 12, 1908, NA,

RG59:2413/127; Straight to Fletcher, March 11, 1908, Straight Papers; Rockhill to Root, April 28, 1908, NA, RG59:2112/27–29.

18. Rockhill to Root, July 16, 1908, NA, RG59:2413/146–148.

19. Marvin, "Recollections of Willard Straight," February, 1922, Straight Papers; Marvin to Bacon, December 7, 1907, Marvin Papers; Straight to Denby, January 1, 1908, Straight Papers; Marvin to Charles Vevier, June 15, 1951.

20. Marvin to Bacon, December 9, 1907, Marvin Papers.

21. Straight Diary, November 26–29 and December 27, 1907, Marvin's Diary, November 29, 1907, and Marvin, "Recollections of Willard Straight," Straight Papers; Marvin to Bacon, December 26, 1907, Marvin Papers; Root to Straight, December 26, and Straight to Root, December 27, 1907, NA, RG59:3275/59–60.

22. Straight to Huntington Wilson, December 30, 1907, and Bland to Straight, January 5, 1908, Straight Papers; "Memorandum of a Contract Submitted by His Excellency Hsu Shao Yi, Governor of Fengtien," January, 1908, Marvin Papers.

23. Marvin to Bacon, April 15, 1908, Marvin Papers; Straight to Huntington Wilson, January 31 and February 23, 1908, and Straight to Phillips, February 28, 1908, Straight Papers.

24. Straight to Marvin, April 14, 1908, Straight Papers.

25. Rockhill Diary, April 14, 1908, Rockhill Papers; Bacon to American Legation, Peking, April 15, 1908, and Bacon to Marvin, April 16, 1908, Marvin Papers.

26. Rockhill Diary, April 18, 1908, Rockhill Papers.

27. Rockhill to Root, April 28, 1908, NA, RG59:2112/27–29.

28. Rockhill to Marvin, July 21, 1908, Marvin Papers; Rockhill to Root, July 30, 1908, NA, RG59:2413/151, 146–148.

29. Phillips to Rockhill, September 19, 1908, Rockhill Papers; Phillips to Adee, October 9, 1908, NA, RG59:2413/146–148.

30. Straight to Harriman, January 30, 1908, Straight Papers.

31. Straight to Harriman, February 16, 1908, Straight Papers.

32. Straight to Fletcher, March 11 and 17, 1908, Straight Papers.

33. Straight to the Secretary of State, n.d., NA, RG84: Peking Legation Archives; Fletcher to Root, July 10, and to Straight, July 14, 1908, NA, RG84: Peking Legation Archives; Commander Irvin Gilles to Admiral Raymond P. Rodger, August 21, 1908, NA, Records of the Chief of Naval Operations (General Correspondence 9348 0).

34. George Kennan, E. H. Harriman (2 vols., New York, 1922), II, 26; Phillips to Rockhill, July 16, 1908, Rockhill Papers.

35. Straight to Tang Shao-yi, August 11, 1908, Straight Papers.

36. F. M. Huntington Wilson, Memoirs of an Ex-Diplomat (Boston, 1945), 105.

37. Phillips to Adee, September 16, 1908, and Adee to Root, September 21, 1908, NA, RG59:2711; Phillips to Rockhill, September 19, 1908, and Fletcher to Rockhill, January 11, 1909, Rockhill Papers.

38. "Notes Transcribed by George Marvin From a Memorandum Written by Bacon," n.d., but approximately late September, 1908, Marvin Papers.

39. Phillips to Rockhill, June 3, 1908, Rockhill Papers.

40. "Notes Transcribed by Marvin From Bacon Memorandum," Marvin Papers.

41. Marvin, "Recollections of Theodore Roosevelt," n.d., Marvin Papers.

42. Jessup, *Root*, II, 34–43; Straight, "Memorandum on the Root Takahira Agreement," November 11, 1908, NA, RG59:16533/6.

43. Herbert Croly, *Willard Straight* (New York, 1924), 276; Straight, "Memorandum Regarding the Present Situation in China," January 7, 1909, NA, RG59:15118/271.

44. Rockhill to Root, December 3, 1908, NA, RG59:16533/46; John G. Reid, *Manchu Abdication and the Powers, 1908–1912* (Berkeley, 1935), 13–15.

45. Roosevelt to Kaiser Wilhelm II, January 2, 1909, in Bishop, *Theodore Roosevelt*, II, 287.

46. Huntington Wilson to Root, December 5, 1908, NA, RG59: 2413/220, endorsing a Memorandum from Straight.

47. Interview Between Mr. Tang Shao-yi and the Secretary of State, December 9, 1908, NA, RG59:2413/218.

48. Root to Straight, December 11, 1908, NA, RG59:2413/213A.

49. Root to Roosevelt, December 18, 1908, in Jessup, *Root*, II, 54.

50. Straight, "Memorandum to Secretary of State Knox," Very Confidential, March 26, 1909, Straight, "China's Loan Negotiation," speech delivered at Clark University, and "Notes on Harriman," Straight Papers; Cyrus Adler, *Jacob H. Schiff* (2 vols., New York, 1928) I, 248.

51. Interview between Tang and the Secretary of State, December 9, 1908, and Straight to Bacon, December 11, 1908, NA, RG59:2413/218 and 226.

52. Miller to Root, December 14, 1908, and Straight, "Memorandum of a Conversation with Mr. A. Wendell Jackson," December 15, 1908, NA, RG59:1140/12.

53. "Memorandum of a Conversation with His Excellency Tang Shao-yi," December 16, 1908, NA, RG59:1140/12; Straight to Schiff, December 15, 1908, Straight Papers.

54. Straight to Schiff, December 18, 1908, and to Harriman, December 31, 1908, Straight Papers.

55. Straight to Harriman, April 30, 1908, Straight Papers.

56. Schiff to Takahashi, August 31, 1908, in Adler, *Schiff*, I, 247; Straight, "Notes on Harriman," and "Memorandum Regarding the Proposal to Secure Control of the Chinese Eastern and the South Manchurian Railways," Straight Papers.

57. "Memorandum of a Conversation with His Excellency Tang Shao-yi," December 19, 1908, Straight Papers; J. O. P. Bland, *Recent Events and Present Policies in China* (Philadelphia, 1912), 315; Schiff to Takahashi, December 24 and 28, 1908, in Adler, *Schiff*, I, 248–249.

58. Straight to Harriman, January 20, 1909, Straight Papers; Bacon to the American Legation at Peking, January 7, 1909, NA, RG59:2413/215; Phillips to Rockhill, January 9, 1909, Rockhill Papers.

59. Straight to Schiff, January 6, 1909, and Straight, "Notes on Harriman," Straight Papers.

60. Straight to Tang Shao-yi, January 20, 1909, Straight Papers.

CHAPTER FIVE

The Jackals and the Lions

Official Washington may have been saddened by Tang's departure for home, but there was one important compensation: William Howard Taft assumed the Presidency of the United States in 1909. In short order, the conditioning that he had experienced in the Philippines and Japan as well as at Shanghai and Vladivostok became manifest. For although American export and investment figures for most parts of the world climbed, trade in China had dropped steadily since 1905. The trends of the times called for encouragement of trade, stimulation of investment, salesmanship, and efficient organization. The new President soon demonstrated his concurrence with these demands when he went before the Congress to state his conception of American foreign relations.

There was, he said, a basic relationship between political and economic interests which the government had to recognize. Representatives of American finance and industry sought investment opportunities and markets. Wherever they went, the government had to follow, providing protection and seeking additional openings for its nationals. For the achievement of this purpose, it was necessary to enlarge and reorganize the State Department in the interests of greater efficiency, and Taft called for Congressional appropriations to carry on the good work.[1] To the officers of the State Department, these words were encouraging though not surprising; they wrote most of Taft's speeches dealing with foreign affairs and thus influenced the conduct of policy.[2]

For his Secretary of State, Taft chose Roosevelt's Attorney General, Philander C. Knox of Pennsylvania, a corporation lawyer who was highly recommended by Elihu Root. Knox had no experience in foreign affairs, though he earlier had encouraged the imperialist oratory of Albert S. Beveridge. Knox had been a candidate for the Republican Presidential nomination and was a political power in his state. Taft respected and appreciated him. Unlike Hay and Root, Knox had no intention of overworking himself in office, and Taft got the impression that his Secretary of State was lazy. The President, nevertheless, openly shared the credit with Knox for the formulation of foreign policy.[3]

Knox chose Huntington Wilson for his chief subordinate as Assistant Secretary of State. Huntington Wilson had labored to rise in the ranks of the diplomatic service. As chargé d'affaires in Tokyo he had been close to the center of events during the Russo-Japanese War and afterward. Ambitious, willing to improve himself for higher position, and eager to take on responsibility, he had managed to secure an appointment in 1906 as Third Assistant Secretary of State. Despite Roosevelt's commendation of Huntington Wilson for his performance in the crisis with Japan, Root had never cared for him. Root had resisted Huntington Wilson's schemes for reorganizing the State Department into geographical sections only to be forced later to permit the experiment when the Division of Far Eastern Affairs was founded. The triumph was recognized by Straight, who asked several times for a Washington assignment to further his own training. Huntington Wilson, in addition, had joined with Straight in urging support of China against Japan, and he sympathized with his colleague's attempt to introduce American capital in Manchuria.[4]

Before Taft entered office, Huntington Wilson was scheduled to go to Argentina as American Minister. The move was regarded as a "kick upstairs" that would make room for William Phillips as Third Assistant Secretary in the new régime. The choice of Phillips for the post rested on his knowledge of the Far East, acquired during his tenure as Chief of the Division of Far Eastern Affairs.

Always the devoted public servant, Huntington Wilson visited Knox before leaving for Buenos Aires and discussed some of his plans for Department reform with the incoming Secretary. Impressed by Huntington Wilson's grasp of organizational problems, Knox appointed him Assistant Secretary of State. Under this arrangement, Huntington Wilson did most of the administrative work, taking time off every day to visit the Secretary at lunch to inform him of the progress of affairs, make suggestions, and carry out orders. The President accepted Knox's selection though he had no love for Huntington Wilson—whose behavior later elicited from the genial Taft the desire to "sit on Wilson and mash him flat." [5]

William Phillips had an important job in the new order as Third Assistant Secretary of State. A Harvard graduate with some diplomatic background from service in the Legation at Peking to add to his experience in the Division of Far Eastern Affairs, Phillips knew of Straight's designs for Manchuria. A cautious man, he was careful not to antagonize hostile factions within the Department, for he had backed Rockhill against Straight and then shifted when Bacon sent Straight to Harriman.

The new broom of the administration swept William Woodville Rockhill out of office as American Minister to China. Taft did not hold Rockhill in such high esteem as did Roosevelt. He resented Rockhill's devotion to scholarly pursuits and judged the Minister to be a mere dilettante whose usefulness was limited at Peking.

He, Rockhill, has not the slightest interest in American trade or in promoting it. He is pessimistic and not optimistic in his views of what can be done, and he is not a man of strength and force of action such as we need at Peking. . . . I regard the position at Peking as the most important diplomatic position that I have to fill, and it is necessary to send there a man of business force and perception and ability to withstand the aggressions of the Japanese, the English, and the Russians. China is very friendly to us, and . . . anxious to encourage American trade and the American investment of capital, because she does not distrust our motives. The opportunities it seems to me, therefore, for the development of the Oriental trade are great if we can only have a man on the ground who realizes the necessity and has the force and pluck and experience to take advantage of the opportunity.[6]

Harriman had just the man for the job. Concerned with keeping a close watch on Chinese affairs, he lobbied quietly to have Straight appointed American Minister to China. He made a personal appeal to the incoming Secretary of State in February, 1909, calling Knox's attention to Straight "because of the special matters which will probably prevail in our relations with Oriental countries." Straight did not engage in job-seeking, and Harriman hastened to clear the Acting Chief of the Division of Far Eastern Affairs of any charge that he had invoked Harriman's assistance. The railway king revealed only that Straight "talked to me some of Eastern matters, because of our meeting out there, and because of the extensive interests which I represent there, and which we are continuing to carry from patriotic motives rather than give up a drop of the old stars and stripes." [7]

Knox promised to pay special attention to Straight's case, but Taft finally gave the appointment to a Chicago business man and world traveler, Charles R. Crane. Crane's business connections fitted in with Taft's conception of the demands of the post in Peking, and the choice was heralded by the press for the same reasons. Crane, who had been impressed by Taft's Shanghai speech, soon became embroiled in a dispute with Knox and Huntington Wilson over alleged indiscreet statements made to the press, and he was recalled before he left the United States.

The Departmental reorganization was very efficient, the acme of administrative decentralization. Taft deferred to Knox, who gave great authority to Huntington Wilson, who in turn was Straight's superior while he was Acting Chief of the Division of Far Eastern Affairs. With the possible exception of Knox, who was still an unknown quantity, all important offices, from Taft down to Straight, were held by men who favored a more active role for the United States in China and Manchuria.

An invigorated State Department took a long look at the state of American interests in China in May, 1909. Phillips stated policy succinctly: "The Department has in view the general extension of American influence in China so that when the commercial interests and exporters of the United States turn their attention more and more vigorously toward securing the markets of the Orient, they will find those of China open to their products and the Chinese public favorably disposed toward American enterprise." He repeated the criticisms made by Rockhill and Straight regarding the failure of Americans to investigate opportunities in China at first hand, but he now saw another avenue of approach through investment of funds. American bankers did show some of the backwardness exhibited by traders, but they were "undoubtedly anxious" to provide loans to China.[8]

Phillips was not guessing or hoping for a miracle. The support given by Huntington Wilson and Bacon to Straight's Manchurian undertakings in the last days of Roosevelt's administration began to show results. The postponed loan negotiations with Tang were revived, but the focus of attention was shifted from Manchuria to China proper. Although the basic ingredients were the same, money and railroads, they were related to earlier railroad loan efforts made by the American China Development Company prior to the outbreak of the Spanish-American War.

The company lost out to a Belgian syndicate in 1896 and 1897 for the rights to construct a line from Peking to Hankow. China promised to borrow money from the firm for another projected road from Hankow to Canton, but American involvement in the Spanish-American War temporarily halted the effort. After the war, the company managed to retain a hold on the Hankow-Canton concession, but the Belgians, seeking to undercut the American position, bought control of the company in the open market. The Chinese, who had no love for the Belgians, argued that the grant to the Americans was made with the express purpose of depriving the Belgian syndicate of the rights to the line.

At this point, J. P. Morgan and Company secured control of the American China Development Company for the United States, raising hopes that China would not cancel the concession now that it was held once again by American interests. Angered and disgusted with American tactics, Peking cancelled the concession, forcing the House of Morgan to consider selling out in order to avoid further difficulty. While the American bankers debated, the King of Belgium, who still retained shares in the concession, appealed to President Roosevelt through Henry Cabot Lodge for the Chief Executive's support of Morgan against the Chinese. Lodge made his case with Roosevelt on grounds of national interest and the preservation of American prestige. He urged the President to persuade Elihu Root, who was advising the House of Morgan at the time, not to recommend sale.

Roosevelt did not want to abandon the project, and he invited the American banker to stay in the field.

> Now, my dear Mr. Morgan, it is not my business to advise you what to do. From the standpoint of our national interests, I take entirely Lodge's view. I cannot expect you or any of our big business men to go into what they think will be to their disadvantage. But if you are giving up this concession, if you are letting the

railroad slip out of American hands, because you think that the Government will not back you up, I wish to assure you that in every honorable way the Government will stand by you and will do all that in its power lies to see that you suffer no wrong whatever from the Chinese or any other power in this matter. I have sent Root a copy of this letter and shall be very glad if either you or he cares to talk to me about it. My interest of course is simply the interest of seeing American commercial interests prosper in the Orient.[9]

A month later, Roosevelt urged Morgan to delay sale of the line, promising to "call a halt, in emphatic terms to the Chinese Government." Late in August, 1905, the President conferred with J. P. Morgan and agreed that the banker should accept an indemnity from China in return for cancellation of the concession. Morgan insisted that the indemnity was large and that if the line was not to be built, then China's payment was greater than any that would be awarded by an arbitral body. Feeling that he had entered the negotiations too late to be effective, Roosevelt was forced to assent, admitting that he could not guarantee protection if trouble came with China.[10]

Peking paid a heavy indemnity to the Americans with money borrowed from the city government of Hongkong after China's gentry failed to produce enough funds. Ever aware of their sphere of influence in China and hoping to acquire the Hankow-Canton concession, the British had acted when rival German bankers offered to lend the money to Peking.

Before the final collapse of the Hankow-Canton venture, Americans attempted to get another Chinese railway concession. In the summer of 1903, the American Minister in Peking, Edwin Conger, learned of plans for a railroad to be constructed from Hankow to Szechuen. Anticipating British competition, Conger applied for American rights to finance the line and asked for a priority if China used foreign funds. The British also had approached Peking, and the Chinese informed Conger that application would be made to Anglo-American interests at the proper time and if native sources of capital were unable to raise funds.

The next year, two American syndicates placed bids for the Hankow-Szechuen Railway. The first offer came from Thurlow Weed Barnes of the Hankow and American Syndicate, an organization of combined British and American capital. Conger referred Barnes' request to the Chinese, but the attempt failed because the Chinese still hoped to finance the road themselves. The second effort came later in the year when Albert Bash, formerly of the American China Development Company, and now representing the China Investment and Construction Company, asked for the Szechuen loan in case China did not raise the funds. Peking's attitude, however, remained the same.

Conger notified Washington of the American applications and reported that representatives of British and French capital were to meet in London in October, 1904, in order to organize a company and merge forces to build and finance the line. Through Conger, they extended an invitation to American interests to join. Conger sent the news to Washington but steadily maintained the priority of American claims. To complicate the situation further, Bash had received earlier an invitation from the British Peking Syndicate to join in the railway loan. This offer was made before the British and the French decided to combine for the Szechuen loan, and Bash had refused, insisting on retaining a one half interest rather than the one third offered by the Anglo-French syndicate. Bash passed this specific information on to Conger, thus explaining the Minister's reiteration of the American claim.[11]

After the French and British interests met, the British Ambassador in Washington asked the State Department if American interests wished to share in the loan arrangement. Washington treated the British query as a new item of information and publicized the opportunity without success-fully arousing American interest. In mid-October, 1905, the British Ambassador informed Secretary Root that the Chinese Central Railways group (the combined British and French groups) was proceeding on the assumption that Americans did not desire participation. Root was reluctant to give the appearance of soliciting concessions for private interests. When he was informed of an application made by Bash to Rockhill for such assistance, he instructed the American Minister not to be overzealous.[12]

Toward the end of 1907 and early in 1908, the Hankow-Canton railway project reappeared on the scene. This time British interests took the lead, though they were pressed hard by the Germans. In return for the loan made to China for the indemnity payment to J. P. Morgan and Company, Peking had promised to give the British a priority on this line. The situation was complicated by an earlier agreement in 1895 between British and German banks to share Chinese business. The accord was short-lived, and three years later, the British and Chinese Corporation (created by the Hongkong and Shanghai Bank and Jardine, Matheson and Company) acquired five railway concessions in the Yangtse Valley from China. The British position, however, was still insecure, for the Germans persisted in seeking to make railway loans to China.

Represented by J. O. P. Bland, the British and Chinese Corporation continued a long-standing attempt to lend money for the Hankow-Canton project. On the lookout for allies, the English first approached the First National and National City Banks in the United States and offered collaboration. The American banks refused, leaving the British still confronted by the Germans, who promptly lent money to China on very easy terms for the construction of the Tientsin-Pukow Railroad. The lax terms of the German loan set a precedent in Chinese railroad history and contrasted with earlier excessive British demands. The loan also coincided with a strong movement in China that opposed foreign control of its railways, and met with the approval of an important faction in Peking that advocated close ties with Germany after Washington rejected Tang's diplomatic overtures.[13]

German tenacity had brought the British to heel, while the French, who had only a minor part in the financing of these roads, merely followed the English. Compelled to recognize the strength of German finance, representatives of the tripartite interests met in Berlin in March, 1909, to draw up an agreement for the sharing of Chinese loan business.

All this reckoned without the desires of the Chinese. In July, 1908, Chang Chih-tung, one of China's leading statesmen, was appointed official overseer of the Hankow-Canton Railway. Hoping to divide the powers and exact the most favorable terms, he negotiated with both British and German interests at the same time that the tripartite banking interests were meeting in Berlin. The Germans had already consented to withdraw their bid for the Hankow-Canton line which they had made on lenient Tientsin-Pukow terms. Much to their distaste, the British had been forced to make a similar offer in order to meet competition. The German promise of retraction prompted the British and Chinese Corporation to wire Bland, ordering him to make a similar withdrawal. It was too late. Several days later, news arrived that the Germans had made an arrangement for the Hankow-Canton line on lenient Tientsin-Pukow terms.

The British at first were not disturbed, for they assumed that the impending Berlin agreement would set matters aright. But the Germans now refused to relinquish the loan contract, claiming that they would antagonize the Chinese. The recently created amity foundered in a sea of recrimination and argument. Seeking a way out of the impasse, the

Deutsche Asiatische Bank suggested that the British and French bankers join them in the Hankow-Canton loan. The result was an involved series of trades. The Germans surrendered the Hankow-Canton loan to the British; the British gave the Hankow-Szechuen loan to the Germans; and the French received the sweepings: a one-third share in both loans and a 5 per cent commission on the purchase of railway materials used in construction. By May, 1909, the details were ironed out, and the three banking groups signed another agreement.

Just at this time, the State Department, impatient for action, became aware of the manipulation that was involved in the projected construction of the two trunk lines, linking together several of China's most important cities and economic regions.[14]

Washington's knowledge of the reactivated Hankow-Canton railroad project first came through private American banking sources who were interested in floating the loan for the road. In the fall of 1908, Selwyn Tait, the manager of the Washington branch of the International Banking Corporation, returned from a trip to the Far East with reports of the scramble for railway loans in China. His firm did a considerable business throughout the Far East and had close ties with the National City Bank. Tait's observations on the possibilities of the situation encouraged his superiors to request Bacon's help in obtaining information from Rockhill in Peking, though the bank carefully made it clear that it did not expect the government to secure the contract for a private American interest. Then it challenged British interests for access to the Hankow-Canton loan and requested Washington's help "to offset this powerful English influence for the benefit of American commerce." This time, Huntington Wilson handled the correspondence with the American bank, and he instructed Rockhill to obtain "for that institution no less favorable an opportunity than is enjoyed by any other competitors." Rockhill was easily put off in Peking. The Chinese promised to admit the United States to future loans, and representatives of the tripartite banks assured him that they welcomed American participation. Rockhill's advices, however, did not jibe with the failure of the International Banking Corporation to enter the Hankow-Canton loan. On three occasions, from January to April, 1909, the British refused to cooperate, an attitude that frankly took account of the fact that the United States was not in "a position to talk actual business," as Tait informed Straight confidentially.[15]

When the Deutsche Asiatische Bank signed a preliminary contract with China for the Hankow-Canton loan, the British were not the only ones who were surprised. The State Department inquired immediately whether any American interests had an opportunity to tender for the loan. Rockhill replied that the International Banking Corporation knew of the Anglo-French negotiations for the loan and would have been welcomed to participation. Phillips immediately sent the Department's inquiry and Rockhill's reply to J. P. Morgan and Company, the last American holder of the Hankow-Canton concession.[16]

Washington's deepening interest in the Hankow-Canton question stemmed from Straight's earlier messages regarding the approach of railroad centralization in China and the fruitful opportunities flowing from this development. The construction of railroads was the chief means of internal development in China, opening the way for greater investment of foreign capital and creating a large market for manufactured goods. Loss of the rights to participate in the loans meant loss of markets and investment outlets. With the signature of the tripartite agreements for the Hukuang Railways (the combined Hankow-Szechuen and Hankow-Canton loans) in May, 1909, Phillips complained that "the failure of the United States to execute its part in the Hankow-

Canton Railway concession becomes more and more important as we see the European powers seizing the opportunity which was once entirely and exclusively in the hands of American capitalists." [17]

But Phillips had a good memory and a talent for salvaging lost situations. He saw that the Hukuang Loan was secured in part by several important charges on China's likin, making it impossible for Peking to fulfill its pledges for abolition of the ancient trade tax as required by the terms of the 1903 commercial treaty with the United States. Several days later, he remembered the Conger correspondence with China in 1903 and 1904 regarding the Hankow-Szechuen railway concession and the British inquiries made in 1905 for American combination with the Anglo-French financial interests in the same railway loan. "I do not, therefore, consider that we have relinquished our rights," he informed Secretary Knox.[18]

Seizing on the likin issue as an excuse, Phillips, Straight, and Huntington Wilson went to work to build a case for American intervention in the Hukuang Loans. While Phillips concentrated on the likin security, Straight expounded on the tactical advantage held by the United States. He related the struggle of the tripartite powers for railway loans in China to their past promises expressing approval of the abolition of likin. If Washington took the lead in demanding the solution of the likin problem, he believed that it would demonstrate American unselfishness in China and the desire to protect trade in the empire.[19]

Huntington Wilson, eager for action, precipitously ordered a note sent to the powers protesting the hypothecation of the likin charges. Phillips, more hesitant, saw a flaw in the procedure.

> It occurs to me also that the Department might be placed in an embarrassing position by such a protest in view of the fact that, should the occasion arise in the future when our banking interests

were invited to participate in a loan to China, I fully believe that they would jump at the opportunity and would gladly accept the likin as security. Would not the United States thereupon be placed in the awkward position of having protested to the foreign powers on account of their adoption of the likin as a guarantee, while we ourselves, in a similar situation, would be powerless to alter the terms of a loan at the hands of American capitalists if our own bankers were willing to make use of the likin for the purpose of securing the loan.

After reading Phillips' word of caution, Huntington Wilson retreated. "We *might* deter our people," he noted, but agreed to shelve the protest.[20]

The delay was only temporary. Phillips' forecast of the entrance of American capital on the scene was no theoretical excursion into the realm of possibility. In March he had sent the Hankow-Canton data to J. P. Morgan and Company. Later in April, before he had restrained Huntington Wilson, and on May 21, 1909, he received assurance that the International Banking Corporation and the National City Bank were willing to undertake Chinese railway loans.[21] Now in possession of a substantial economic interest to back policy, Huntington Wilson and Straight disregarded Phillips' hesitance and sent a protest to Peking on May 24, 1909. The note argued that the United States held a joint claim with Great Britain for the Hankow-Szechuen section of the Hukuang Railways and charged that the British had bartered it away to the Germans in exchange for sole rights to the Hankow-Canton section.[22]

Washington's telegram launched the American bid for inclusion in the Hukuang Loans. The Chinese were reluctant to reopen the negotiations, and they put off Rockhill three times before the Minister managed to get an interview. Although Peking welcomed American participation in principle and gave hope that the Szechuen portion of the loan might be reconsidered, China was in a hurry to sign the agreement with the tripartite banks. Phillips and Huntington Wilson maintained that the United States never had withdrawn officially from the Szechuen project and that American rights rested upon China's assurances. Fletcher, who took over after Rockhill's departure from the Chinese capital, admitted that the Conger correspondence which formed the basis of Washington's claim was none too favorable to the American cause. But the Chinese recognized the Conger assurances as valid, thus permitting Fletcher to plead Washington's case.[23]

China signed the Hukuang Agreement with the tripartite banks on June 6, 1909, but Washington continued the fight. Knox mulled over the likin question raised by Phillips and devised a way out of the dilemma. He made a positive tool of Phillips' fear that American bankers would accept the likin as loan security and added it to Straight's contention that the likin question involved economic considerations granted by a political treaty. If this was true, then the United States legitimately claimed a hold on the likin revenues, as did the other powers. American bankers could accept the likin as part of the loan security without any difficulty while the various governments discussed ways and means of abolishing the onerous tax. Knox's contention actually postponed attempts to settle the likin question until the loan negotiations were completed. The American objection to the likin was "based more upon a question of policy than upon one of right," ran a memorandum sent to Knox, "and can be disposed of by the mere statement that the government is at perfect liberty to change its policy at any time it sees fit to do so." [24]

Throughout June and early July of 1909, Washington kept after Peking. The Chinese were placed in a familiar position. Hemmed in by American desire on one side and by tripartite resistance on the other, China agreed to American participation if the other powers consented. It was a neat way of throwing the burden back on Washington, one which the State Department gladly shouldered.

Once again, the United States blared out the call of the open door to Britain, France, and Germany. Whitelaw Reid, American Ambassador to Great Britain and an expansionist of the Mahan-Roosevelt-Lodge school, presented Knox's point of view to Earl Grey, Britain's Foreign Secretary. Reid invoked the open door, declared that the United States had not relinquished its Chinese railroad rights in 1905, and suggested that a common front by the United States and the tripartite powers "would be highly desirable, both in creating a community of interests and in affecting the Oriental imagination." Only on the last count did his superiors ask him to walk softly, cautioning that the race question "might be verbally and confidentially communicated" if it helped achieve the desired end.[25]

Toward the end of June, 1909, the British consented to American entrance in the loan if it did not endanger the Hukuang Agreement. The British chargé in Washington felt that the delay caused by American demands was "humiliating." Huntington Wilson, in charge of the campaign in Washington, taunted the British by pointing out that Germany had upset the loan, not the United States. Was it not all a matter of politics? [26]

The Assistant Secretary also had interviewed the German Ambassador and contended that the governments had the power to compel their financial interests to admit the Americans to participation. "I remarked," Huntington Wilson recalled, "that everyone who knew how these things are done in China was well aware that all the bankers are absolutely dependent upon their Governments to secure them these opportunities and that therefore their Governments had upon them a strong hold and could easily influence their action." [27]

Washington's diplomatic exchange with Berlin was cordial. Germany's entrance into the loan scheme for the Hankow-Canton line had aroused jubilance in Berlin, but the Germans did not stubbornly insist on their rights, and they acquiesced in American entrance to the loan. The French, according to Ambassador Henry White, who was stationed in Paris, were difficult to sway and needed strong government persuasion.

Having taken steps in China and Europe, Washington turned next to New York. The protest telegram that had been sent to Peking on May 24 was prompted by the willingness of the International Banking Corporation and the National City Bank to handle the Hukuang Loan. But these were not the only financial interests involved in the State Department's desire to present a substantial front to the other powers. While Phillips cooperated with the International Banking Corporation, Straight worked along similar lines but with another group of bankers.

Straight's temporary tour of duty in Washington ended in March, 1909, but the Department gave him oral instructions to continue studying ways and means of introducing American capital into China and Manchuria.[28] With the Tang memorandum as a basis, he was "in constant touch" with Harriman through the winter and early spring of 1909. Harriman was still attracted to Manchurian railway affairs, an interest that preceded Washington's excitement over the Hukuang Loan. When Knox became Secretary of State, Straight brought him up to date on Harriman's Manchurian plans and accented the support promised to the financier's venture by Bacon and Root.[29]

Straight also maintained important relations with Jacob Schiff. Initial fears that Tang's political position had been undermined by developments in Peking proved groundless, and Straight expressed his readiness to help Schiff. The banker required no urging from Straight, asserting his "readiness to deal with Manchurian and Chinese matters." [30] Schiff wanted to keep a channel open to China, and Straight gave him some advice:

You ask what should be done by you to assure the desired connections with the Chinese Government. It seems to me that the only way in which you can obtain a hold in China is to appoint a competent person who will represent you at Peking and in the Far East generally and who will keep you fully informed regarding the developments in the financial situation.

The assistance of such a man, were he rendered the support which I feel quite confident our Government will extend to American financiers interesting themselves in the flotation of Chinese loans, would enable you to compete at least on equal terms with the French, Germans, and British who at Peking have active and extremely intelligent agents, men well versed in Chinese affairs. . . . The British and Continental Financiers are anxious to obtain Chinese loans. . . . The visit of Mr. Tang to this country and his political schemes afforded Americans what, had his mission not been so suddenly terminated, would have been an extraordinary opportunity. Once he is back in Peking . . . it will be difficult . . . to keep private his American connections. . . . This, of course, is my own private and unofficial opinion, but, as you know, I am keenly interested in this project and anxious that American interests should be extended in China.[31]

Evidently impressed by Straight's suggestion, Schiff, in early May, 1909, offered Straight a position as Kuhn, Loeb's representative in China to complete the loan negotiations undertaken with Tang. Straight did not take up the offer at this time.[32]

Shortly after the news of the Hukuang Loan arrived in Washington, Straight helped in the task of creating a banking group that would substantiate the American claim for a share in the loan. "At this time," he recalled, "I was working with Mr. Robert Bacon as well as Mr. Harriman." The House of Morgan, interested in Chinese loan possibilities, was thinking of sending a man to Peking to search out opportunities for investment. In order to avoid any competition between American financiers and desirous of presenting a strong front to the European banks, the State Department went to Wall Street "for a group of American bankers who would politically serve its purposes." By June 3, Huntington

Wilson wired Peking of the formation of an "American financial group of great strength." [33]

The members of the American Group that signed articles of organization on June 11, 1909, were J. P. Morgan and Company, the National City Bank, Kuhn, Loeb and Company, the First National Bank, and Edward Henry Harriman. Washington's invitation to the bankers did not promise any immediate rewards, and it stressed the patriotic virtue of preserving the China market as an outlet for the products of American industry. [34]

At first glance, the American Group appeared to be united on the basis of a general extension into China at the request of the State Department. Confusion and difficulty, however, were foreshadowed by the circumstances that gave rise to the creation of the Group and the divergence of the aims of its components. The National City Bank, through its associate, the International Banking Corporation, was actively in the China field before the American Group was formed. The House of Morgan was not a newcomer to the Chinese loan scene, and Phillips' overture merely revived its old interest. Kuhn, Loeb and Company stood midway between an interest in China proper and in Manchuria. Schiff looked to the future, for "sooner or later China and her finances must be thoroughly reorganized," he wrote. "It is well to pave the way now for participation at that time." On the other hand, Schiff worked closely with Harriman in Manchuria. In both areas, Kuhn, Loeb and Company had been active long before June, 1909. Thus, as Straight explained, the State Department laid the Hukuang business "before the bankers already interested in the loan proposed by Mr. Tang Shao-yi and the American Group was organized." [35]

And it was Harriman who issued the modest pronouncement that "I originated the China matter." He knew what he was talking about, for it was his influence on the Department of State and on Straight that fired up American enthusiasm for activity in Manchuria. Of the five separate elements that made up the American Group, only the First National Bank had shown no interest in China or Manchuria prior to the assembly of the American Group. If this, together with Straight's role is kept clearly in mind, then the government's initiative in forming the American Group should be set within a context of preparatory activity by the American financiers. On June 9, Straight resigned his position in the State Department and prepared to travel to Peking via Europe as representative of the American Banking Group.[36] It was a symbolic change of occupation for the ex-Consul General.

Washington carefully released the news to its representatives abroad, and Huntington Wilson informed Taft that the State Department had begun executing the policy which the President had enunciated to Knox. Taft directed the Assistant Secretary to notify China "in the most emphatic way" that the United States insisted on admission to the Hukuang Loan. If China refused, "we can only regard it as an unfriendly act." [37]

The State Department's apparent success was marred by the bitter protests of those interests that were not included in the American Group. The International Banking Corporation raised an outcry against the Department's handling of the loan effort. Selwyn Tait had been in constant touch with William Phillips, furnishing arguments justifying American claims for participation in the loans and prodding the Department to action. Anticipating Washington's intervention, the corporation sent a representative to China and requested aid from the American Legation.

Phillips, perhaps unwittingly, had encouraged the corporation by expressing the wish that a group of American bankers should get together on behalf of the American investment interest.[38] When the International Banking Corporation learned that the House of Morgan and the National City Bank were forming such an organization, it sought the opportunity to act as the American Group's agent. J. P. Morgan and Company thought it inadvisable to have two different American representatives in China. Hoping to be appointed agent for the American Group, the corporation withdrew.[39]

Events in China moved swiftly. Five days after the formation of the American Group, Fletcher wired that the tripartite bankers' representatives in Peking were recommending American participation. The chargé stressed the need for quick action and urged that the group's representative rush to Peking for signature of an agreement before the situation changed. Straight was not ready at the time, and Washington authorized Fletcher to sign the agreement for the American Group.

By this time, the fortunes of the International Banking Corporation had changed. The American Group refused to appoint the International Banking Corporation as its agent in the loan business, and Tait's superiors condemned Fletcher's signature for the American Group as an unjustified activity by the State Department. General Thomas Hubbard, President of the corporation, angrily denounced the refusal of the American Group to cooperate, and he indirectly accused Washington of acting as the commercial representative of J. P. Morgan and Company. In retaliation, Hubbard offered to take the whole Hankow-Szechuen loan from China for his firm and demanded State Department support.[40]

Having already made its commitment, the State Department explained that since the corporation had previously withdrawn such a request, it could not comply with Hubbard's desires. Washington had no other choice, particularly since it believed that Hubbard's bank had been working in conjunction with J. P. Morgan. Hubbard remained dissatisfied and brought the question out into the open. He attacked the State Department in a public speech in September, 1909, for supporting an American banking monopoly in China and accused Washington of deliberately soliciting Chinese loans for the American Group. "We certainly do appear in our own eyes in this instance to have simply been the jackals of the lions of Wall Street," Tait wrote Huntington Wilson.[41]

More criticism was directed at the State Department by the China Investment and Construction Company. The company had demonstrated a desire to participate in the Hankow-Szechuen loan, but Root's refusal to be aggressive in its behalf and its own stubborness in not accepting a reduced share blocked any chance of success. When the Hukuang news broke, Albert Bash stepped forward and claimed that since his company had been involved in the Conger correspondence which had been the basis for the American claim to the Hankow-Szechuen line, it should receive Department support.[42]

Washington was embarrassed by Bash's claim but managed to extricate itself after investigation showed that the China Investment and Construction Company was ill-equipped to take up the task of furnishing loans to China.[43] Henry Hoyt, the Department's solicitor, found little evidence to justify the company's claim and in a later report revealed the underlying reason for Washington's rejection. "To have taken up the Bash claim," Hoyt wrote, "or to have insisted that the group of American bankers now ready with the actual capital should admit the Bash syndicate to their enterprise, would inevitably have meant that no American interests at all would have participated in the loan. It was little short of a miracle anyway that the opportunity was secured." [44]

The way was now clear for Straight's jaunt to Europe and China in order to make certain that the "miracle" was not a mirage. In his own person, Straight bore the China-Manchuria equation. The State Department and part of the

American Group operated on the assumption that the Hu-kuang Railroad Loan for China proper was the principal task. While sharing this view to some extent, Straight was too closely tied to Harriman to be able to work freely of his strong Manchurian assumptions. Soon the Manchurian rail-road scheme, pushed by Straight and Harriman, disentangled itself from the Hukuang Loan.

NOTES

1. *Papers Relating to the Foreign Relations of the United States, 1906–1913* (Washington, 1909–1920), *1909,* XV–XX.
2. F. M. Huntington Wilson, *Memoirs of an Ex-Diplomat* (Boston, 1945), 200.
3. Archibald W. Butt, *Taft and Roosevelt, The Intimate Letters of Archie Butt* (2 vols., New York, 1930), II, 717, 719; George Hill to Whitelaw Reid, December 12, 1909, Reid Papers; Taft to Knox, October 9, 1910, Knox Papers; *New York Times,* May 3, 1910.
4. Philip C. Jessup, *Elihu Root* (2 vols., New York, 1935), II, 30, 105, 112; Straight to Edwin V. Morgan, April 5, 1907, and Straight to Huntington Wilson, May 10, 1908, Straight Papers; Roosevelt to Root, July 13, 1907, *The Letters of Theodore Roosevelt,* ed. Elting E. Morison (8 vols., Cambridge, 1951) V, 717.
5. Fletcher to Rockhill, January 11, 1909, Rockhill Papers; Roosevelt to the State Department, December 12, 1908, Morison, *Letters of Roosevelt,* VI, 1420; Huntington Wilson, *Memoirs,* 173, 175, 180; Jessup, *Root,* II, 250; Butt, *Taft and Roosevelt,* I, 372.
6. Taft to Rollo Ogden, April 24, 1909, and Taft to Henry S. Brown, April 1, 1909, Taft Papers.
7. Straight, "Notes on Harriman," and Harriman to Knox, February 5, 1909, Straight Papers.
8. Memorandum by William Phillips, May 10, 1909, Knox Papers.
9. Jessup, *Root,* II, 51, 432; Roosevelt to J. P. Morgan, July 18, 1905, Roosevelt Papers.
10. Roosevelt to J. P. Morgan, August 17, 1905, Roosevelt to Rockhill, August 29, 1905, Roosevelt to King Leopold of Belgium, August 31, 1905, Roosevelt Papers.
11. Bash to Huntington Wilson, June 20, 1909, NA, RG59:5315/282–283.
12. *Foreign Relations, 1909,* 147–148, 149, 150; Phillips to Knox, June 10, 1909, Knox Papers; Root to Rockhill, October 21, 1905, in Jessup, *Root,* II, 54.
13. J. O. P. Bland, *Recent Events and Present Policies in China* (Philadelphia, 1912), 245; Westel W. Willoughby, *Foreign Rights and Interests in China* (2 vols., Baltimore, 1927), II, 1063–1069; Fletcher to Root, Feb-

ruary 28, 1908, NA, RG59:5315/73–74; Fletcher to Root, January 17, 1908, *Foreign Relations, 1908,* 200–201.

14. Rockhill to Knox, March 13, 1909, NA, RG59:5315/192; Casenave, "Recollections of Willard Straight," and Straight, "Memorandum on the Hukuang Loan Negotiations," Straight Papers; Tait to Phillips, April 14, 1909, NA, RG59:5315/236.

15. Tait to Rockhill, September 24, 1908, Rockhill Papers; Paul Morton to Bacon, November 30, 1908, Tait to Bacon, December 3, 1908, Adee to Morton, December 5, 1908, and Rockhill to Root, December 28, 1908, NA, RG59:5315/146, 147, 174–175; J. Selwyn Tait, "American Possibilities in the Far East," *Journal of the American Asiatic Association,* 10 (February, 1910):22–23; Tait to Straight, March 23, 1909, NA, RG59:5315/234.

16. Rockhill to the Secretary of State, March 10, 1909, Knox to the American Legation, n.d., Rockhill to the Secretary of State, March 22, 1909, and Memorandum by William Phillips, March 22, 1909, NA, RG59:5315/187, 189.

17. Memorandum by Phillips to Knox, n.d., attached to a letter from Tait to Phillips, April 16, 1909, and Phillips to Knox, May 13, 1909, NA, RG59:5315/206, 236; Memorandum by William Phillips, May 10, 1909, Knox Papers; Bureau of Trade Relations, Department of State, September 15, 1909, "Memorandum Relative to American Trade Possibilities in the Far East," Knox Papers.

18. Phillips to Knox, May 18 and 21, 1909, NA, RG59:5315/207, 208–209.

19. Memorandum by Willard Straight, April 23, 1909, NA, RG59:788/224.

20. Huntington Wilson to Phillips, May 11, 1909, Phillips to Knox, May 6, and to Huntington Wilson, May 19, 1909, NA, RG59:788/266, 227, 267; Memorandum by Phillips, May 10, 1909, Knox Papers.

21. Tait to Phillips, April 25, 1909, and Memorandum by Phillips, May 21, 1909, NA, RG59:5315/237, 208–209.

22. Knox to the American Legation at Peking, May 21, 1909, sent on May 24, 1909, NA, RG59:5315/208–209; Straight Diary, May 24, 1909, Straight Papers; Fletcher to Knox, June 4, 1909, NA, RG59:5315/349.

23. Huntington Wilson to Rockhill, June 4, 1909, *Foreign Relations, 1909,* 148; Memorandum by Phillips to Knox, n.d., Knox Papers; Fletcher to Knox, June 4 and 9, 1909, NA, RG59:5315/349, 407–411.

24. Knox to Fletcher, June 12, 1909, *Foreign Relations, 1909,* 159–160; Lewis Einstein to Knox, October 17, 1910, Knox Papers; E. C. Baker to Phillips, August 30, 1909, and Phillips to Baker, same date, NA, RG59:788/277, 229–230; "Memorandum on the Chinese Loan," September 30, 1909, Knox Papers.

25. Reid to Knox, June 11, 1909, and Knox to Reid, June 12, 1909, NA, RG59:5315/228.

26. Memorandum by Huntington Wilson, June 28, 1909, NA, RG59:5315/307.

27. Memorandum by Huntington Wilson, June 19, 1909, NA, RG59:5315/295.

28. Straight to the Assistant Secretary of State, March 17, 1909, NA, RG59:2711/30; Carr to Straight, May 1, 1909, NA, RG59:2711/30A.

29. Straight to Knox, March 26, 1909, Straight Papers.

30. Straight to Schiff, March 18, 1909, Straight Papers; Schiff to Straight, March 19, 1909, in Cyrus Adler, *Jacob H. Schiff* (2 vols., New York, 1928), I, 248.

31. Straight to Schiff, March 27, 1909, Straight Papers.

32. Straight, "Notes on Harriman," and Straight Diary, May 5, 1909, Straight Papers.

33. Straight, "Notes on Harriman," Straight Papers; Huntington Wilson, *Memoirs,* 215; Huntington Wilson to the American Legation at Peking, June 3, 1909, and Huntington Wilson to Reid, White, and Hill, June 7, 1909, NA, RG59:5315/212, 217.

34. Thomas W. Lamont, *Henry P. Davison: The Record of a Useful Life* (New York, 1933), 165, 157.

35. Schiff to Takahashi, June 15, 1909, in Adler, *Schiff,* I, 250; Willard Straight, "American Friendship For China," *Journal of the American Asiatic Association,* 12 (November, 1912):298.

36. Harriman to James Stillman, July 2, 1909, in Anna R. Burr, *James Stillman* (New York, 1927), 268; Straight to the Assistant Secretary of State, June 9, 1909, Straight Papers.

37. Memorandum by Huntington Wilson, June 19, 1909, NA, RG59: 5315/296; *Journal of the American Asiatic Association,* 9 (July, 1909): 162.

38. Tait to Phillips, May 27 and June 3, 1909, Phillips to Tait, June 12, 1909, and Tait to Phillips, June 4, 1909, NA, RG59:5315/239–240, 241, 271A, 242.

39. Tait to Phillips, June 5 and 10, 1909, and Tait to General Clarence Edwards, June 7, 1909, NA, RG59:5315/243, 218–220, 244.

40. Hubbard to Tait, June 16, 1909, Tait to Knox, June 17, 1909, Hubbard to J. P. Morgan, Jr., June 17, 1909, and J. S. Fearon to Tait, June 19, 1909, NA, RG59:5315/264–265, 266–267, 268–269.

41. *Far Eastern Review,* 4 (April, 1910):523; Knox to Tait, June 18, 1909, Memorandum by Huntington Wilson, July 1, 1909, and Tait to Huntington Wilson, September 22, 1909, NA, RG59:5315/266–267, 332, 517.

42. Bash to Knox, June 16, 1909, and Bash to Huntington Wilson, June 20, 1909, NA, RG59:5315/260, 282–283; *New York Herald,* July 2, 1909; *Wall Street Journal,* February 16, 1910.

43. Straight to Reid, July 12, 1909, Reid Papers; Reid to Grenfell, July 12, 1909, Bash to Huntington Wilson, July 1, 1909, and Hoyt to Knox, November 17, 1909, NA, RG59:5315/378–380, 316–319, 591.

44. Hoyt to Knox, October 18, 1909, NA, RG59:893.77/881.

CHAPTER SIX

Harriman, Straight, and the American Group

Somehow, George Marvin could not shake off his teaching experience at Groton. The American bankers regarded Straight as an infant prodigy, but they also thought enough of Marvin to appoint him Secretary of the American Banking Group, with headquarters in New York. Standing in front of huge maps of China hung on the walls of the conference room, he met the bankers and informed them about the country in which they were prepared to invest large sums of money. Pointer in hand, Marvin traced existing and projected railroads across China's rivers and plains. He introduced the vocabulary of the Old China hand; his students learned that a "go-down" was a warehouse and that "shroffs" were cashiers. The bankers, he considered, were representative of the types found in any classroom. George Baker, the aging head of the First National Bank, floundered beyond his depth. Frank Vanderlip of the National City Bank said little and gave the impression that he knew the answers. Henry P. Davison of the House of Morgan did his homework assiduously in order to preside at the meeting of the directors. Paul Warburg of Kuhn, Loeb and Company was a star pupil, for he knew that Szechuen was a province and the Yangtze a river.[1] Only Edward H. Harriman played hooky.

Reinforced by the formation of the American Banking

113

Group, Washington continued to assert American demands for entrance to the Hukuang Loan. Huntington Wilson magnanimously surrendered the American claim to 50 per cent of the Hankow-Szechuen section for 25 per cent of the whole loan and equal rights for the purchase of railroad materials to be used in construction of the railroad. In his view, the United States asked for nothing "less than concurrent, simultaneous, equivalently guaranteed equal sharing by the American Group," and he made the point clear by threatening to repair "the breach of faith" suffered by American interests by cancelling the remission of the Boxer indemnity.[2]

This threat made the Chinese pause temporarily, and they held off final signature of the loan until the tripartite bankers settled terms with the American Group. The Germans opposed the grant of an equal share to the Americans and made a counteroffer of 25 per cent of the Hankow-Szechuen section alone. Impatient at the wrangling, Peking gathered its courage and insisted that the United States accept the German suggestion, lashing out at Huntington Wilson's conception of the American claims. China denied Washington's accuracy in basing its position on one-half of the Hankow-Szechuen section. In the case of the Hankow-Canton section, Peking was even more emphatic. The memory of the American China Development Company's past activities was still fresh, and China refused to recognize any American claim for this section of the proposed railroad trunk system.

Henry Fletcher, now in charge of the American Legation at Peking, had succeeded in delaying a final Hukuang agreement. Working through personal contact and leaving "as little evidence of 'pressure' as possible," he had high hopes for American claims. But the Chinese were aroused. Throughout the country, antipathy toward foreigners and provincial opposition to the administrators of the central government stiffened Peking's resistance. Fletcher's feeling of security vanished as the Prince of Ching, head of the Foreign Office, heatedly indicted the American record in the Hankow-Canton negotiations and presented an ultimatum: either the United States must accept a one-quarter share in the Hankow-Szechuen section or receive nothing at all.[3]

Strong measures were necessary. Taft intervened personally by sending his now-famous telegram of July 15 to the Chinese Regent, insisting upon American entrance to the loan. In an accompanying dispatch, Secretary Knox placed all the responsibility on China if American wishes were thwarted and offered to have American bankers assume the financing of the entire loan. Confronted by such determination, Peking had no choice, and orders went out from the Imperial Palace to admit the United States. "I think that quite a diplomatic victory," Taft rejoiced. Later, after poking the Chinese Minister in the ribs knowingly, he assured the envoy that "we only want your trade" and the opportunity to participate in the councils of the powers when Chinese matters are being discussed.[4]

While Washington grappled with China and the powers on the diplomatic front, Straight prepared to go to Europe for conferences with the tripartite bankers. Before his departure, he paid his respects to Roosevelt at Oyster Bay and was thoroughly briefed by Taft, Knox, Huntington Wilson, and Henry P. Davison, the Morgan partner in charge of the American Group. Eight days before Taft wired the Chinese Prince Regent, Straight arrived in London.

His reception was far from cordial. The European bankers were excited, and the Germans, whose efforts in China had finally gained a seat for the Deutsche Asiatische Bank among the financial powers, exhibited considerable nervous strain. Straight's first meeting with the tripartite group was a "stormy one—characterized by recriminations and innuendo and unmitigated by any measure of personal sympathy

or understanding." The tripartite bankers demanded documents that verified American claims, but Straight was not
able to produce them at the moment. The taut atmosphere
was intensified by the American Group's claim for a one-
quarter share in the whole loan. The reluctant Europeans
flatly refused, frightening Straight into the conviction that
the whole loan was doomed to collapse.[5]

The opposition of the Europeans moved the members of
the American Group to consider their position and function.
They were businessmen seeking a concrete proposition, and
they were willing to accept less than an equal share. Straight's
disheartening reports from London softened their insistence
upon an equal division of the loan, and they notified the
State Department that a 20 per cent share was agreeable.
Huntington Wilson refused. If the bankers accepted an un-
equal share in the loan, Washington's assertion of equal
status with the other powers in China would be weakened.
The Assistant Secretary refused to back down, and he asserted that if the American Group did not adhere to Washington's claims for equal opportunity, the State Department
would "seek other instrumentalities to secure proper American recognition." A step back by the bankers was a step
down in prestige for the American Government, the steward
of American interests, which "alone has any rights in this
matter." [6]

"A note privately for your ear," whispered George Marvin,
the peacemaker. J. P. Morgan, Jr., Henry Davison, Frank
Vanderlip, and Jacob Schiff felt that Washington need not
have the "slightest uneasiness" regarding the "attitude or
future deportment of the Group." The bankers were patriots,
and they had no intention of going against Washington's
wishes. The flurry of disagreement was smoothed over, but
Marvin and Straight urged Huntington Wilson to accept a
compromise in order to avoid a hopeless deadlock "that
would last forever." [7]

Straight then took to the road, visiting Hamburg, Berlin, and Paris and talked to the bankers interested in the negotiations. His London experience led him to despair of genuine international banking cooperation in China, and his conclusions were not altered by the end of his trip. Even the dream of Chinese railroad centralization under American auspices was affected by the hostility that he encountered from Europe's financial houses. He was persuaded that an agreement with them for future business in China was not desirable. After all, he reasoned, the American Group was powerful in its own right. Kuhn, Loeb and Company and J. P. Morgan and Company had outlets and connections in London, Hamburg, and Paris. Any agreement with the tripartite banks, moreover, was bound to stir up the resistance of the Chinese, who did not enjoy the prospect of being hemmed in by a financial ring.[8]

In Peking, Fletcher had suggested an increase of the whole loan by 12.5 per cent, thus providing for an equal American share, but no solution or agreement appeared imminent. Straight noticed a weakening of the British position and began playing with the idea of an Anglo-American financial alliance, working in conjunction with France and Russia. It was an idea, however, that developed from other considerations.[9]

Complex as they were, the Hukuang negotiations were not enough to keep Straight busy in London and on the continent. He still tended Harriman's fires, keeping warm the Manchurian projects that had occupied his attention in Mukden and Washington from 1907 to 1908: the Manchurian Bank, the purchase of the Chinese Eastern Railway from Russia, the construction of a railroad to link up with the Trans-Siberian Railroad. He gave his time to Hukuang affairs, but he was impatient to get on with Manchurian business. August 19, 1909, found him in Peking, seeking a solution for Harriman's railroad plans. Although the trip to

China was "ostensibly to secure participation for American interests in the Hukuang Railway loan," he wrote, "in reality my mission was to carry through Mr. Harriman's plans of securing an interest in railway construction in Manchuria, to obtain the link for his round-the-world transportation system. No one I think was familiar with his plans." [10]

Straight, however, had a good idea of Harriman's intentions. When he first arrived in England, Dr. Rutherford Harris of Pauling, the firm that had met defeat in the Hsinmintun-Fakumen deal, approached him. Engaged in the never-ending quest for railroad contracts, Harris asked that Pauling be made the construction arm of the American Group and proposed to use American funds and materials for future enterprises.

A week later, Straight discussed the matter with Lord ffrench, his old friend in Manchuria who still worked for Pauling. ffrench denied that his firm had accepted cooperation from a Japanese syndicate, backed by high officials in Tokyo, for the construction of the Chinchow-Tsitsihar line. It was an obvious reminder that Tang had promised construction rights for this railroad to the British before he went to the United States in 1908. ffrench asserted, as he had before, that Downing Street backed the construction of the Chinchow-Tsitsihar line provided Japan did not protest.[11] And if Japan objected? It was an unasked question, for J. O. P. Bland now joined the reunion, rounding out the friendly trio of planners and manipulators of the machinery of international politics and finance in Manchuria.

Bland was no longer employed by the British and Chinese Corporation because of his mishandling of the Hankow-Canton negotiations at the time the Germans successfully entered the Hukuang project. He was, nevertheless, still the confident interpreter of international affairs, still virulently anti-Japanese and anti-German. Together with ffrench, he reported the existence of strong English opposition to

Anglo-German financial cooperation in China. France obviously did not enjoy its weak financial position in China, while Russia, with no financial position in China proper at all, was restive.

The thing to do, Bland believed, was to admit Russia to some participation in Chinese investment schemes and secure diplomatic support from St. Petersburg. This would drive a wedge into Anglo-French-German financial arrangements in such matters as the Hukuang Loan. Britain, always the friend of the United States, together with Russia and France (Germany's European rivals), would then join the United States in the creation of a new financial alignment.[12]

Straight was impressed with the logic of the scheme. True, the Bland-ffrench outline contemplated Russian entrance to the Hukuang Loan; but Straight, who thought in terms of Manchuria, felt that Russia still had a measure of economic and political power in the region. He agreed with ffrench that a small participation in the Chinchow-Tsitsihar line should be given the Russo-Asiatic Bank, perhaps the handling of Pauling's account. Thus Straight modified his original aim for sole American handling of Chinese loans. But his approval of a Russian role in Chinese finance was due also to other influences. In mid-July, 1909, Straight had seen Harriman.[13]

Although stricken with illness, Harriman sailed for Europe in May, 1909. This was a month before Straight went to London and while the members of the newly formed American Group were receiving briefings from George Marvin. In Paris, Harriman spoke with Eduard Noetzlin, the French banker, who was Schiff's personal contact with Russia's government and financial experts. Directly in the background of these conversations were the unsuccessful Schiff-Wilenkin negotiations in the fall of 1908 for the combined purchase of the Chinese Eastern Railway and the South Manchurian Railroad.

Conditions appeared favorable for another Russian effort to sell the Chinese Eastern Railway. Finance Minister Kokovtsov planned to visit Manchuria in the fall of 1909 in order to examine the Russian railroad holdings which were causing so much difficulty for St. Petersburg.[14] Economically, the railroad was a drain on the Russian treasury, and political relations with Washington were tense because of the actions of the railroad administrators in attempting to impose their control over the Harbin municipality in the late spring of 1907.

Russian administrative confusion and rumors of a possible sale of the Chinese Eastern Railway to Japan had alerted Fred Fisher, the American Consul General in Harbin. As concerned for American trade in Northern Manchuria as his colleague Willard Straight in the south, Fisher protested against Russia's attempt to override its railroad jurisdiction through control of Harbin. Fearing that any Russian success would embolden Japan to take similar measures in the south, Straight supported Fisher.[15]

Washington followed the advice of its consuls and rejected St. Petersburg's request that Fisher be restrained. The State Department argued that not only was the open door being violated, but that Japan, Russia's former enemy, stood to profit more from the Harbin action than Russia. Determined not to make an issue of Harbin while the United States had difficulties with Japan, Secretary Root called on Britain for assistance, only to receive weak replies from London.[16] Seeking a way out of the impasse, Straight had recommended that Harbin be made an international settlement, but the proposal did not receive effective support from the other powers. There the matter rested until May, 1909, when Russia and China signed an agreement over Harbin, one which Washington later refused to recognize.[17]

All this did not concern Harriman, who wanted to establish a connection with the Trans-Siberian Railroad. Noetzlin informed him that Russia desired to cooperate for the financing of a railroad on the right bank of the Liao River running north from a Chinese deep water port. If this was not feasible, the French banker held open an opportunity for Harriman to assist in improving Russia's present holdings in the Chinese Eastern Railway. The Russians merely awaited a proposition; meantime China's fear of Japan practically guaranteed Peking's approval for any competitive line that would weaken the strength of Japan's grip on the Manchurian railway system.[18] Harriman rose to the occasion and fired up Straight's predilection for large-scale political and financial maneuvers.

When Straight visited the railroad magnate at Bad Gastein, he found the latter "down on his luck," but definitely still active. Harriman explained Noetzlin's proposition to Straight and laid his plans with the ex-Consul General. Japan became the primary target, as Harriman intended to box the South Manchurian Railroad between two competing railways. The Russian overture reopened the possibility of purchasing the Chinese Eastern Railway, which, if connected to a newly constructed line running north from a deep water port, would hamstring the Japanese.

"Once an agreement had been reached with the Russians and the right for the construction of a north and south line secured from China," Straight wrote, "we would have been in a position to negotiate with the Japanese. If they had been willing to make some arrangements regarding joint operation of the South Manchurian Railway it would have been unnecessary to construct another north and south line. If they were unwilling to make such an agreement, the construction of another north and south line operating in conjunction with the Russian road would have placed them in a very embarrassing position." [19]

As it then stood, Harriman returned to his original proposition with Japan of 1905. He and the Japanese empire were to enter into a mutually beneficial partnership. Harriman could reach Europe; Japan would have money and American know-how to operate its railroad. If Tokyo refused—and the opposition to the Hsinmintun-Fakumen Railroad and the rejection of Schiff's offer in 1908 indicated that no change in attitude was forthcoming from Tokyo—Harriman stood to gain and Japan to lose. China? With Straight doing the work, Harriman was helping China to preserve its hold on Manchuria by installing an American interest in the area. Russia, harassed by internal administrative dissension, financial difficulty, and fear of Japan, held the key to American success. Noetzlin's move was a saving action that repaired the broken link with Russia caused by Schiff's rebuff of Wilenkin. It was, in fact, a continuation of Wilenkin's conversations with Schiff in 1908.

There were three things that Harriman had to do in order to assure smooth execution of his plans. He had to have Straight directly on the scene in China; he had to jog Noetzlin and the Russians; and he had to reveal his plans to the American Group in which he had a share. On the first two counts, he was decisive; on the last he was indefinite.

Harriman sent Straight on a hurried trip to Peking. "I intend talking to both Mr. Morgan and Mr. Schiff on my return," he notified Straight, "but I want you to be prepared with the Chinese end of it, so that a quick decision may be had in case the Russians materialize." Since Straight's trip to Peking was ostensibly to work on Hukuang matters, it shadowed his mission for Harriman.[20]

Much impressed by Bland's analysis of the Russian situation, Straight brought Bland and Harriman together in Paris. Bland repeated his views on Russia, and Harriman promised to transmit them to the American Group when he arrived home. But before Harriman left Europe, he exhibited the impatience of a sick man trying to make one last coup. "I have not time to work out combinations and groups and

alliances, and mix diplomacy with business. Let us try and
have, if anything, a plain straight-forward transaction."
Those were his orders to Noetzlin. He wanted a proposition
from the Russians, one that was contingent upon China's
consent and the physical possibility of a new north-south
line in Manchuria that could be used either as a transportation link or as a weapon to threaten the Japanese and force
them to submit.[21]

While Straight was still with him at Bad Gastein, Harriman
wrote his colleagues in New York. Straight's account of the
American Group's difficult relations with the European
bankers gave him an opening. "I fear that you will all be
disappointed in the outcome of Chinese matters," he advised
Davison. He urged the American bankers to exercise patience, and he cautioned the Group not to expect too much
in the short time it had operated in the China field. Then, in
an extremely guarded fashion, he prepared New York for
his Manchurian venture.

> I want to use Straight for some purposes of my own (not busi-
> ness), for which he will have plenty of time, and do not want
> anyone to know of it. In arranging with him for it I would like
> you to speak to Mr. Morgan and he and you to consent and so
> advise Straight. I want it without any conditions, and only Mr.
> Morgan and you to know. Of course nothing shall interfere with
> his obligations to the Group, and I will pay any expense attached
> to my things. I would have done this whether or no the Group
> had taken Straight up. Please read this to Mr. Morgan.
> I fear the European group will resort to measures in China
> which will not be creditable in methods of construction and deal-
> ing generally with the Chinese. I hope for purely American in-
> fluence in some one thing, so we can show them how to do it
> right, and thus get a real and lasting American influence.[22]

With this accomplished, Straight went on to Peking, and
Harriman made preparations to return to the United States.
Now aware of Harriman's negotiations with Russia through
the personal agency of Noetzlin, Straight thought that it
would "be well to follow pretty sympathetically any move to

introduce Russia into the financial situation," but he feared antagonizing the Hongkong and Shanghai Bank and the Deutsche Asiatische Bank, the two financial institutions with loan obligations in China. Russian entrance might engender British and German hostility since their loans would have to be converted. If they refused, the ultimate centralization of China's railroads under the aegis of foreign finance which now included American interests would be blocked.[23] Now that Harriman was moving into Manchuria, it was a chance that Straight was willing to take.

On the way to Peking, Straight stopped off in St. Petersburg and confirmed Bland's information regarding Russia's willingness to participate in the international banking group. Even though he noted the existence of some strife between the Russian Finance Ministry and the Ministry of Foreign Affairs, he believed that Russia would be amenable to joining the new financial arrangements shaping up in China and would sell the Chinese Eastern Railway.

Tokyo, however, was not St. Petersburg. Japan's power in Manchuria had increased steadily, and in the summer of 1909, it forced the Chinese to settle several important Manchurian mining and railway questions. It was quite obvious to Peking that the Russian position in Northern Manchuria compounded the danger created by Japan in the southern section of the region. Despite past disappointments, the Chinese sought salvation through American economic aid.[24]

As early as March, 1909, Japan made overtures to China for construction of a line west of Fakumen to connect with the South Manchurian Railroad, promising in return to permit construction of the Hsinmintun-Fakumen Railroad. Tokyo's bid was poorly timed and ill conceived; if anything, China wanted Japan blocked. Resolving to run its own line into Mongolia, Peking concentrated on the construction of a road from the port of Hulutao going north to Chinchow, Taonanfu, Tsitsihar, and on to Aigun, near the Amur River.

This proposed line had the virtue not only of encouraging colonization of China's northern frontier with Russia but also of freeing trade from the Russian and Japanese transportation monopoly in Manchuria. It also would have opened Mongolia to agricultural and mining development.

In Washington, R. S. Miller of the Division of Far Eastern Affairs and at Peking, chargé Fletcher believed that the contemplated road would neutralize Russia and Japan in Manchuria, particularly since foreign funds would be required to finance construction. "It would be very interesting if the American syndicate would take up this railway also," Miller wrote. "Being further west than the Fakumen line, it might be put through without arousing serious opposition from the Japanese, especially if supported by American influence." [25]

None of this was news to Straight, but the Chinchow-Aigun proposal, the tense political atmosphere in Manchuria, Harriman's railroad plans, Kuhn, Loeb's interest in financing China's purchase of Russia's and Japan's Manchurian railways, Bland's political analyses regarding Russia, and Pauling's desire for construction contracts were reshaped, juggled, and manipulated by Straight in a course of action that not even his mentor, Harriman, would have recognized. Willard Straight set out to synthesize the haphazardly organized but related Manchurian railroad and financial schemes that had sputtered and then flashed since 1905.

The Chinese were in a "blue funk" by the time he arrived in Peking. True to the tradition established by Straight, Frederick D. Cloud, his successor as Consul General in Mukden, "drilled" into the Chinese the conviction that Manchuria's security required American economic support. Straight immediately opened the Manchurian question with imperial officials in Peking and promised to visit Mukden "at the earliest possible date." [26]

The Chinese officials in Peking were conservative and

feared Tokyo. They needed funds for the centralization of railroads in China proper. Perhaps Straight was interested? No, that must be postponed, Straight declared. Conditions in Manchuria differed from those existing in China proper, and the Chinchow-Aigun Railroad was a business proposition, as Harriman insisted. Operations in China proper were enmeshed in complicated political and financial relations, the untangling of which required more time than was available at the moment.[27]

While he lobbied with Chinese officials in Peking, Straight made an agreement with ffrench, who was on the scene. Pauling had rights to the line from Chinchow to Tsitsihar acquired from Tang in 1908, and Harriman had the rights to the line from Tsitsihar to Aigun which Straight had received from Tang in the late summer of 1907. Straight and ffrench pooled forces and combined both sections into a single operation under the control of an Anglo-American syndicate. Pauling would build the road using American engineers and materials, and the American Group would finance the entire construction. This Anglo-American syndicate would be controlled by a Chinese-American group, and any financial participation by outsiders would require China's consent. If granted, such participation would be limited to no more than 40 per cent, thus keeping financial control in American hands.

Taking his cue from Bland and Harriman, Straight informed Kuhn, Loeb and Company of a touchy subject. A small percentage given to the Russo-Asiatic Bank assured Russian political support. But it was justified since it opened Manchuria and Mongolia. "This is a rare opportunity," he wrote. Straight also broke the news to J. P. Morgan and Company, adding that the Americans and Englishmen on the Board of Directors would control policy and that the Chinchow-Aigun Railroad offered "an excellent chance for extension into Siberia as well," a prospect that jibed well with Morgan's interest in Russian investment.[28]

Next he hurried off a letter to Harriman, who was to explain the scheme to the members of the American Group. Considerable explanation was needed. Straight's agreement with ffrench assumed that diplomatic support from London would be forthcoming, while Harriman and Bland were certain of backing from St. Petersburg and Paris. But the problem of Germany and Japan remained. The Germans were members of the tripartite banking group in the Hukuang Loan; the Japanese had power in Manchuria. Through the Chinchow-Aigun scheme, London could be used as an effective buffer against its Asiatic ally, Japan. But Germany occupied a vital position. If Berlin's bankers entered Manchuria, they would split the Anglo-French-Russian combination which the American Group, through its hold on the Chinchow-Aigun Railroad, was in a position to control. Straight suggested that Harriman call on Max Warburg in Hamburg, Kuhn, Loeb's close European associate, to persuade the German Foreign Office not to demand a share.[29]

Straight was certain that Harriman would explain to the American Group the larger scope of the enterprise that included the Chinchow-Aigun Railroad. He assumed that his own letters would arrive in time to amplify the situation and wired for permission to negotiate an agreement with China. New York appreciated the "attractive features of the Manchurian proposition," but believed it "unwise" to take it up before the Hukuang Loan was concluded. The American Group was interested and asked for further information as well as a copy of any proposed agreement. That was all.[30]

Straight found the American bankers' response unsatisfactory, and he wired Harriman that the Chinchow-Aigun road was the first step in the new scheme proposed by Bland. If a German interest had to be admitted, it should be the firm represented by Max Warburg. This would stifle any complaints by the German Foreign Office that its interests were being ignored and offset the rumors passed around by the Deutsche Asiatische Bank that Americans were not seriously interested in China. In keeping with Harriman's desires and his own beliefs, Straight thought that the American State Department should be kept out of the affair unless Japan raised opposition. Having learned that political means for economic ends reacted against her, China was interested only if the negotiations steered clear of governmental interference; thus the actual business interests concerned had to take the lead.[31] But Straight's telegram was wasted.

Harriman died on September 10, 1909. He had been the one man who was determined to work in the Manchurian field. The burden of execution now fell on Straight, who played a complicated role. Hired by the American Group seeking railway loans in China proper, he had diverted his energies to Harriman's projects in Manchuria. Not content with this, Straight had then made Harriman's plan the core of a larger project, without much certainty that even Harriman approved of it. Impulsively, Straight pressed on; he negotiated with China and incurred German hostility without the approval of the American Group whom he represented. Harriman's death had deprived him of a champion in New York; there was nothing else to do but go on.

Manchurian officials in Mukden, desirous of signing an agreement, anxiously awaited Straight. "Our people cannot expect me to discuss a question of this sort without committing them to a certain extent," he complained. On September 15, 1909, he wired New York for authority to sign the Chinchow-Aigun agreement and wrote a long letter to Jacob Schiff, who had been in touch with Harriman six days before Harriman's death.[32] The letter to Schiff was necessary because New York's refusal to pursue the Chinchow-Aigun plan convinced Straight that Harriman had not explained matters to his colleagues. The virtues of the proposition were so obvious to Straight that he could only think that the bankers did not have a clear grasp of its nature.

Cognizant of Schiff's anti-Russian attitude, Straight emphasized activity in Manchuria and Mongolia rather than Siberia, though he did mention the latter. Straight's argument depended on several premises. First, Russia and its allied French economic interests fretted over the entrance of German interests into the Russo-Chinese Bank. The only way to vitiate this unwelcome influence was either to "inject new life" into the bank or extend Russian financial activities to China and Manchuria. Russian finance could check Japan in Manchuria, while its financial cooperation in China proper would have a wholesome effect in restoring St. Petersburg's waning prestige in the Far East. Anglo-American-French capital was an effective means of achieving both ends, and St. Petersburg's support was promised to insure diplomatic protection for Manchurian and Mongolian enterprises.

The best opportunities were in these two regions. Americans could "act as partners and not lenders alone," for the tight international political situation drove China to accept "more favorable terms than could be secured elsewhere." The antiforeign popular sentiment that harried loan schemes in China proper was absent. What concrete actions should be taken? Straight had a five-point plan.

First, the cooperating Anglo-American interests (Pauling and the American Group) should follow through on the Chinchow-Aigun Railroad project by admitting the Russians in a minor financial role. Next, the Sino-American-British Company (controlled by the American interest) that operated the Chinchow-Aigun line should purchase the Chinese Eastern Railway from Russia. There was room here for a political coup, because Russia, wary of Japan, would draw up a political agreement with the United States, similar to the Root-Takahira agreement. This would protect St. Petersburg against Tokyo, facilitate the transfer of the Chinese Eastern Railway, and eliminate the Harbin issue, thus giving China sovereignty and administrative control in Manchuria. Japan would then be forced to follow suit—the fourth step in Straight's outline—or be charged with bad faith for refusing to fulfill the provisions of the Portsmouth Treaty and the Komura Agreement with China.

The final blow for American interests would be struck with the revival of the Manchurian Bank scheme which had been discussed as a combined Chinese-American enterprise. "The success of the project," Straight wrote Schiff, "would mean the development of Manchuria and Mongolia under American and British auspices, would ensure to us an entry into Siberia, and would go far to preserve the peace of the East by practically neutralizing Manchuria its danger spot."

The diplomatic means for checking Tokyo were available. Straight viewed the Russo-Japanese Treaty of 1907, the Anglo-Russian accord, and the Root-Takahira Agreement as bonds that would make Tokyo's opposition to a Russo-American entente "hardly a diplomatic probability." If Japan maintained its obstructionist tactics, it could be brought over by some financial participation, or embarrassed by reminder of its 1905 negotiations with Harriman, or threatened by "judicious manipulation of the American and European attitude" toward the conversion of Tokyo's war loans.

In sum, then, Straight proposed to establish American financial supremacy in Manchuria and Mongolia and effect entrance into Siberia. Germany and Japan were "the only disturbing factors," he believed. There was a chance to persuade the Germans to cooperate he thought, but the Japanese "must be forced by diplomacy into line." In order to heighten Schiff's interest (and in keeping with the trend of the times), Straight concluded with a rousing finale. He hoped that the banker would consider this scheme "in connection with our transcontinental railways, Pacific shipping, and the development to follow the completion of the Panama Canal."

It was an American project with elements which Straight carefully kept apart. He discussed the purchase of the Chinese Eastern Railway with Fletcher and with Edward T. Williams, who was on his way back to Washington to take charge of the Division of Far Eastern Affairs. To his cohorts, Bland and ffrench, he mentioned only Russia's participation in the Chinchow-Aigun Railroad.[33]

Having revealed his expanded conception of the Harriman railroad project, Straight continued his talks with the Chinese. He suspected some Chinese officials in Peking of collaborating with Japan, but the pro-American element at the capital urged him to consult with the Manchurian administration. A week after dispatching his important letter to Schiff, Straight arrived in Mukden and found the government officials there waiting to close an agreement with him.

Although he was handicapped by lack of authorization from New York and by the absence of Lord ffrench, who was to initial the contract for the British interest, Straight took an important step. On October 2, 1909, he signed a preliminary agreement for the construction of the Chinchow-Aigun Railroad. The risk was really not so great, he explained, for if the American Group refused to accept the contract, it would be simple to "get out by insisting on impossible terms." By committing the Manchurian Viceroy and Governor, the American Group had established its claim.[34]

Once they had acted, the Manchurian officials became uneasy. The regrets expressed by the Viceroy, "whose feet were very cold," angered Straight. The time had come for a "showdown," he declared. "I had come out for Manchurian business on the assumption that China could do her part. If she could not, I might as well quit," he admitted. But if Japan did oppose the railroad, would the United States fight, the Chinese still wanted to know. Yes, they were assured, but first China must issue an imperial edict that would validate the preliminary agreement of October 2 and create a vested American interest in Manchuria. Then and only then was American diplomatic support available. "It is much like surf riding this Manchurian game," Straight wrote to Davison. "One has to seize the right wave or run the risk of being upset altogether." He promised not to act without authority again, but stated that political uncertainty in Manchuria had made the contract possible and there was no alternative.[35]

The American Group did not find the water as rough as it had been earlier, but neither did it want to venture too far out. New York accepted the contract with the qualification that it relied on Straight's assurance that the Group could retreat if necessary. The bankers were willing to consider the Manchuria-Mongolia-Siberia enterprise, but neither it nor the Chinchow-Aigun line was to take precedence over the Hukuang Loan. No one told this to Bland, who had returned with important news from St. Petersburg in mid-October, 1909, after meeting with Russian officials.[36]

The Russians agreed to admit American and English capital to Siberia. The way was open for an Anglo-American syndicate to finance and construct a line from Irkutsk, the capital of Siberia, to Kalgan in Mongolia. St. Petersburg offered an additional plum in return for Anglo-American aid against Japan. Mining concessions, agreements for future railway construction, and a contract for the construction of a stretch of railroad from Stretensk to Nicolaevsk on the strategic Amur Railroad were further examples of a Russian desire to link up with an Anglo-French-American financial combination.

Bland's news added considerable substance to the Siberian part of the large proposition. The Kalgan line to Irkutsk and the combined trackage of the Chinchow-Aigun Railroad and the Chinese Eastern Railway provided two outlets for

Siberian produce. "We should be able to gain the very thing the Russians fought for," Straight exulted, "by playing Russia and China against Japan, and holding the Japanese down on the 'open door' declarations." Once again he explained the relationship of the political question to the economic picture, hoping to bring the American Group around to his point of view.

"I have already written that I believe Manchuria, Mongolia, and Siberia to offer the best field for the activities of the Group. China proper is now too much ridden by the gentry whose anti-foreign predilections have not yet been tempered by good sense and a realization of their own inability without foreign money to develop the country. The time will come when this fact will be recognized. For the present, however, I believe that our efforts should be made to get a strong hold on the development of the Russian Far East and of these Chinese dependencies, using the advantage which our political position has given us." [37]

A day later he thrust the Manchurian Bank scheme into his already overcrowded railroad bundle, recommending that provision for the bank be made in the final railroad agreements. And now that the Irkutsk-Kalgan line had emerged as a possibility, he thought of linking it to the Chinese-owned Peking-Kalgan line and building a branch line to the Chinchow-Aigun Railroad. [38]

The next move was toward Russa. Noetzlin and Bland had been the bearers of tidings from St. Petersburg up until November, 1909. It was now incumbent on Straight to approach the Russians, but time and Washington caught up with him. So swiftly did the State Department travel that its onward rush carried it past Straight, who vainly waved for reduced speed. In 1911, the debris still littered the diplomatic and financial landscape.

NOTES

1. George Marvin, "Willard Straight," *Japan,* 13 (November–December, 1924):33–45.

2. Huntington Wilson to Hill, June 25, 1909, *Papers Relating to the Foreign Relations of the United States, 1906–1913* (Washington, 1909–1920), *1909,* 166; Huntington Wilson to the American Legation in Peking, June 19, 1909, NA, RG59:5315/299.

3. Fletcher to Huntington Wilson, July 14, 1909, NA, RG59:5315/473; Prince of Ching to Fletcher, July 14, 1909, *Foreign Relations, 1909,* 171.

4. Archie Butt to Clara, July 18 and November 21, 1909, in Archibald W. Butt, *Taft and Roosevelt, The Intimate Letters of Archie Butt* (2 vols., New York, 1930), I, 145–146, 215; Taft to G. W. Painter, September 6, 1909, Taft Papers.

5. Straight to J. P. Morgan and Company, July 8, 1909, and Straight to Huntington Wilson, July 11 and 10, 1909, NA, RG59:5315/355–356, 400, 376; Straight to Harriman, July 12, 1909, Straight Papers.

6. Marvin to Huntington Wilson, July 8, 1909, NA, RG59:5315/344; Huntington Wilson to Reid, Hill, and White, July 9, 1909, *Foreign Relations, 1909,* 171.

7. Marvin to Huntington Wilson, July 10, 1909, NA, RG59:5315/246; Schiff to Cassel, July 20, 1909, in Cyrus Adler, *Jacob H. Schiff* (2 vols., New York, 1928), I, 252; Straight to Huntington Wilson, July 11, 1909, and Marvin to Huntington Wilson, July 12, 1909, NA, RG59:5315/400, 350.

8. Straight Diary, July 25–31, 1909, Straight to Harriman, July 23, 1909, Straight to J. P. Morgan and Company, August 1, 1909, and Straight to Huntington Wilson, August 3, 1909, Straight Papers.

9. Straight to Harriman, August 2 and 3, 1909, and Straight to J. P. Morgan and Company, August 1, 1909, Straight Papers.

10. Straight, "Notes on Harriman," Straight Papers.

11. Straight to J. P. Morgan and Company, July 16, 1909, and Straight, "Memorandum of a Conversation with Lord ffrench," July 22, 1909, Straight Papers.

12. Straight Diary, July 28, 1909, and Straight to Harriman, August 2, 1909, Straight Papers.

13. Straight, "Memorandum of a Conversation with Lord ffrench," and Straight Diary, July 19–22, 1909, Straight Papers.

14. Noetzlin to Harriman, August 14, 1909, Straight Papers.

15. Fisher to Rockhill, February 19, March 26, May 3, and July 6, 1907, Rockhill Papers; Fisher to Fletcher, December 20, 1907, Phillips to Huntington Wilson, February 6, 1908, and Straight to the Assistant Secretary of State, January 2, 1909, NA, RG59:4002/3–10, 2, 11.

16. Root to Reid, April 11, 1908, NA, RG59:4002/2; Root to Reid, May 22, 1908, Root Papers; Root to Adee, June 19, 1908, in Philip C. Jessup, *Elihu Root* (2 vols., New York, 1935), II, 52–53.

17. Memorandum by Willard Straight, November 18 and December 11, 1908, NA, RG59:4002/2, 110; Fisher to the Assistant Secretary of State, August 29, 1908, and Phillips to the Secretary of State, February 19, 1909, NA, RG59:4002/127, 142.

18. Noetzlin to Harriman, August 14, 1909, Straight Papers.

19. Straight, "Notes on Harriman," Straight Papers.

20. Harriman to Straight, August 18, 1909, and Straight, "Notes on Harriman," Straight Papers.

21. Straight to Harriman, August 7, 1909, Harriman to Straight, August 18, 1909, and Harriman to Noetzlin, August 18, 1909, Straight Papers.

22. Harriman to Davison, July 21, 1909, Straight Papers.

23. Straight to Harriman, August 2, 1909, and "Memorandum Concerning the Purpose of the Manchurian Administration," n.d., but drawn up by Straight, Straight Papers.

24. Straight Diary, August 5, 7, and 10, 1909, and Straight to Harriman, August 8 and 23, 1909, Straight Papers.

25. Frederick D. Cloud to the Assistant Secretary of State, March 20, 1909, and Fletcher to Knox, July 29, 1909, NA, RG59:5315/198–199, 420; Fletcher to the Secretary of State, January 24, 1910, NA, RG59:893.77/840.

26. Cloud to Straight, August 18, 1909, Straight Papers; Cloud to the Assistant Secretary of State, August 20, 1909, and Fletcher to Knox, August 23, 1909, NA, RG59:5767/87,89; Straight Diary, August 20, 1909, and Straight to Cloud, August 22, 1909, Straight Papers.

27. Straight Diary, August 24 and 25, 1909, Straight Papers.

28. Straight, "Notes on Harriman," and Straight Diary, August 22, 1909, Straight Papers; Straight to Kuhn, Loeb and Company, September 4, 1909, NA, RG59:5315/483–486; Straight to J. P. Morgan and Company, September 5, 1909, Straight Papers.

29. Straight to Harriman, September 6, 1909, Straight Papers.

30. Straight to Kuhn, Loeb and Company, September 6, 1909, and J. P. Morgan and Company to Straight, September 8, 1909, NA, RG59:5315/483–486, 492–493.

31. Straight to Harriman, September 9, 1909, and Straight to J. P. Morgan and Company, September 10, 1909, Straight Papers.

32. Straight Diary, September 14 and 15, 1909, Straight Papers; Adler, Schiff, I, 117.

33. Straight to Schiff, September 19, 1909, and Straight to J. P. Morgan and Company, September 21, 1909, Straight Papers.

34. Straight Diary, September 20 and 30, 1909, Straight to J. P. Morgan and Company, September 23 and October 22, 1909, and Straight to ffrench, October 2, 1909, Straight Papers; Straight to J. P. Morgan and Company, October 3, 1909, NA, RG59:5315/587–590.

35. Straight Diary, October 9, 10, and 11, 1909, and Straight to Davison, October 11 and 14, 1909, Straight Papers.

36. J. P. Morgan and Company to Straight, October 8 and 22, 1909, and Straight to J. P. Morgan and Company, October 19, 1909, Straight Papers.

37. Straight to Davison, October 14, 1909, Straight Papers.

38. Straight Diary, October 15, 1909, and Straight to J. P. Morgan and Company, October 19, 1909, Straight Papers.

CHAPTER SEVEN

Neutralization and the Chinchow-Aigun Railroad

"Not a sympathetic man . . . manners of a Russian bureaucrat . . . reactionary . . . considerable conceit . . . overbearing . . . martinet . . . unable to control his antipathy in discussing the policy of the United States in the Orient." [1]

Thus ran an American diplomat's description of Alexander Iswolsky, Russia's Foreign Minister during the period of the American attempt to put through the Chinchow-Aigun Railroad, the first step in Straight's grandiose plans for American activity in Manchuria, Mongolia, and Siberia. Iswolsky's attitude and manner, however, were less important than Russia's formidable position in the pre-World War I international political alignment. Russia, Great Britain, and France opposed Germany in Europe. China and Russia confronted Japan in Manchuria. Straight believed it vital to prevent a merger of Berlin and Tokyo, and the Anglo-French-Russian combination was an important factor to this end. He also realized that if London backed British interests active in Manchuria against Japan, Tokyo would turn toward St. Petersburg. The Russians, therefore, were the weak link and required a diplomatic alternative in order to resist a Japanese overture. And the expected result? By taking advantage of China's fear of Russia and Japan in Manchuria, and Russia's fear of Japan and Germany, the American Group stood to "secure the greatest measure of profit." [2]

Now that a connection with St. Petersburg became important in his plans, Straight thought of approaching Russia but delayed until he had a Chinese imperial edict that ratified the Chinchow-Aigun preliminary agreement of October 2, 1909. While he waited, he wired New York for permission to make arrangements with the Russian Minister in Peking for future financial cooperation in Manchuria and Mongolia when the edict was issued. Alert to the fact that an important diplomatic question was involved, Davison dutifully forwarded Straight's message to the State Department.[3]

Four days later, the American Group responded favorably to the admission of the Russians with a "nominal participation" and instructed Straight to await issuance of the edict. Enmeshed in the details of the Hukuang negotiations, New York appreciated more fully Straight's chain of messages and letters regarding the Chinchow-Aigun Railroad. The Group now agreed with its representative that "plans and terms will be more favorable and more easily handled in Manchurian business than can be hoped for in China proper." [4]

It was a signal victory for Straight. Through New York's commitment to the Chinchow-Aigun road, he successfully transferred the American Group's interest to Manchuria. Thus he made the State Department's instrument the overseer of Harriman's earlier project which he had transformed into the larger plan for Manchuria, Mongolia, and Siberia. Straight's scheme now took hold in Washington.

The settlement of Manchurian questions by China and Japan late in the summer of 1909 alerted the State Department to the seriousness of the situation. E. Carlton Baker of the Division of Far Eastern Affairs viewed the turn of affairs in Manchuria as an infringement of American economic interests. Tokyo, he noted, was bent upon control of Man-

churia's trade, railways, and mineral deposits. Japan's statesmen had drawn up an imperial program as a response to
their conviction that meager resources and a large population
at home required *Lebensraum* in Manchuria. There was, in
addition, need for a strategic buffer against Russia in the
Far East. Clearly it was up to Washington to do something,
and the course of action that it undertook was directed by
considerations arising from the American Group's swing-
over into Manchuria.

As early as August, 1909, the State Department had
knowledge of Straight's activities. Before leaving Europe for
Peking, he had outlined to Huntington Wilson the difficulties
of the Hukuang Loan and had introduced Harriman's Russian cooperation proposition. Straight dwelt heavily on the
necessity of admitting Russia to the banking combination in
Europe in exchange for St. Petersburg's political support of
American enterprises in Northern Manchuria and Mongolia.[5]

A little over a month later, Washington learned of Tokyo's
overtures to ffrench and the possibility of a successful Japanese protest against the Chinchow-Aigun line. The source
of information was Straight, who felt that there was no need
for concern. Lord Grey, Britain's Foreign Minister, had
promised to support construction of the line as far north
as Taonanfu. Of course, the Foreign Secretary had warned
that extension of the line past Taonanfu to Tsitsihar might
justify a Japanese protest on the grounds that it prejudiced
the South Manchurian Railroad, but Straight brushed this
aside, asserting that such a claim would not have any political
or geographical basis. In addition, Straight cited a familiar
formula to Huntington Wilson: Japanese objections would
be a violation of the open door that checked an Anglo-
American enterprise. If Washington took a strong stand on
the issue, the British lion might be encouraged to roar louder
at its Japanese ally.

Still worried about the Sino-Japanese settlement of Manchurian questions, chargé Fletcher insisted on September 23, 1909, that Washington exact a statement from Japan regarding its intentions in Manchuria, particularly since Straight was discussing the Chinchow-Aigun project with China.[6] Two days later, Straight gathered up the loose ends for Huntington Wilson.

> The Manchurian projects are of course very important and if carried through should be of far reaching consequences. My own idea is that once we have the Chinchow-Aigun line started we should open negotiations with the Russians for the Chinese-Eastern Railway, secure the withdrawal of Russia's claims in the Railway settlements and the removal of the Railway guards. This done we will be in a position to force Japan, particularly since she wants to revise her treaties and convert her war loans, to withdraw her guards and her administrative claims, thus restoring Manchuria in fact as well as name, to China, and virtually neutralizing the country. With the Manchurian Bank in running order we should then with China and our associates, British or German or French as the case might be, be able to undertake the commercial and industrial development of this region.[7]

Straight's mention of the railway settlement dispute with Russia came at an opportune time, for both nations were deadlocked on the Harbin issue. Washington viewed Russia's claims as an unwarranted assumption of power and a dangerous precedent for Japan's exertion of similar claims in South Manchuria. St. Petersburg wavered between fear of Japan and uncertainty about the United States. Chained to its stake in Manchuria, the Russian bear growled at the United States and Japan, waiting for someone to step forward with a pacifying gift.

Word came to Washington from St. Petersburg late in September, 1909, of the increased interest shown by Russian public opinion in the Far East, particularly after China and Japan had signed their Manchurian agreement. Iswolsky and Kokovtsov clashed over the proper policy to follow, and Montgomery Schuyler, the American chargé in the Russian capital, felt that the time had come for "informal discussions" between the two governments regarding a possible Russian-American political agreement that would block Japan.[8]

Rockhill, now the American Ambassador to Russia, had been busy in the Russian capital, too. He found Iswolsky nervous over the Sino-Japanese agreement and learned that several officials in the Foreign Office had received the Tsar's approval for a settlement of the Harbin issue along lines laid down by the United States. St. Petersburg wanted to placate Washington in order to reach a larger agreement with the United States on the whole Far Eastern question. The Ambassador asked for instructions. "This seems to insure Russian cooperation if and when we find it necessary to move for the open door in Manchuria," commented Alvey A. Adee, Third Assistant Secretary of State, after he read the dispatches from St. Petersburg. The order went out to Rockhill: "Be receptive." [9]

Reviewing the dispatches from Schuyler and Rockhill, the State Department added them to the information already on hand. Washington now knew of the full import of the Chinchow-Aigun Railroad and the importance of Russian support; it was aware of Japan's increasing grip on Southern Manchuria and the danger to the Chinchow-Aigun line if Japan protested; and it kept in mind Fletcher's suggestion for forcing a statement from Tokyo regarding its claims in Manchuria. The wheels of policy began to turn as the State Department realized that the political situation in Manchuria had become "critical." [10]

Secretary Knox, assisted by Huntington Wilson, assumed active command. Information furnished by the American Group and by Schuyler at St. Petersburg brought him up to date on Harriman's negotiations with Noetzlin regarding the sale of the Chinese Eastern Railway. Schuyler reported the existence of a strong feeling in "certain quarters" of the Russian government favoring sale of the line to American capitalists. "Assume receptive attitude," replied Huntington Wilson.[11]

Knox next turned to Harriman's 1905 discussions with Japan for the sale of the South Manchurian Railroad and learned of the dead railway magnate's plans for his world-wide transportation system. Paying scant attention to Tokyo's cancellation of the project and acting as if the proposals were still alive, the Secretary inquired about the status of the Chinese imperial edict that was to ratify the Chinchow-Aigun agreement of October 2, 1909. The American Group wired Straight, discovering that he had heard through un-official sources in Peking that it had been issued. That was all Knox needed.

Harriman's dealing with Japan and with Russia indicated that both nations were anxious to rid themselves of railway responsibilities in Manchuria. In addition, possession of the Chinchow-Aigun contract by the American Group gave the United States a substantial interest in Manchuria and there-fore the right to make suggestions regarding the future of the region. Late in October, 1909, Knox informed Davison of a proposal for the neutralization of Manchuria's railways, ad-mitting that it was somewhat "ideal." The American Group saw a great advantage in the plan, but had several reserva-tions regarding its implementation.

> We feel, however, that it is most important that nothing should be said or done until the Imperial Edict on the Tsitsihar line is issued, and I feel that we should also have the Manchurian Bank scheme settled in our favor, not that we would hold it out, but that it would give us a stronger position. Of course if this plan is adopted we would be in a very strong position, as it would have originated with us and we would have the bank and the Tsitsihar line to trade with.[12]

In spite of Davison's contention that action be postponed until the necessary edict was issued officially, the State De-partment sent a neutralization note to Great Britain on November 6, 1909, confidentially though incorrectly informing London that the Chinchow-Aigun contract had been signed and ratified. Knox outlined the plan as a single scheme with one alternative for the preservation of the open door in Manchuria and China's retention of sovereignty in the area. The American Secretary proposed that an international syndicate lend money for the purchase of all of the Manchurian railways on China's behalf and exercise supervision over them during the term of the loan. The plan required the cooperation of China, Japan, and Russia, the "reversionary and the concessionaires" of the Manchurian lines and Great Britain and the United States, whose "special interests rest upon the existing contract relative to the Chinchow-Aigun Railroad."

If London found this unsatisfactory, Knox urged Great Britain to join the United States in diplomatic support of the Chinchow-Aigun Railroad. He invited the participation of the powers in the financing and construction of this line and any future lines, as well as in the acquisition of rights to furnish funds for China's purchase of "such existing lines as might be offered for inclusion in this system." It was, wrote Huntington Wilson, a "practical policy," certain to have "an excellent diplomatic effect," whether it "was actually adopted wholly, or in part, or not at all." The Assistant Secretary's estimate was correct on the last count. Overoptimism led him to misjudge the powers' diplomatic reaction to the offer.[13]

Clearly, neutralization was directed at forcing Tokyo's hand in Manchuria. The strategic aim of a prior transmittal of the note to Great Britain was to secure support for British interests and pave the way for London to present the proposition to its Japanese ally. If Tokyo refused to participate, then Japan would be branded an anti-open door power in Manchuria. But Washington's proposal also fell directly in line with Straight's plans for establishing the American claim in Manchuria via the Chinchow-Aigun Railroad.

The very term neutralization indicated something more than the setting up of an international stewardship of Manchuria's railroad system. It had been used by Straight, by E. T. Williams, and by Fletcher to mean competition with the South Manchurian Railroad that would lower the value of the line to Japan.[14] Although Washington couched its statement in the diplomatic terminology of the open door, the background of its proposal made it a bid for American economic supremacy in Manchuria. By virtue of its acceptance of the Chinchow-Aigun project, the American Group had become heir to the Harriman-Straight blueprint for Manchuria, and it stood to benefit or lose as Washington's effort proved to be either a success or a failure. And Washington failed miserably because it played a poor hand with Russia.

The State Department did not respond eagerly to Straight's suggestion for admittance of the Russians to the Hukuang Loan in order to create a financial combination in China that would exclude Germany and Japan. When St. Petersburg attempted to feel out Washington's attitude toward Russian participation, Fletcher and Phillips thought it possible on the basis of the open door, but Knox took a different position as he pondered over St. Petersburg's overture.

The Secretary differentiated between loans growing out of China's national interests and those that were based on China's credit, supporting "enterprises of a more or less private nature." In no mood to tamper with the fates after his arduous struggle for American admission to the Hukuang Loan, Knox back-pedaled and threw out a suggestion to his subordinates. It "would hardly do to agree that business developed and made possible through the energy of our own people, or of the people of any other country, should . . . be equally divided with those who have no hand in bringing it forward." The State Department informed the Russian chargé in Washington, Baron Krupensky, that the United

States thought it "might not be practicable" to support Russia directly, but "abstention from opposition was virtually equivalent to moral support." Krupensky understood a diplomatic rejection. "We cannot rely on the active support of America," he wired Iswolsky.[15]

It was not a serious matter, for Russia had little capital to export. It did mean something to Iswolsky, who as early as March, 1908, had made speeches in the Duma preaching friendship with Japan. Shortly after the Sino-Japanese settlement, Prince Ito, one of Japan's elder statesmen, planned a visit to Harbin in order to explain to the Russians the purpose of his country's treaty with China. Ito obviously sought to consult with representatives of the Tsar's government regarding the American effort to move into Manchuria. He hoped to effect a rapprochement with Russia and thus ward off any external pressure upon Japan to sell its rights to the South Manchurian Railroad. Angered by the conflict at Harbin with China and the United States, Iswolsky refused to utter any soothing statements that would quiet China's fears of another Russo-Japanese treaty. At the same time, Russia's Finance Minister, Kokovtsov, who had promised Noetzlin that he would recommend sale of the Chinese Eastern Railway to American interests, left for Manchuria to inspect the railroad property and report on its condition to the Tsar.[16] Instantly, Harbin became the focus of attention in the Far East.

Straight, Bland, and Fletcher brooded over the likelihood of a pact. The Ito-Kokovtsov meeting "boded no good," Straight noted, "if the Russians were such damned fools as to make an arrangement with Japan." He was confident that the American Group had the inside track with Russia and minimized the possibility of a Russo-Japanese agreement. Washington shared the same view, despite warnings that were sent from Mukden, Peking, and St. Petersburg at the very time the State Department was preparing its neutralization proposals.[17]

On November 1, the Russian Minister to China, Ivan Korostovetz, returned to Mukden from Harbin and conferred with Fletcher. Korostovetz, favoring cooperation with the United States, hinted strongly that Japan had approached Russia at the Harbin meetings. He pointed out that Kokovtsov could not oppose Iswolsky's pro-Japanese policy unless Washington gave definite assurances to St. Petersburg. Fletcher intimated that Russian participation in the Chinchow-Aigun Railroad was contemplated, but fearing a leak to Japan, he held back any other information. Instead, the American chargé stiffly informed the Russian Minister that certain enterprises would be presented to Russia which the United States would support, whether or not St. Petersburg worked with Tokyo.

Straight followed Fletcher's lead, assuming that Russia was "playing off both sides against the middle." In his talks with a representative of the Russian Finance Ministry, he expressed the American Group's willingness to cooperate with Russia, assist in China's purchase of the Chinese Eastern Railway, and set up a cohesive transportation system in Manchuria. But no one had political rights in the enterprise, Straight declared. Even if Japan was admitted to the Chinchow-Aigun project, it had to be on a commercial basis. "I said the same thing applied [to Russia]" Straight noted, "and that our position was just and whether we had to meet Russo-Japanese opposition singly or in cooperation it made no difference." [18] It was a bold statement, based more on bravado and inflated conceptions of strength than on an objective knowledge of conditions.

For on November 6, the day Knox's neutralization note went to Great Britain, Iswolsky decided to work with Japan. In one of his frequent interviews with the Foreign Minister,

Rockhill learned of Iswolsky's fear of a Japanese attack. He frankly revealed Tokyo's overtures to Rockhill, and "in the absence of any acceptable suggestions for settling the Harbin question," and China's refusal to accept the Russian preliminary regulations governing the city, Russia had no choice but to consider Japan's proposals.[19]

Washington's concentration upon tying up Japan and its slighting of Russia weakened the pro-American faction at St. Petersburg, depriving Kokovtsov of any substantial weapons with which to combat Iswolsky. In large measure, the overblown estimate of Russia's dependence upon the United States was due to Straight's insistence that Russia would come along. Still, there was Great Britain, Japan's ally; if London approved of neutralization, then Tokyo would have to retreat.

Great Britain, however, saw the Far Eastern situation in a different light than did Washington. Facing Germany in Europe, London worked for the Anglo-Japanese alliance in order to prevent the diversion of its own energy to Asia. As long as the Japanese link existed, British diplomats refused to run counter to Tokyo's wishes. It was an outlook that directly contradicted Straight's analysis. While the Hukuang negotiations dragged on, the Foreign Office, though agreeing in principle with neutralization, suggested postponement of the project until financial cooperation in China proper had become a reality. As for the Chinchow-Aigun line, London suggested that the United States help persuade China to admit the Japanese! The French backed the British stand.[20]

London also coupled its support of Tokyo with support of Russia. After Knox released the neutralization proposal to the other powers on December 17 to 21, British diplomacy attempted to spare "Russian susceptibilities" and demonstrate its good intentions as peace broker between St. Petersburg and Tokyo in order to fortify the anti-German bloc in

Europe. With Britain committed to Japan and Russia on the basis of its own position in European politics, the American effort collapsed.

With almost tragic persistence, Washington continued its dispute with Russia over the Harbin municipality. Adoption of the neutralization plan would eliminate the issue, the State Department claimed—a point of view that Iswolsky did not accept in view of American diplomatic ineptitude. Three days after he sent the initial neutralization note to Great Britain, Knox issued a formidable set of instructions to Rockhill: prevent the consummation of a Russo-Japanese agreement, discover Russia's intentions with respect to the sale of the Chinese Eastern Railway, and make "shrewd and discreet use" of the neutralization memorandum sent to London.[21]

Approving of neutralization as "a good scheme if it can be carried through," Rockhill discussed the matter with Iswolsky. The Foreign Minister commended it *"en principe"* and asked for a confidential memorandum.[22] Rockhill understood the coercive relationship of the Chinchow-Aigun Railroad to the neutralization program and asked for permission to strengthen his overtures to Iswolsky by mentioning the existence of American and British railroad interests in Manchuria. The Minister's request caught the State Department in the lull caused by Britain's consideration of Knox's proposals, and it ordered Rockhill not to issue any written or formal statement confirming the acquisition of the concession by Anglo-American interests. But tempted by the possibilities of the Chinchow-Aigun line as a persuasive measure to soften Russian resistance, it suggested: "on your own responsibility refer to such reports as indicating that such a concession if granted, might be used as a nucleus for a broader plan." These cloudy instructions to Rockhill were complicated by Huntington Wilson's message to "omit as a matter of propriety" any written reference to the unpublished edict sanctioning the Chinchow-Aigun Railroad agreement. Rockhill followed orders and held back the Chinchow-Aigun alternative when he presented the neutralization proposal to Iswolsky.[23]

The Russian Foreign Minister, already unsympathetic to the United States, learned from other sources of the alternative embodied in the Knox note. Why did Russia have to go elsewhere to discover the complete proposal, he thundered at Rockhill. Acting on the assumption that the validity of the Chinchow-Aigun claim depended on the publication of an imperial edict, Rockhill wired Washington for confirmation. It was too late. Angered at Rockhill's "stupidity" in presenting the proposition to the Russians in a fragmentary form, Huntington Wilson overlooked his own murky instructions and threw the blame on Rockhill. Yet, he still hoped for an agreement with St. Petersburg on January 10, 1910. The next day Russia and Japan presented almost identical notes rejecting the proposal.[24]

Stung by Iswolsky's opposition to an American-Russian *rapprochement,* the American bankers and Huntington Wilson thought seriously of attempting to secure Iswolsky's removal from office. J. P. Morgan and Company received a wire from its French banking associates inquiring about the possibility of closer ties between Washington and St. Petersburg. Certain Russian groups, it was learned, preferred to work with the United States rather than with Japan and were in a position to influence their government. Obviously Iswolsky stood in the way. The American Group telephoned the news to Huntington Wilson, who drafted instructions to Rockhill authorizing him to seek an audience with the Tsar for a protest against Iswolsky's anti-American attitude. Home on leave from St. Petersburg, Montgomery Schuyler managed to dissuade the Assistant Secretary, and nothing came of the move.[25]

If Washington's relations with Russia were tragic, its neutralization explanations to Japan were almost comic.

Ambassador Thomas J. O'Brien understood very little concerning Washington's intentions to "smoke out" Japan. He displayed his lack of familiarity with the true state of affairs by informing Tokyo that the Chinchow-Aigun Railroad promised to offer strong competition to the South Manchurian line, the very fact that Washington had played down in its diplomatic correspondence. Puzzled, in addition, by Tokyo's comment that China had not yet ratified the Chinchow-Aigun agreement, O'Brien "could not quite believe that the Department would have treated the agreement as concluded unless the essential steps to make it binding upon the Chinese government had first been undertaken." [26]

Too late, much too late, Washington brought its Ambassador up to date. The State Department admitted that American bankers had requested support for the Chinchow-Aigun line, which would affect "somewhat" Russian and Japanese railroad holdings in Manchuria. Officially, the United States backed the open door principles that had received the approval of the powers in the past.[27]

It was an approach, however, that permitted Tokyo to deny American allegations regarding the state of affairs in Manchuria. Neutralization violated the Portsmouth Treaty and the Treaty of Peking, Japan claimed, and in no way did it promise efficiency or economy of operation of Manchuria's railroads. Friendly Japanese informed O'Brien that American inquiries should have been conducted discreetly in order to avoid harmful publicity if Japan rejected neutralization. "There is an almost complete misunderstanding of the simple purpose that you had in view," O'Brien reported.[28] It was the most significant understatement of the whole controversy.

Japanese intransigence embittered Jacob Schiff. When Baron Takahashi wrote him that the proposals were "premature" and of a "partial nature," Schiff censured Japan for its ingratitude to those Americans who had financed its war against Russia. He disclaimed any prior knowledge of Knox's proposals, a direct contradiction of Davison's statement that the American Group had been informed of the project late in October, 1909. Schiff supported Knox completely by invoking the 1905 Harriman negotiations and claiming that the action agreed to by Japan at that time was the same as outlined by Knox in 1909. He had kept Tokyo fully informed of all steps taken by the American bankers for the purchase of the Chinese Eastern Railway and South Manchurian Railroad properties. He repeated his old warning that Russia was Japan's true enemy, just when the State Department and the American Group hoped to soothe the Russians.[29]

Confused and a bit at sea because of the failure of neutralization and harassed by the reopening of the immigration question with Japan, Taft called on his old mentor, Theodore Roosevelt, for advice. Still intent on advancing American interests in the Pacific, the President was reluctant to "neglect our opportunities." To Roosevelt, however, the main question was Japanese immigration. Tokyo's sensitivity regarding Manchuria must be respected, he counselled. The United States should not ruffle Japan, for any other course of action required the support of a large army and navy. And the open door? Roosevelt dismissed it as a doctrine that had no validity when any nation decided to violate its tenets.[30]

Knox disagreed with his former chief. "Why the Japanese *need* Manchuria any more than does China who owns it now, or why it is any more 'vital' to them than it is to China is not apparent," he complained. The open door meant "fair play" for American commerce and China's territorial integrity, Knox argued. It was time to invigorate old formulas and put them to work.[31]

Taft heeded the advice of his Secretary of State, and willfully misunderstood Roosevelt's position, refusing to see that Roosevelt admitted American weakness in Manchuria. In line with his own proclivities, the President felt that the United States would not antagonize Japan in Manchuria but also would not retreat from the assertion of American rights under the open door formula. In this way, according to Taft, the United States had taken only "the natural and proper steps to foster and promote" its competitive interests in Manchuria.[32]

This was precisely the reason for failure, for the background of economic affairs in Manchuria made Washington's action a bid for American financial supremacy. Knox was not bluffing. He was convinced that he argued from a position of power because of the American Group's claimed rights to the Chinchow-Aigun Railroad and the Manchurian Bank. If Russia and Japan had accepted his political overtures for the neutralization of Manchuria, they would have opened the area to American economic exploitation and have been forced to do business on terms laid down by the American Group. Impatient with "diplomatic generalities," Knox was defeated by diplomacy. He depended too much on Great Britain and failed to recognize the strength of the diplomatic ties that bound London to both Tokyo and St. Petersburg. But the Chinchow-Aigun Railroad still remained, and Straight was determined to advance the project despite Washington's mauled diplomatic overtures to the powers.

From February to June, 1910, Straight's reaction to Knox's neutralization diplomacy ranged from approval to reproof. Hopeful of concentrating on the construction of the Chinchow-Aigun Railroad, a project "much nearer [his] heart," Straight nevertheless was glad to see Russia and Japan "pretty well smoked out by the Knox Proposals." Yet, by early summer, he strongly criticized the Secretary's handling of the scheme, asserting that the American Group should have done the "scouting" while the State Department made the "mass plays." [33] This shift in Straight's views in these five months sharply demonstrated the American Group's failure to make the Chinchow-Aigun Railroad a reality.

Japan had learned of the Chinchow-Aigun project in the early stages of Straight's negotiations with China and requested participation. Peking delayed its response to Tokyo, while Straight, acting on ffrench's assurance that Great Britain's support would counter Japan, tried to conclude an arrangement. Although he managed to sign a preliminary agreement for the line, Tokyo's opposition made the Chinese hesitate and cautiously feel their way. Just at this point, Great Britain suggested Japan's admission to the Chinchow-Aigun Railroad. Anxious to appease London, Knox indicated that both the American and British interests "at the proper time" and in "consultation with their Governments" would make "such equitable arrangement as may be found due, which however it seems premature to attempt now to make precise." [34]

It was a vague declaration that indirectly pledged the American Group to admit the Japanese, but not until Britain had soothed its ally. Nevertheless, it was a diplomatic pledge, and it forced Straight to juggle his estimates of the situation and come up with a satisfactory answer.

Aware that he could not resist Washington, Straight was now willing to accept Tokyo's participation in the project, but only in a manner that would render the Japanese harmless. For if neutralization failed, Japan's intrusion in the Chinchow-Aigun Railroad would threaten American control of the line. As Straight saw it, the task ahead was to secure the Chinchow-Aigun edict and then offer Japan only a part of the 40 per cent of non-Anglo-American capital in the enterprise. This would insure continued control by the American Group and Pauling. Taking his cue from Davison's desire to have the project in hand before neutralization was proposed, Straight sought "something definite that we could trade on." Later, the Chinchow-Aigun line might be discarded for another road that could be built in case Russia and Japan agreed to neutralization.[35]

Indeed, Straight did not object to Japan's admission to the Chinchow-Aigun line. In order to justify its participation, Japan would have to advance a business proposition, thus opening negotiations on a commercial rather than on a political basis which would weaken Tokyo's bargaining power. On the other hand, Straight wrote, if the American Group admitted Japan, it would lose much of its influence with China. Yet there was a saving grace in this procedure. A Japanese approach to China only heightened the tension between the nations, and the more China feared Japan, he concluded, "the better the terms that we shall be able to secure."

The American Group, hoping for postponement of Japan's admission until after the ratifying edict had been published, was content to follow Washington's lead, and Fletcher received instructions to join with the British Minister in urging China to admit Japan.[36] Seen in this light, Knox's hazy promise to the British allowed the American Group to maneuver the Chinese against Japan without exposing itself to attack. But Washington also had to reveal the neutralization proposition to Peking, and as Straight negotiated for publication of the all-important edict, Fletcher informed Peking that the purpose of neutralization was to unify Manchuria's railways "under Chinese control and under the financial leadership of American and British interests."

Straight was "astonished" that Knox had acted before the appearance of the edict. To urge Japan's admission to the Chinchow-Aigun line laid the United States open to the charge of deserting China and would justify cancellation of the whole project by Peking. The Chinchow-Aigun edict was necessary to tie China to the United States. Once it had ap-

peared in public print, Straight proposed to offer neutralization to China. Only then did he want to approach Tokyo,
offering American terms, compelling Japan's acceptance of
neutralization, and proving to China the value of American
support.[37] Knox's premature release of neutralization, however, made a brittle diplomatic situation in Peking, forcing
Straight and Fletcher to engage in a carefully staged playlet
with Chinese officials.

Avoiding any mention of Japan's admission to the Chinchow-Aigun line, Fletcher received China's acceptance of
neutralization in principle. Then, accompanied by the British
Minister, he visited his Russian and Japanese colleagues in
Peking. Korostovetz doubted Japan's acquiescence but the
Japanese Minister suggested a merger of American, British,
Russian, and Japanese interests in the neutralization program. That was all Straight and Fletcher needed. Both men
hurried back to the Chinese Foreign Office and suggested
issuance of the Chinchow-Aigun edict and Japan's admission
to participation in the line.

As expected, the Chinese angrily inquired the reasons for
Japan's admission. Fletcher parried the thrust, stating that
it was a question of permitting Tokyo to save face in order
to gain support for neutralization. The American chargé
pointed out that China could force Japan to accede by "making a competitive loan which would detract from the value
of the S.M.R.R. [South Manchurian Railroad]." Then
Straight stepped forward in his capacity as representative of
the American Group, pleading for China's issuance of the
edict so that the Group would have the "necessary 'pied à
terre' to push the larger enterprise." Neutralization was
worthless without the Chinchow-Aigun edict, Straight explained, for "without this we had no standing," and Japan
"could give us the horse laugh." In a fitting climax, Fletcher
returned and "cursed and growled a little," informing Peking's officials that the American government did not care for

the neutralization project but that it was a good opportunity for China and she could "take it or leave it." [38]

Straight's optimism soared, for Washington had instructed Fletcher to get China's ratification of the necessary edict and the Chinese promised to hurry matters. "Strangely enough," he mused, "events are now shaping themselves much as they did after the China-Japan War—by foreign pressures Japan is likely to be robbed of the fruits of her victory." [39]

Soon Straight met the same disappointment with Britain that Washington was experiencing. The Russo-Japanese rejection of neutralization immobilized China, exposing the flabby nature of British support of the Chinchow-Aigun line. Without informing Washington, London suggested that China consult Japan and Russia before proceeding any further. Sent to the British Foreign Office for an explanation, Ambassador Reid received Lord Grey's apologies for not notifying Washington of London's advice to China. The Russians had reminded the Foreign Secretary of an agreement of 1899 that pledged noninterference with each nation's railway concessions in the Yangtse Valley and North China. Grey, pleading ignorance of the extension of the Chinchow-Tsitsihar line to Aigun, and "considering the general delicacy of the situation," informed Peking of the Russian attitude.[40]

While Reid queried London, Knox explained the diplomatic context of the bungled neutralization proposals and the purposes of the Chinchow-Aigun alternative to a hostile officialdom in St. Petersburg. Kokovtsov was angry with China for designing a railroad to cross the tracks of the Chinese Eastern Railway without informing him. He did not appreciate being kept in ignorance of Peking's willingness, influenced by American representations, to admit Japan to the Chinchow-Aigun line. Iswolsky countered Washington's explanations with an offer to cooperate in the construction of a railroad from Kalgan to Kiakhta, the project that Bland had brought back from the Russian capital when he and

Straight had developed the large Manchurian-Mongolian-Siberian enterprises in 1909. In this way Iswolsky hoped to eliminate completely American railway influence from Manchuria by using the Kalgan-Kiakhta road as a diversion, thus sidestepping the political implications involved in the Chinchow-Aigun line.[41]

Russia's obstinacy was partly attributable to Japan's response to the Chinchow-Aigun proposal. Like St. Petersburg, Tokyo wanted to be consulted, but cleverly offered to retract its opposition if it was admitted. This action left the Russians frightened and confused, for they were close to agreement with Japan regarding Manchuria. In addition, St. Petersburg was upset by the Chinchow-Aigun line, about which it had learned little from China and the United States. Tactically, Russia found itself in the position of incurring "all the odium" if the Chinchow-Aigun line was defeated.

Always prepared to piece together the bric-a-brac of his Manchurian schemes, Straight stood by his earlier insistence that Russia was the soft spot in the anti-American bloc in Manchuria. From Korostovetz, he learned of Russia's intention to obstruct the Chinchow-Aigun line, but the Russian Minister, pro-American in his sympathies, hinted that American interests might make a fresh overture. Straight reported to his superiors in New York, suggesting that such an approach be devoid of political overtones and that the offer to Russia be made by commercial interests within the framework of a business proposition. If China signed a final Chinchow-Aigun loan agreement and concurred in Russian and Japanese participation, then the American Group and Pauling would hold the whip hand by virtue of the initiative that they had exercised. And, in order to insure Anglo-American control, Straight hoped to make the Chinchow-Aigun Railroad as "Chinese as possible" on the surface but with special privileges provided for the American Group and Pauling in a secret agreement with China. Assisted by ffrench and

Fletcher, Straight began to formulate a plan which "if carefully handled" would give the Anglo-American combination "two railroads instead of one." [42]

He received Korostovetz's approval of Russian participation, and he conferred with the Peking manager of the Russo-Chinese Bank, promising American assistance for the Kalgan-Kiakhta line if Russia did not insist upon a heavy share in the Chinchow-Aigun Railroad. He persuaded a leading Chinese official to approve of the Kalgan-Kiakhta line, Russia's participation in the Chinchow-Aigun Railroad, and the initialing of the final Chinchow-Aigun agreement. At the same time, he informed the American Group of his plan of procedure, requesting the bankers to contact Noetzlin once again in order to mollify Russia's officials. If the scheme succeeded, Straight intended to visit St. Petersburg for talks with Russia's bureaucrats in order to conclude the details of a project which he regarded "as a pleasant roller under the Japanese and Russians." [43]

Straight still needed the final Chinchow-Aigun agreement from China. Handicapped by interference from Japan and strife between the Chinese central government and the Manchurian administration, he and his assistants negotiated with various Chinese officials during March and April, 1910. After days of delay, vacillation, and the removal of the negotiations from Peking to Tientsin, a final agreement was signed on April 30, 1910.[44]

Straight made his preparations for the all-important trip to St. Petersburg even before the conclusion of the agreement, but a difference of opinion between the American Group and the State Department necessitated a postponement. Involved in negotiating controversial diplomatic questions with Russia, Rockhill insisted that the "commercial side" was of "no importance," an estimate that prompted the American Group to order Straight to bypass St. Petersburg and continue directly home for consultations. For

Washington, after learning from Rockhill that Kokovtsov was waiting for a report from a survey party sent out to examine the Chinese Eastern Railway, preferred to wait before approaching Russia again. The State Department wanted to dispose of St. Petersburg's objection to the Chinchow-Aigun line and the Kalgan-Kiakhta counterproposal. Once this had been accomplished, it was willing to stand aside for direct negotiations between the American Group and Russia's Finance Ministry.[45]

Embittered by its experience in the neutralization episode and determined to keep aloof from direct business negotiations, the State Department had resisted a Russian overture carried by Wilenkin in the spring of 1910. Kokovtsov proposed sending Wilenkin to Washington in order to do something about the Manchurian railroad situation despite the ill-feeling raised by the neutralization controversy. Rockhill thought that Wilenkin's trip would resurrect neutralization this time "not as a governmental suggestion but a private one, presented by the financial group in the United States which is interested in it." Kokovtsov, Rockhill added, "would make attractive terms to capitalists of our country." [46]

Late in April, 1910, Wilenkin arrived in the United States, hoping to come to terms with Schiff, an expectation shared by Straight. Wilenkin conferred with Rockhill in Washington and with Secretary Knox, who was not "impressed" by Kokovtsov's representative, and nothing came of these meetings. Although a member of the American Group, Schiff still sustained his opposition to Russia.[47]

Straight arrived home in June, 1910, and held several conferences with Knox, Huntington Wilson, and members of the Division of Far Eastern Affairs, all of whom rejected Wilenkin and were determined to hold back with regard to Russia. But the American Group wanted action. It regarded the Kalgan-Kiakhta project as a means of maintaining contact with the Russians and expressed willingness to proceed with the first section of the Chinchow-Aigun line if Washington protected its rights to the remainder.

Straight argued that either the United States had to ignore Russia and go ahead with the line or else take steps to remove Russia's opposition. Washington refused to assign any diplomatic status to any mission to St. Petersburg undertaken by Straight and warned that he went "to talk on his own responsibility." The Division of Far Eastern Affairs, recalling the disaster that resulted from launching the neutralization scheme without possessing the edict for the Chinchow-Aigun line, urged him to be frank with the Russians and not conceal the fact that although the final agreement was signed, it had not been ratified by China.[48]

In a real sense Straight's trip to Russia duplicated Wilenkin's mission to the United States. Straight was acting unofficially, he represented an attempt to place economic interests in the forefront of American-Russian relations, and yet he operated in an atmosphere of diplomatic approbation. As it turned out, he also hit a stone wall of opposition.

Straight journeyed to a country that was fearful of Japan, angered by American diplomacy, and annoyed with American-inspired resistance by China in the Harbin question. The unabated tension between Russia and the United States over affairs in Manchuria coincided with French and British efforts to harmonize relations between St. Petersburg and Tokyo in order to focus Russia's attention on Europe. Just as Straight arrived in St. Petersburg to persuade Russia that American overtures were more reliable than those made by Tokyo, the Manchurian allies of 1907 were drawing closer together.[49]

Straight made appointments with Russian officials with the help of the American Embassy and conveyed the impression to friendly sections of the Russian press that he was more than just a representative of the American Group. "Before my trip to St. Petersburg," he was quoted as saying,

"I saw the Secretary of State in Washington." But his first interview with Korostovetz, who was home on leave from his post in Peking, demonstrated the futility of the mission. Korostovetz had promised Straight to work for an American-Russian *rapprochement,* but he delivered a discouraging report on Russia's attitude. Straight's preparatory talks with Korostovetz stood him in good stead in his conversations with Iswolsky. The Russian Foreign Minister gave him a tongue lashing, attacking American procedure and purpose in the neutralization and Chinchow-Aigun proposals. "I don't understand what you Americans are up to anyway," he complained. "What do you want?" If it was business, Iswolsky asserted, there was the Kalgan-Kiakhta line. "I think you are playing politics," he concluded.[50]

Straight kept himself in check, aware that the Foreign Minister was attempting to cover his own resolution to come to terms with Japan. Nevertheless, the American Group's representative asserted China's right to cross the tracks of the Chinese Eastern Railway at Tsitsihar and continue north to Aigun. Straight managed to elicit nothing from the Foreign Minister, with the exception of the scolding that he received for Washington's sins of commission.

Kokovtsov's reception of his mission was milder, but of equal futility. Disappointed with Wilenkin's failure in Washington and saddled with the responsibility of the Chinese Eastern Railway, the Finance Minister stated that the Chinchow-Aigun line threatened Russia's railway interests in Manchuria and might be seized by Japan if Russia cooperated in its construction. With Kokovtsov, Straight acted the businessman. Americans were involved in the Chinchow-Aigun line, he declared because they "had to take business where [they] could find it." As for any Japanese attempts to take over the road, Straight pointed out brashly that the United States "in order to protect its bondholders, could hardly acquiesce in such seizures."

Other Russian officials, having little power of decision, were more friendly. Count Witte, also without influence, was lavish with advice. Russia had no money to help build the road. "You go ahead," he prompted Straight, "build your railway. They can't stop you and won't try. Confront them with a fact then you can come here and talk if you like."

Straight left St. Petersburg on June 26. The newspapers carried his final impressions of his negotiations. "I have been very courteously received by M. Iswolsky and M. Kokovsteff [Kokovtsov]. While talking with these remarkable political gentlemen, I received the most favorable impression for our enterprises. Up to the present, nothing is finally decided, but what I have heard enables me to return to America with a light heart." [51]

Straight's heart was heavier than he admitted, but his mind threw off the burden of defeat as he formulated ideas for saving the situation. There were three alternatives, Straight explained to the American Group. First, support China and build the Chinchow-Aigun Railroad. This course of action would block future American enterprise in Russia and give rise to the probability that China would show itself ungrateful and not "appreciate and reward" American efforts. Second, join Russia in the Kalgan-Kiakhta line. This would mean loss of China's friendship as well as the American reputation for fair dealing. Even St. Petersburg would not respect a nation that deserted China to follow a policy "so frankly utilitarian and selfish." Third, adopt a middle course and attempt to reconcile Chinese and Russian interests. The latter, Straight wrote, appeared to be the best course of action.

Thus, China must be persuaded to ratify the final Chinchow-Aigun loan contract and begin construction of the first section of the line from Chinchow to Taonanfu, an area in which Russia had no voice and Britain had promised diplomatic support. St. Petersburg would be placated by promises not to continue the line north of Taonanfu and an offer to take up the Kalgan-Kiakhta road. Straight, however, wanted to nudge Russia with a Chinese steamship line on the Sungari River that would connect with the railroad from Chinchow to Taonanfu. At the same time, he believed in continuing the agitation for construction of the railroad line from Taonanfu to Aigun. This might squeeze the Chinese Eastern Railway sufficiently to force its sale to China, a tactic that Harriman had attempted earlier with Japan and the South Manchurian Railroad.

In keeping with the new approach of having the American Group take the initiative, Straight hoped to prevent a repetition of the neutralization fiasco. The State Department would be held in reserve for emergencies and "remain largely in the background." Washington's task was to insist on the open door and the protection of the rights of its nationals. The American Minister at Peking would urge China to ratify the final Chinchow-Aigun edict, while Ambassador Reid held Britain to its pledge of support to Pauling. The job of the American embassies at St. Petersburg, Tokyo, Berlin, and Paris was to keep the powers "in good humor and ignorant of the broader significance of the plan." [52]

The setback that he experienced in Russia did not dishearten Straight, and he tried to stiffen the courage of the American Group. "But I believe still, notwithstanding what may seem to be the discouragements of the Russian situation, that we hold the whip hand and stand to profit in the long run by the very situation we have created by your debut into the choice international society of crooks that dances attendance on the Peking Court. We will win in the end all along I think for I feel convinced that we are the only people who are honest, and prepared to give everyone a 'square deal.' " [53]

But another blow fell on July 4, 1910, when Russia and Japan announced the signature of a pact. Knox's neutralization proposals actually drove both countries together, and they promised mutual consultation, in protection of the *status quo,* and cooperation in Manchurian railway development. A secret convention was drawn up that provided for the delineation of spheres of interest and influence in Manchuria and Mongolia.

China was shattered by the July announcement. Peking had not replied to Russia's demand for consultation in the Chinchow-Aigun road, preferring to wait for word of Straight's achievement in St. Petersburg. While the Japanese and the French inspired rumors that Washington had deserted China, the Chinese Foreign Office sought vainly for the members of the American Legation, all of whom had gone to Peitaiho, a seaside resort located a hundred miles from Peking. After receiving official notification of the Russo-Japanese Treaty, the Chinese "made such representation" that the recently appointed American Minister, William J. Calhoun, returned, surveyed the situation, and wired Washington. Then he went back to the beach.[54]

The State Department adopted the leisurely pace of its Minister in China and announced that its policy was unchanged, that there was no need for panic, and that the next move was up to the American Group. It was an answer that "appealed only to the Chinese sense of humor" and discouraged any hope of practical assistance from the United States.[55] For Huntington Wilson realized that Washington had offended Russia and lost the confidence of China, a situation created largely by dependence upon British support. Unless London gave effective backing to Pauling, the State Department refused to move. By throwing responsibility upon the American Group and asserting that there was little more to be done, Washington implicitly acknowledged the bankruptcy of its own policy and set the stage for a clash with the American Group.

The government's inaction touched off the dissatisfaction

of the American bankers both with the State Department and each other. J. P. Morgan, Jr., surrendered hope of any success for the Chinchow-Aigun Railroad because of the opposition of the other powers, whereas some members of the American Group blamed the House of Morgan for expenditures incurred in China that had not shown any concrete returns. With its business acumen dampening its ardor to work with the government, the American Group threatened to withdraw from the whole China field, an eventuality that finally raised dust at the State Department.[56]

Huntington Wilson hurried to New York, "fearing a horrible loss of prestige" and the demise of the open door in China. He critically lectured the American Group on the spasmodic nature of its attempts in China and urged it to stay in the field. In return he promised to keep the Chinchow-Aigun line project open and bring in Germany, hoping to shock the British into a more steadfast position. The bankers were not placated, and the Assistant Secretary had to call on Knox. "Jolly them, congratulate them on the Hukuang loan success, appreciate their patriotism and point out the need of patience," he advised the Secretary of State. "If it comes to retreat," he added, "it should not be difficult by intelligent and patient cooperation to make the movement an orderly one and to throw the blame on Great Britain." [57]

President Taft added his plea to that of the Assistant Secretary after learning of the American Group's reluctance to continue its effort. "I beg of you that you go to New York at once and invite the members of the syndicate to confer with you before they shall take the final step which will defeat entirely our international purpose," he wrote. The Division of Far Eastern Affairs put in a word, too. "Our policy in Manchuria has won us the ill will of Russia, irritated Japan, and failed of support in France and Great Britain," E. T. Williams noted. Any turning back now would incur

China's enmity also, he pointed out to the Secretary of State.[58] Knox went to New York.

Irritated by the American Group's stated refusal to go ahead with the Chinchow-Aigun line, which gave the impression of a decision made without Washington's consent or knowledge, Knox met Schiff, Davison, and Straight on September 3, 1910. The conference resulted in a semblance of agreement. The Group agreed to wait for Washington to make some arrangement with the powers and promised to go ahead with the government's support if an agreement did not materialize. Knox and the American Group refused, however, to build the line, section by section, a procedure advocated by Straight. But Straight's influence was shaken by differences that he had with the State Department. Huntington Wilson felt that Straight had arrogated diplomatic functions to himself and blamed the trip to St. Petersburg for the failure of the Chinchow-Aigun Railroad negotiations.[59]

The root of the difference between the two men lay in the poor execution of the neutralization scheme and its effect on the Chinchow-Aigun Railroad. Straight justly claimed credit for the neutralization project, but only if carried out by the bankers. Washington's action was hasty, was overly dependent upon the "vague" and "guarded acquiescence" that came from London, and was a poor bluff. By advancing it through diplomatic channels, it gave Iswolsky rather than Russia's Finance Ministry the power of control. Straight was candid about the whole proposition.

"In other words his [Knox's] proposition meant that if the Russians and Japanese didn't feel inclined to share their loaf, as they were calmly invited to do, with guests whom Mr. Knox had requested to have a square meal at some one else's expense, he would be very glad to have them assist him in baking another . . . which would make their brand look rather unhealthy." [60]

Straight, however, thought Knox "more creditable even if less sophisticated" than Lord Grey, for the British followed a "cold-footed trimming policy" and had not "played the game." He attacked the Russo-Japanese agreement of July, 1910, as a creation of the British Foreign Office, which "deemed it necessary to give these pirates a free hand in the Far East" in order to ward off Germany.[61]

It was a severe defeat. Every step taken by the American Group and the State Department was accompanied by great expectations but brought severe disappointments. This failure might have deterred any further effort in Manchuria, but the financial situation in China proper became dominant as the direct American intrusion in Manchuria waned. Yet the ghost of Tang's 1908 mission to the United States hovered over the tangled negotiations between the powers. And it was a loan for Manchuria that helped to clarify relations among the powers, their bankers, and China, stimulating a revival of large-scale currency reform for China. Once again, the State Department and its chosen instrument, the American Group, fared forth in search of a stronger position in China.

NOTES

1. Swenson to Knox, March 1, 1910, NA, RG59:893.102H/280.

2. Straight to J. P. Morgan and Company, October 19, 1909, Straight Papers.

3. Straight Diary, October 19, 1909, and Straight to J. P. Morgan and Company, October 29, 1909, Straight Papers; Davison to Knox, November 1, 1909, NA, RG59:2122/99 3/4.

4. American Group to Straight, November 5, 1909, Straight Papers.

5. Fletcher to the Secretary of State, September 5, 1909, and E. Carlton Baker, "General Memorandum Regarding the Recent Chinese-Japanese Agreements Respecting Manchuria," October 7, 1909, NA, RG59:5767/62,143; Straight to Huntington Wilson, August 3, 1909, NA, RG59:5315/469.

6. Fletcher to the Secretary of State, September 17 and 23, 1909, NA, RG59:5767/110–111, 74.

7. Straight to Huntington Wilson, September 25, 1909, Straight Papers.

8. Edward H. Zabriskie, *American Russian Rivalry in the Far East*

(Philadelphia, 1946), 151; Schuyler to Knox, September 22, 1909, NA, RG59:8594/3.

9. Rockhill to Knox, October 2, 1909, Adee to Hoyt, October 17, 1909, Hoyt to Adee, October 8, 1909, and Huntington Wilson to Rockhill, October 19, 1909, NA, RG59:8594/4.

10. Chandler Hale (for Secretary Knox) to Cloud, October 14, 1909, NA, RG59:5767/87.

11. Schuyler to the Secretary of State, October 25, 1909, and Huntington Wilson to Schuyler, October 30, 1909, NA, RG59:2157/2.

12. Huntington Wilson to the American Embassy at Tokyo, October 30, 1909, NA, RG221/117A; O'Brien to Knox, November 1, 1909, NA, RG59:221/120–121; Straight, "Notes on Harriman," E. T. Williams, "Recollections of Willard Straight," and Davison to Straight, November 6, 1909, Straight Papers.

13. "Commercial Neutralization of the Railways of Manchuria," Department of State, Division of Information, Series D, Number 7, Manchuria, No. 4, Knox Papers; Huntington Wilson to Elbert F. Baldwin, January 19, 1910, Huntington Wilson Papers.

14. Memorandum by E. T. Williams, December 5, 1910, and February 4, 1911, NA, RG59:893.51/1404, 1410.

15. Aide Memoir, October 4, 1909, NA, RG59:5315/536A; Knox to Phillips, October 6, 1909, Knox to Hoyt, October 8, 1909, and Memorandum of an interview between Krupensky and Adee, October 7, 1909, Knox Papers; Memorandum from the office of the Assistant Secretary, October 21, 1909, NA, RG59:5315/560; Krupensky to Iswolsky, October 4 and November 8, 1909, in Anatole Kantarovich, *Amerika v Borbe za Kitai* (Moscow, Satsegiz, 1935), 237, 228.

16. Schuyler to Root, March 28, 1908, NA, RG84: Peking Legation Archives; Rockhill to Knox, October 2, 1909, NA, RG59:8594/4; Straight, "Notes on Harriman," Straight Papers.

17. Straight Diary, October 19, 1909, Straight to J. P. Morgan and Company, October 25 and 29, 1909, Straight Diary, October 26, 1909, and J. O. P. Bland, "Recollections of Willard Straight," Straight Papers; Fletcher to the Secretary of State, October 19, 1909, NA, RG59:4002/256; Schuyler to the Secretary of State, October 21, 1909, and Cloud to the Assistant Secretary of State, October 25, 1909, NA, RG59:19038/2, 4.

18. Straight Diary, November 2, 17, and 19, 1909, and Straight to J. P. Morgan and Company, November 10, 1909, Straight Papers; Fletcher to Knox, November 6, 1909, NA, RG84: Peking Legation Archives.

19. Rockhill to the Secretary of State, November 6, 1909, NA, RG59: 4002/255; Schuyler to the Secretary of State, December 15, 1909, and Greene to the Assistant Secretary of State, December 17, 1909, NA, RG59:19038/3, 11.

20. Reid to the Secretary of State, November 9 and 26, 1909, NA, RG59:5315/572, 601; John G. Reid, *Manchu Abdication and the Powers, 1908–1912* (Berkeley, 1935), 69.

21. Reid, *Manchu Abdication,* 61 and 70; Rockhill Diary, December 31 and January 19, 1909, Rockhill Papers; Knox to the American Embassy at St. Petersburg, December 30, 1909, and Huntington Wilson to Rockhill, January 3, 1910, NA, RG59:4002/204, 261; Knox to the American Embassy at St. Petersburg, November 9, 1909, NA, RG59:5315/574A.

22. Rockhill Diary, November 10 and 13, 1909, Rockhill Papers.

23. Rockhill to the Secretary of State, November 13, and Knox to Rockhill, November 16, 1909, NA, RG59:5315/584; Huntington Wilson to Rockhill, December 15, 1909, Rockhill Papers; Zabriskie, *American Russian Rivalry*, 156–157, Paul A. Varg, *Open Door Diplomat—The Life of W. W. Rockhill* (Urbana, 1952), 104–106, William A. Williams, *American-Russian Relations, 1781–1947* (New York, 1952), 68 ff.

24. Zabriskie, *American-Russian Rivalry*, 156, 163; Rockhill Diary, December 25, 1909, Rockhill Papers; Huntington Wilson to Knox, January 20, 1910, Huntington Wilson Papers; Reid, *Manchu Abdication*, 93; *Papers Relating to the Foreign Relations of the United States, 1906–1913* (Washington, 1909–1920), *1910*, 249–251; Rockhill Diary, January 21, 1910, Rockhill Papers.

25. Herman Harjes to J. P. Morgan and Company, January 19, 1910, Knox Papers; Schuyler to Rockhill, February 15, 1910, Rockhill Papers.

26. O'Brien to Fletcher, December 24, 1909, and January 14, 1910, NA, RG84: Peking Legation Archives.

27. State Department to the American Embassy at Tokyo, January 14, 1910, Knox Papers; O'Brien to Fletcher, January 27, 1910, NA, RG84: Peking Legation Archives.

28. O'Brien to Knox, January 21, 1910, Knox Papers; O'Brien to Knox, January 24 and 25, 1910, NA, RG59:893.77/786–787; O'Brien to Fletcher, February 3, 1910, NA, RG84: Peking Legation Archives.

29. Takahashi to Schiff, January 20, 1910, and Schiff to Takahashi, February 24, 1910, enclosed in Paul Warburg to Knox, February 24, 1910, NA, RG59:893.77/809½.

30. Taft to Roosevelt, December 2 and 6, 1910, and Roosevelt to Taft, December 8 and 22, 1910, Taft Papers.

31. Knox to Taft, January [n.d.] 1911, suggesting a reply to Roosevelt's letter of December 22, 1910, and Knox to Taft, December 19, 1910, Taft Papers.

32. Taft to Roosevelt, January 17, 1911, Taft Papers.

33. Straight to Carr, February 15, 1910, and Straight to Davison, June 29, 1910, Straight Papers.

34. Straight to J. P. Morgan and Company, September 16, 1909, and Straight Diary, August 26 and 27, September 27, and October 17, 1909, Straight Papers; Fletcher to the Secretary of State, October 26, 1909, and Reid to the Secretary of State, October 20, November 26, 1909, NA, RG59:5315/559, 601, 562; "Memorandum, The Chin-Ai Railway Project," January 16, 1911, NA, RG59:893.77/1107; Knox to Reid, December 14, 1909, *Foreign Relations, 1910,* 236; Knox to Reid, November 6, 1909, NA, RG59:5315/559.

35. Straight to J. P. Morgan and Company, January 10, 1910, and Straight Diary, January 17, 1910, Straight Papers.

36. Straight to J. P. Morgan and Company, October 29 and December 17, 1909, Straight to Davison, December 3, 1909, American Group to Straight, December 8, 1909, Straight to Griscom, December 9, 1909, and Straight Diary, December 15 and 16, 1909, Straight Papers.

37. Straight to J. P. Morgan and Company, December 17, 1909, and Straight to Davison, December 20, 1909, Straight Papers.

38. Straight Diary, December 31, 1909, and January 3, 4, and 7, 1910, and Straight to J. P. Morgan and Company, December 31, 1909, Straight Papers.

39. Straight Diary, January 6, 8, and 9, 1910, and Straight to J. P. Morgan and Company, January 10, 1910, Straight Papers.

40. Straight to Bland, January 10 and 23, 1910, and Straight Diary, January 11 and February 15, 1910, Straight Papers; Fletcher to Knox, January 24 and February 7, 1910, NA, RG59:893.77/850, 867; Reid to Knox, February 18, 1910, NA, RG59:893.77/807.

41. Rockhill to the Secretary of State, February 25 and March 5, 1910, and "The Chin-Ai Railway Project," January 16, 1911, NA, RG59:893.77/852, 825, 1107; Williams to Rockhill, March 11, 1910, and Rockhill Diary, February 24, 1910, Rockhill Papers.

42. Straight Diary, January 12, 25, February 11, 15, and March 3, 7, and 12, 1910, Straight Papers; Fletcher to the Secretary of State, February 25, 1910, NA, RG59:893.77/892; Straight to J. P. Morgan and Company, Straight to Davison, February 16 and 28, 1910, Straight to Huntington Wilson, March 3, 1910, and Straight to Marvin, March 15, 1910, Straight Papers.

43. J. P. Morgan and Company to the Secretary of State, February 28 and March 8, 1910, and Straight to J. P. Morgan and Company, March 4, 1910, NA, RG59:893.77/821, 832, 880; ffrench to Pauling, March 9, 1910, NA, RG59:893.51/106½; Straight to Davison, March 12 and 25, 1910, and Straight to J. P. Morgan and Company, February 28 and April 18, 1910, Straight Diary, March 30 and April 15, 1910, and Straight to Bland, April 17, 1910, Straight Papers.

44. Straight Diary, March 4–14 and April 3–25, 1910, Straight to J. P. Morgan and Company, March 9, 16, 18, and 28, 1910, Straight to Davison, March 25, 1910, and Straight to J. P. Morgan and Company, April 18, 1910, Straight Papers; Straight to J. P. Morgan and Company, April 30, 1910, NA, RG59:893.77/914.

45. Straight to Davison, April 25, 1910, and Straight to Schiff, April 24, 1910, Straight Papers; J. P. Morgan and Company to the Secretary of State, May 4, 1910, NA, RG59:893.77; Unsigned report to the Secretary of State, March 31, 1910, Knox Papers; "The Chin-Ai Railway Project," NA, RG59:893.77/1107.

46. Rockhill to the Secretary of State, March 26, 1910, "Extra Confidential," NA, RG59:893.77/1006½; Einstein to Knox, June 27, 1910, NA, RG59:793.94/150.

47. Straight to Schiff, April 4, 1910, Straight Papers; Rockhill Diary, May 18, 1910, Rockhill Papers; R. S. Miller to Rockhill, June 14, 1910, NA, RG59:4578; Schiff to Takahashi, March 8, 1910, Cyrus Adler, *Jacob H. Schiff* (New York, 1928), I, 256; Williams to Rockhill, June 14, 1910, Rockhill Papers.

48. Huntington Wilson to Davison, June 3, 1910, NA, RG59:893.77/947A; Straight to Davison, June 8, 1910, Straight Papers; Williams to Rockhill, June 7, 1910, Rockhill Papers.

49. ffrench to Pauling, May 23, 1910, and Menocal to J. P. Morgan and Company, May 31, 1910, NA, RG59:893.77/982, 987.

50. Post-Wheeler to the Secretary of State, June 26, 1910, ffrench to

Pauling, May 23, 1910, Menocal to J. P. Morgan and Company, May 31, 1910, and Straight to J. P. Morgan and Company, June 28, 1910, NA, RG59:893.77/1007, 982, 987, 1011.

51. Post-Wheeler to the Secretary of State, June 26, 1910, NA, RG59: 893.77/1007.

52. Straight to J. P. Morgan and Company, June 28, 1910, NA, RG59: 893.77/1011.

53. Straight to Davison, June 28, 1910, Straight Papers.

54. Morgan, Grenfell and Company to J. P. Morgan and Company, July 6, 1910, Memorandum by R. S. Miller, July 6, 1910, and J. P. Morgan and Company to Straight, July 6, 1910, NA, RG59:893.77/1005; ffrench to Straight, July 8, 1910, NA, RG59:893.77/1043; Menocal to J. P. Morgan and Company, July 12, 1910, NA, RG59:893.77/1045.

55. Menocal to J. P. Morgan and Company, July 27, 1910, NA, RG59: 893.51/143 3/4; Menocal to Morgan, August 10, 1910, NA, RG59: 893.77/1060.

56. Straight to McKnight, July 20, 1910, Straight Papers; Morgan, Grenfell and Company to J. P. Morgan and Company, July 21, 1910, Knox Papers; Huntington Wilson to Davison, July 13, 1910, and J. P. Morgan and Company to the Secretary of State, June 24, 1910, NA, RG59:893.77/ 1011, 988; Huntington Wilson to Knox, July 15, 23, and August 8, 1910, Huntington Wilson Papers; R. S. Miller, Memorandum of a conversation with Davison, July 22, 1910, Knox Papers.

57. Huntington Wilson to Knox, August 12 and September 1, 1910, Huntington Wilson Papers; Williams to McKnight, August 9, 1910, Straight Papers.

58. Taft to Knox, September 1, 1910, Taft Papers; E. T. Williams, "The Chin-Ai Railway Project," August 28, 1910, NA, RG59:893.77/1058.

59. Memorandum of a meeting in New York City with Schiff, Davison, and Straight, September 3, 1910, NA, RG59:893.77/1074; J. P. Morgan and Company to Menocal, September 6, 1910, NA, RG59:893.51/160½; ffrench to Straight, September 5, 1910, Morgan, Grenfell and Company to J. P. Morgan and Company, September 6, 1910, and J. P. Morgan and Company to Morgan, Grenfell and Company, September 6, 1910, NA, RG59:893.77/1075a; Straight to Davison, February 13, 1911, Straight Papers.

60. Straight to Bland, July 16, 1912, Straight Papers.

61. Straight to Huntington Wilson, March 3, 1910, Straight to Davison, March 25, 1910, and Straight to Bland, April 17, 1910, and August 1, 1912, Straight Papers.

CHAPTER EIGHT

China's Currency and Manchuria

The winds of rumor that blew steadily in China always seemed to bear news from Manchuria, and much of the gossip that reached Straight's ears dealt with British and German designs on the Manchurian loan field. In the fall of 1909, he heard that the British-controlled Hongkong and Shanghai Bank was engaged in financial negotiations with Manchurian officials. A few months later, his good friend Lord ffrench "intimated" that China was disgusted with the international complications arising from the Hukuang negotiations and sought to compensate the Deutsche Asiatische Bank with a Manchurian loan. Then the Germans innocently queried Straight about Manchurian affairs, asserting that the British were well aware of his ambitions for the United States in Manchuria. The American Group's representative grew tense. "There is apparently something in the air."

Straight had good reason to be wary. The Chinese imperial government's enthusiasm for the Chinchow-Aigun line was inhibited by its uncertainty of Japan's reaction and the degree ← End of support that it could expect from the United States. Peking, however, decided to launch a general developmental scheme for Manchuria, an intention that dovetailed neatly with the ambitions of the American Group.[1]

But the European bankers stood in the way because of their hold on the Hukuang Loan. Although they dickered unhappily with the American Group for participation in the project located in China proper, their contact with Peking's bureaucrats placed them in a position to secure lending opportunities whenever they developed. Thus the American Group's head start in Manchuria, as well as its financial success in China proper, was threatened. More conversant with the Manchurian phase of the Group's activity than anyone else and spurred on by the rumors emanating from the Three Eastern Provinces, Straight hastened to establish the American claim.

He reminded the imperial government that the Tang memorandum gave the United States a priority on loans for Manchurian development, a project in which Harriman and Schiff had shown great interest. Convinced that China's aim was to pit the foreign banking groups against each other, Straight held to his consistent theme that the United States had been in the field first and that its financial representatives proposed to admit the other bankers "at the proper time" and "if China so desired."

Straight was angered by China's tactics, and he urged the American Group to file the Tang memorandum with the State Department as a precautionary measure for the strengthening of its claim. For if China was successful in stirring up the rivalries of the competing interests, the Tang document would permit the American Group "to make conditions regarding future cooperation" with the European bankers. Reluctant as he was to share Chinese business with the other groups, Straight was prepared to accept the formation of an international financial combination that "would scarcely be in accordance with American past policy." Nevertheless, such action would compel the Chinese to adopt a "more reasonable attitude" and inaugurate a "definite financial policy." [2]

The issue remained in the background throughout the winter and spring of 1910 because of the maneuvering and diplomatic hand-wringing over the neutralization proposals. It was brought forward again in September in order to counter Russian and Japanese obstruction to neutralization and the Chinchow-Aigun Railroad, Washington's tepid support of China, and the vigorous agitation waged by Manchurian officials for loan funds. As Knox and Huntington Wilson pleaded with the American bankers to remain in the field, the Viceroy of Manchuria, acting on his own initiative, practically reached a final agreement with the Hongkong and Shanghai Bank for a loan of twenty million taels.

Immediately an almost farcical exhibition of zealous concern for the safety of the American position took place in Peking, New York, and Washington. The representative of the American Group, D. A. Menocal, filed a protest with the American Minister in Peking, William J. Calhoun, reminding him of the Tang memorandum and requesting diplomatic intervention by the United States. Unfortunately, Menocal's hasty action paralleled an overture made by the tripartite bankers to the American Group for financial cooperation in China. Hoping to keep negotiations on a business level, New York ordered Menocal to hold off his protest to the American Minister and then informed the Hongkong and Shanghai Bank of its intention to admit the British bankers to Manchurian loans once China had recognized American priority.[3]

It was too late to stop Calhoun's official protest to the Chinese Foreign Office, but Peking saved the day. China rejected the American demand based on the Tang memorandum, creating a delay that permitted the State Department to catch up with the American Group for a joint protest to Peking and mutual consideration of foreign participation in Manchurian business.[4] The American Group was placed in an uncomfortable position. Although the British insisted that their Manchurian loan rights stemmed from the loan that they made to China in November, 1908, while Tang was en route to the United States, they still indicated a willingness to cooperate with the American bankers. Trapped by China's refusal to recognize the Tang memorandum and the British offer to share in the loan, the American Group attempted to delay the negotiations.[5]

The State Department was in an even more distressing situation because of its commitment to the American Group. Calhoun learned that the Tang memorandum never had been offered for imperial sanction or even filed with China's official documents. Sincerely believing that the British had a stronger claim, the American Minister urged cooperation with the Hongkong and Shanghai Bank and reluctantly obeyed instructions from Washington to follow up his earlier protest. Calhoun also realized the danger of having the United States accused of an attempted monopolization of Manchurian loans, a consideration that made him hope for a swift conclusion of the loan by the American Group. Yet in his final estimate of the situation, he agreed with Straight that acquisition of the Manchurian loan would help persuade the European bankers to work together with their American counterpart, an accomplishment that would also secure diplomatic cooperation. "By virtue of our position," he informed Washington, "we would be the natural leader." [6]

Thus Calhoun's desire for the United States to be the "natural leader" fell in with the American Group's wish to control Manchurian financial affairs. Relations between Washington and New York, however, were still strained. Straight requested information from Huntington Wilson as to Washington's future policy in Manchuria. Still smarting from the humiliation of having to humble the State Department before the bankers, the Assistant Secretary coldly replied: "The diplomatic negotiations were our business and the diplomatic and business ends must be kept separate." Then, in perhaps the lowest tone of voice ever inscribed on paper, Huntington Wilson agreed to cooperation between the

American bankers and the Hongkong and Shanghai Bank.

With diplomatic support from Washington assured, New York toughened its approach to China, instructing Menocal not to discuss any loan terms unless the Chinese were prepared to offer strict control provisions for loan expenditures and supervision in the contract.[7] Shortly afterward, in an effort to break up the talks between Peking and the British, the American Group announced its willingness to share the loan with the tripartite financial group. The loan was not an end in itself and had no great interest for the American Group; but once the American-claimed financial position in Manchuria was threatened, the project became a device to avow the supremacy of American rights and gain access to international money markets for the sale of bonds. Acting for the American Group, J. P. Morgan and Company wired its London associates: "As you know Chin-Ai is already in our hands and rights Manchurian Bank loan are ours under Tang Shao-yi note. While we will not ourselves propose cooperation Tripartite Banks we shall be pleased accept proposals from them and share with them Manchurian Bank loan and Chin-Ai project. We feel internationalization of loans essential to any such agreement." [8]

The haughtiness of this demand overshadowed the humility of the American position. In the context of the effort to enter the Chinese investment field, the setbacks suffered in the Chinchow-Aigun and neutralization plans, the need for a European market for the sale of bonds, and the irritated state of relations between Washington and New York, Morgan's statement demonstrated not strength but weakness. It remained for China to offer a way out of the impasse that resulted from the self-conscious arrogance of the American bankers and State Department.

The Chinese revived the long-awaited scheme for currency reform as part of a larger program of general reform in China. It was designed to strengthen the empire against foreign avarice and internal dissent that incited the provinces against the imperial government.

Currency reform had a history that began with the Sino-American Commercial Treaty of 1903 and similar treaties that were signed with the other powers at the same time. The powers had long hoped to assist their trade interests in China by stabilizing the nation's currency. Tang had used currency reform in 1908 as bait to attract American diplomatic aid for Manchuria. With the approval of Root and Roosevelt and the cooperation of Straight, actual conversations had begun with Kuhn, Loeb and Company. It was a desperately needed reform, one which the Division of Far Eastern Affairs thought was "pressing," particularly in view of China's financial straits, its ambitions to promote economic reform and development, and if the empire was "to increase her indebtedness to foreign capitalists." [9]

After surveying the mangled remains of the State Department's Manchurian policy, Huntington Wilson seized on the currency issue as a means of restoring American prestige in China and urged "some practical movement" for the abolition of likin, revision of the Chinese tariff, and currency reform. A month later, China took up the Secretary's invitation and made it an excuse for a more fundamental action.

Another Chinese emissary was on the way to Washington and Berlin, seeking diplomatic protection from foreign encroachment, loans for Manchuria, and the reform of the empire's currency. Here was an opportunity to press for the open door again, Huntington Wilson thought, for an American loan would give meaning to an American diplomatic declaration. Were American bankers interested in a large currency loan? China wished to negotiate with an agent sent to Peking for this special task, and Calhoun suggested someone "preferably with Morgans." [10]

The State Department was happy to conduct a large financial project through the snares of international diplomacy in order to recoup its shattered pride and reputation. It decided that, as a basic condition for its consent, China must appoint an American advisor to superintend the reform. The other powers ultimately would be allowed to participate.

Three weeks after Washington's quarrel with the American Group over the Manchurian fiasco and a day after Huntington Wilson had told Straight not to interfere in diplomacy, the Assistant Secretary personally presented the currency proposition to New York. The bankers "seemed interested and reasonable and on the whole the meeting was satisfactory." They realized "that it was the best proposition so far made," and they appreciated "its potentialities for eventual international cooperation, for the Manchurian bank and ultimately for the Chin-Ai Railway." Buoyant now that Washington was directing things once more, Huntington Wilson gave Straight a "rather blunt talking to in the matter of mixing in the diplomatic end of these affairs," and informed Calhoun of the bankers' readiness to undertake the currency loan.[11]

By this time, Peking had decided to include the Manchurian loan in the currency scheme and expressed the desire to negotiate only with the United States. Calhoun understood China's tactics. By employing American capital, Peking hoped to ward off the Anglo-French-German bankers. Yet Calhoun wanted to maintain the United States in the favorable position of friendship with both China and the tripartite bankers. He approved of American cooperation with the English, the French, and the Germans but hoped that China's dependence upon American aid would result in the creation of a strong American vested interest as a "positive factor in the financial situation." Calhoun had not been in China very long, but he had become an old China hand.

The American Group agreed to discuss the matter with China provided that the Manchurian Viceroy suspended all independent loan negotiations.[12] In order to prevent a news leak that would spoil New York's advantage, time now became precious. Responding to the bankers' request for assistance in concluding an agreement with China, Washington added its influence and on October 27, 1910, an agreement for a fifty million dollar Currency Reform and Industrial Development Loan for Manchuria was signed. China permitted the American Group to share the loan with its European associates but specified that only the American Group had the right of signature and the issuance of bonds.[13]

Once again Manchurian considerations affected American relations with China. Perhaps the outlines were not as distinct as in the Hukuang and Chinchow-Aigun loans, but they stood out despite the obscurity afforded by the greater scope of the Currency Reform Loan.

The bitterness of the dim days of early 1910 faded in the warm light of cordiality. "I personally desire to congratulate you," Davison wrote Knox, for "if our hopes are realized, the results of your labors will be most important, beneficial, and far-reaching to our commercial interests." The American Group, Schiff added, was only a willing instrument for the furtherance of the State Department's policy. The "question of pecuniary gain" was "only a second consideration with the bankers," who principally sought to enhance American prestige in the Far East.

There was good reason for the American Group's haste in concluding the agreement with China. Its banking rivals were making life uncomfortable with their skepticism of the Group's ability to handle Chinese loans, and they accused the United States of seeking economic and political benefits in the Far East without assuming any financial responsibilities. The charges were not completely unfounded. Recognizing the strength of the tripartite bankers, Straight hoped to maintain independence of action for the American Group in order to weaken its European opponents and play "German against English, and even strain the Entente Cordiale." [14]

Nevertheless, financial cooperation among the powers was necessary, and in early November, 1910, the four banking groups met in London to confer on future financial operations in China. Although the American Group viewed internationalization of bond issues on the basis of equality as all-important for any loan success, it did not wish to include the Chinchow-Aigun project and the Currency Reform Loan in any future arrangement. New York did not intend to deprive the tripartite interests of participation in the Currency Reform Loan but had to bear in mind China's injunction that only the American bankers take the lead and sign the agreements. It was "unwise not to maintain in China at least the idea of independent negotiations," the American Group declared; otherwise, Peking would turn to bankers not associated with the four groups in order to avoid encirclement in a bankers' ring.[15]

The London conference was not a meeting of "mutual admiration societies," but on November 10, 1910, the bankers formed the first International Banking Consortium for China. The new organization was not concerned with the Hukuang Loan, which had been covered by an agreement previously, in May, 1910, or with the Chinchow-Aigun line which was exempted as an item of Consortium business. Only the Currency Reform Loan came under the control of the Consortium, with the American Group pledged to secure China's consent for the participation of the British, French, and German interests.

The decision was the best that the American Group could gain, but despite Ambassador Reid's assertion that New York had been given a "free hand" in the Chinchow-Aigun Railroad and the Currency Reform Loan, Straight was far from overjoyed. He understood the difficulty of playing an independent role in Chinese finance in order to pacify Peking while the American Group worked together with the European bankers. "I suppose we can never expect absolute sincerity from our new partners," [16] he wrote. But any expression of doubt regarding the integrity of the American Group's associates was beside the point. The United States had joined the bankers' ring in China. This step negated the possibility of securing an independent position for American interests in China and undermined Peking's purpose in dealing with the American Group.

And it was the State Department that bore the brunt of China's anger. Influenced by the tie to its bankers, Washington notified the powers of China's intention to fulfill its treaty obligations for currency reform. It also had secured Peking's acquiescence for quadruple sharing of the loan. The powers, however, wanted joint control of the loan funds, a demand certain to arouse China's opposition and endanger American control of the whole reform.

Peking, moreover, was beset by other troubles which gave it no choice but to protest. In May, 1910, the quadruple banks finally had managed to agree on sharing the Hukuang Loan equally. The news raised a storm of opposition among the gentry of the affected provinces who objected to the imperial government's supervision of the projected lines and Peking's intention to use foreign funds for the construction of the whole system. Two months before the foreign bankers had consolidated forces for the Hukuang Loan, trouble had already occurred. The Manchu dynasty was in "serious straits," Fletcher reported. A "very general spirit of hostility to the investment of foreign capital" that existed bore "the potentiality of an anti-foreign crusade." Rioting broke out in Changsha, while the Hukuang provinces became the scene of vociferous agitation against Peking's cooperation with the Consortium.[17]

The harassed imperial regime was further vexed by bank failures in Shanghai and, in order to bolster its sagging credit structure, had to borrow foreign funds to prevent bankruptcy. Washington heard talk of revolution, and Russo-Japanese consultations over the fate of Manchuria and Mongolia deepened the crisis. The Manchu government was forced to convene a parliament that raised a cry for internal reform. The agencies of the imperial government, particularly those in charge of financial affairs, became frightened, and the Ministry of Finance was reluctant to accept loan terms and conditions which the opponents of the government considered onerous.[18]

Shaken by a threat from without and unrest from within, the international bankers' London agreement sent China's officials to the American Legation to express their fears of the effect that the Consortium would have on the country. Calhoun attempted to pacify the Peking bureaucrats by patiently explaining the intricacies of high finance. He outlined the function of the international stock exchanges and justified the American acceptance of British, French, and German participation in the Currency Reform Loan in terms of the need for European bond markets and outlets. The lectures did little good. The Minister had to admit that the Chinese were "hard to deal with" and felt their hopes for American support were "destroyed." [19]

Discussions held in Washington with Liang Tun Yen, China's envoy, confirmed Calhoun's report. In their talks with Liang, Knox and Taft (who freely asserted that "China took all the time of the Department") insisted on having an American advisor as overseer of the Currency Reform Loan. Fletcher had suggested it as early as April, 1910, and the State Department repeated the demand throughout the summer. Now that he confronted Liang, Knox took up the same issue.[20]

Anxious to discuss political matters, the emissary promised to wire Peking for information and turned to the business at hand. Did Washington wish to lead a movement to have all disputes between China and the powers referred to The Hague in order to permit Peking to carry out internal reform unimpeded? No, it was impractical, Knox replied, and he raised the advisor question and the Currency Loan again. It was a discouraging pattern that was repeated in three conferences with Knox and one with President Taft. Both knew that Liang wanted to resurrect the Sino-American-German alliance scheme that was partially responsible for Tang's 1908 mission, but the United States refused to make a political commitment to China.[21]

Washington's obsession with the advisor demand aroused Straight's ire against the State Department. After attending the Consortium meeting in London, he had agreed on the need for an American advisor, fearing interference in the loan from the other members of the Consortium. At the time, the suggestion fell in with the State Department's wishes but a difference of opinion soon developed when Straight returned to Peking and saw the situation at firsthand. The American Group's representative distrusted the whole reform movement and minimized the importance of China's recently created parliament, feeling that representative government had no place in the Far East. Still, he feared the reforms more for their effect on the loan negotiations than for their intrinsic importance to the Chinese body politic. "These Voxes Populi when they get together will above all things wish to mix in finance," he notified the American Group, "and that is the quarter from which we must expect much trouble." [22]

Washington's claim for an American advisor was certain to prompt the American Group's partners to make a similar demand. By their insistence the powers would then add strength to the antiforeign and antigovernment uproar in China. To avoid this ominous trend of events, Straight now advocated that the appointment of the advisor be made part of the actual loan agreement. In this manner, he hoped to prevent encroachment on this important post by the other banks and head off a clash of rivals. Straight managed to persuade Calhoun to postpone sending a request for an American advisor to the Chinese Foreign Office. Washington, angry at Straight's interference, ordered Calhoun to carry out instructions.

Upon receiving orders to restrain himself, Straight blew up at the State Department. He inveighed against the State Department's bureaucrats for their incompetent handling of the situation, feeling that they had no "clear idea of what should be done, could be done, or what they themselves wanted." Their rigid policy stifled Calhoun, was "not intelligent," and though he thought that some of the "premises" were good, "the execution was rotten." He complained of the lack of contact with the American Group and with Washington and of having "to read between the lines." [23]

Straight's rage led to recklessness, and he suggested that Fletcher be appointed Assistant Secretary of State in place of Huntington Wilson, whom he blamed for the Department's diplomatic failures. He also played with the idea of rejoining the State Department as Chief of its Division of Far Eastern Affairs. Although the mood passed quickly, he held to his conviction that Washington was merely repeating its earlier clumsiness in China.[24]

Even as Straight wrote, Washington set in motion an attempt to modify its approach toward the other powers without retreating on the advisor question. It was Russia and Japan, however, not Straight, who influenced the Department. Both powers were concerned with the Manchurian provisions of the Currency Reform Loan and, having decided to act together when their interests were threatened, began to move against the loan.

At Peking, Lewis Einstein, Secretary of the American Legation, pointed out that while Russia was a danger to China, it was Japan who was potentially a greater source of trouble. Manchuria was coveted by Tokyo, Einstein declared. If Tokyo unleashed a successful policy of territorial annexation, it would be the beginning signal for total dismemberment of the Chinese empire by the powers, a greater disaster than the loss of Manchuria. Anxious to avoid conflict with the Russians and Japan and strongly implying that the United States concentrate its effort in China proper rather than Manchuria, Einstein wanted Washington to assure Tokyo and St. Petersburg that their position in Manchuria was not being challenged.

Einstein was merely the Secretary of an American Legation and not the American Secretary of State. He overlooked certain vital aspects of American policy in China which created an attachment to Manchuria. Knox and Straight viewed the Currency Loan not only as a major project that would enhance the grip of American finance on China, but as a means of furthering the stalled Chinchow-Aigun Railroad and Manchurian developmental schemes. Knox maintained a strong interest in the Manchurian portion of the Currency Loan, asserting that it was "the objects of this part of the loan which were the moving consideration which induced this Government to transmit to the American bankers the proposal to include it with the currency loan." [25]

Though viewing cooperation with Great Britain, France, and Germany with considerable distaste, Straight still regarded the London agreement of November, 1910, as a means of directing the power of the Consortium against Russia and Japan. "The hope of pulling the Chin-Ai out of the fire is the principal argument we can use with the Chinese in favor of joint signature of the Currency loan," he informed Davison. "With the Chinchow-Aigun agreement and the rights on the Currency loan in our hands, we are playing for the very stake which Russia and Japan went to war about. It's a very big game and its consequences, if played well or badly, will have the most far-reaching effect on Far Eastern politics and on the American position on the Pacific." [26] As long as Washington and New York eyed Manchuria from behind the rampart of the Currency Loan, they also had to confront Russia and Japan. And both St. Petersburg and Tokyo watched American activities with great interest.

News of the preliminary signature of the loan prompted Japanese inquiries and requests for participation. The American Group had no great objection, though it was cognizant of China's reluctance. Yet Washington took up the responsibility of learning just how much of a share Tokyo desired. "It will require the nicest discretion," Knox wired Schuyler, now stationed at the Japanese capital, "to ascertain their wishes without possibly encouraging them to ask for more than could be obtained." When the Japanese indicated their acceptance of an offer to join in the loan, Knox informed Schuyler that he was prepared to urge China to admit Japan but "without right to joint signature" and on "an equal footing with Russia and others not parties to the London Agreement." [27]

Knox's desire to place Japan on an equal status with Russia exposed his intention merely to grant a token participation to the two powers that controlled Manchuria. Despite the objections of Kuhn, Loeb and Company, the American Group magnanimously offered Russia a 5 per cent slice of the loan, a share similar to the one proposed by Straight for Russian cooperation in the Chinchow-Aigun Railroad negotiations of 1909–1910. Once again, American representatives queried Eduard Noetzlin as to the chances of bringing Russia into the loan. At the same time, the French bankers, responsive to the demands of their nation's pro-Russian foreign policy, asked New York to invite St. Petersburg. The British, as was their habit by this time, supported both Russia and Japan. [28]

Russia, however, retained its sensitivity regarding Manchuria and blamed American policy for shoring up the Chinese. Late in 1910 and early in February, 1911, St. Petersburg accused Peking of not carrying out commercial treaty obligations and threatened a show of force. Japan, Britain, and France, linked by diplomatic agreements to the Russians, stood by their ally. Then, while the Russians menaced the Chinese, they reformed the Russo-Chinese Bank into the Russo-Asiatic Bank with the evident intention of reentering the field of Far Eastern finance. Coupled with the news of Noetzlin's refusal to accept 5 per cent of the Currency Loan, these developments gave point to Straight's observation that this renewal of Russian activity denoted a "new phase in Far Eastern politics." [29]

Worried that Washington's obdurate stand on the advisor question and Russian and Japanese opposition would block the Currency Loan, Straight pressed for a more flexible American attitude on the appointment of an advisor. He suggested that China ask the State Department to recommend an advisor and that Washington accept the request without stipulation of that official's nationality. Having gone this far, the American Group could then settle the final loan terms with China and admit the other bankers, whose participation would be used to repel Russo-Japanese demands for a share. With this danger eliminated, Washington and the other powers would be free to decide on the choice of an advisor.[30]

Wilting under the heat of Russian threats, China was amenable, and Calhoun requested permission to act on Straight's plan. Knox and Huntington Wilson saw the advantage of the crisis caused by St. Petersburg, but they still demanded an American advisor and notified the other powers to that effect. Official stubborness inflamed Straight again, and he leveled a critical barrage at the State Department's policy which was "most ill-conceived" and would "nullify" anything that might have been accomplished.[31]

Straight and the American Group hoped to maintain the initiative in the Currency Loan, but Washington's almost pathetic determination to secure an American advisor prevented conclusion of the loan negotiations. The force of events was inexorable. Russia continued to crowd China, and a rival banking group composed of Russian, English, and Belgian capital entered the loan field. In order to protect the American Group's position, Washington had no choice but to accept Straight's proposal. The American Group ordered Straight to waive the demand for an advisor and ordered him to proceed with the negotiations. "You will appreciate importance and our desire to retain leadership in negotiations," the Group wired Straight.[32]

Spurred on by a variety of motives, the negotiations dragged on to a conclusion. The Consortium feared competition from the Anglo-Russian-Belgian syndicate; Straight was hostile to the Japanese, whom he attacked as the force seeking to destroy China; and the European members of the Consortium suspected American intentions. The American Group gave Straight a free hand, and the State Department followed suit, though Straight felt no elation over Washington's acquiescence. Throughout March, 1911, Straight and Calhoun negotiated to have a neutral advisor appointed by the bankers rather than the affected governments in order to avoid political complications. Despite a last minute delay, the agreement was signed on April 15, 1911.

The Chinese Currency Reform and Industrial Development Loan was signed by the members of the four-power Consortium with the dual purpose of reforming China's currency and promoting industrial enterprise in Manchuria. Peking provided the Consortium with a statement of the proposed currency reform, a list of specific Manchurian industrial enterprises, and a breakdown of the apportionment of funds. The Consortium also agreed to furnish advances for the various projects included within the scope of the loan.

Tired but exultant, Straight informed the Group that the agreement was the "first tangible result of the new policy inaugurated by Secretary Knox and Mr. Wilson some two years ago." Certainly, he added meaningfully, it would "justify to the Group the wisdom of its venture in China," particularly as it placed the United States on an equal footing with the British, French, and Germans who had "been entrenched here for the last 30 years." [33] The American Minister, on the other hand, repulsed by the "timidity, cupidity, and stupidity" exhibited during the course of "one of the most tortuous and difficult proceedings" in which he had ever participated, took to his bed, a victim of a near nervous breakdown.[34]

Difficulties cropped up almost immediately. In May, 1911, China asked for an advance which was granted over France's objections. It was Japan's fault, Straight charged, for Tokyo had urged Russia to influence Paris. The causal sequence of the French objection, however, was less important than the fact that the Currency Loan was rendered ineffective by other events. The Chinese Revolution of 1911, the negotiations for the Reorganization Loan, and the successful Russo-Japanese move to enter the Consortium engaged the attention of Washington and New York. Although the Manchurian aspect of China's loans still dogged the American Group's effort in China proper, the Currency Loan proved to be the advance notice of the final test to face the United States in China.

NOTES

1. Straight Diary, September 13 and December 7–14, 1909, Straight Papers; Fletcher to the Secretary of State, December 7, 1909, NA, RG59: 5315/618.
2. Straight to J. P. Morgan and Company, December 17, 1909, and Straight to Huntington Wilson, December 19, 1909, Straight Papers; Straight to J. P. Morgan and Company, December 13, 1909, NA, RG59: 2112/98.
3. Menocal to J. P. Morgan and Company, September 1 and 2, 1910, NA, RG59:893.77/1063, 1082; Menocal to Calhoun, September 2, 1910, NA, RG84: Peking Legation Archives; J. P. Morgan and Company to Menocal, September 2, 1910, NA, RG59:893.77/1063.
4. Calhoun to the Secretary of State, September 3, 1910, NA, RG59:

893.77/1052; Huntington Wilson to Knox, September 7, 1910, and Memorandum of a telephone conversation with E. T. Williams, September 8, 1910, Huntington Wilson Papers; J. P. Morgan and Company to the Secretary of State, September 8, 1910, NA, RG59:893.77/1061; Huntington Wilson to Knox, September 12, 1910, NA, RG59:893.51/146A.

5. Menocal to J. P. Morgan and Company, September 12 and 16, 1910, NA, RG59:893.77/1087, 1070; J. P. Morgan and Company to the Acting Secretary of State, September 15, 1910, and J. P. Morgan and Company to Menocal, September 15, 1910, NA, RG59:893.51/147; J. P. Morgan and Company to Menocal, September 16 and 17, 1910, NA, RG59:893.77/1070; Memorandum by R. S. Miller, September 16, 1910, and Huntington Wilson to the American Legation at Peking, September 18, 1910, NA, RG59:893.51/118.

6. Calhoun to the Secretary of State, September 14 and 29, 1910, NA, RG59:893.51/118, 120.

7. Huntington Wilson to Knox and Straight, September 21, 1910, NA, RG59:893.77/1076, 1075b; J. P. Morgan and Company to the Secretary of State, October 3, 1910, NA, RG59:893.51/136.

8. J. P. Morgan and Company to Morgan, Grenfell and Company, September 30, 1910, and to E. C. Grenfell, October 1, 1910, NA, RG59:893.51/136; Morgan, Grenfell and Company to J. P. Morgan and Company, October 1, 1910, and E. C. Grenfell to J. P. Morgan and Company, October 3, 1910, NA, RG59:893.51/136; J. P. Morgan and Company to E. C. Grenfell, October 3, 1910, NA, RG59:893.77/1082.

9. Straight to Griscom, December 8, 1910, Straight Papers; E. T. Williams to Rockhill, March 11, 1910, Rockhill Papers.

10. Huntington Wilson to Knox, July 27, 1910, Knox Papers; Calhoun to Knox, August 25, 1910, NA, RG59:893.00/437; Huntington Wilson to Knox, September 1, 1910, Huntington Wilson Papers; Calhoun to the Secretary of State, September 22, 1910, NA, RG59:893.51/122.

11. Memorandum by R. S. Miller and Memorandum of the Currency Loan given to the American Group by Huntington Wilson, September 24, 1910, NA, RG59:893.51/126, 267; Huntington Wilson to Knox, September 26, and to Calhoun, September 28, 1910, NA, RG59:893.51/127, 122.

12. Calhoun to the Secretary of State, October 1, 2, 5, and 11, 1910, NA, RG59:893.51/137, 134, 198, 199; J. P. Morgan and Company to Knox, October 5, 1910, NA, RG59:893.51/142.

13. Menocal to J. P. Morgan and Company, October 13, 1910, NA, RG59:893.51/156; J. P. Morgan and Company to Knox, October 14, 1910, NA, RG59:893.51/156; Knox to the American Legation at Peking, October 18, 1910, NA, RG59:893.51/158; Calhoun to the Secretary of State, October 27, 1910, NA, RG59:893.51/168.

14. Davison to Knox, October 28, 1910, and Schiff to Knox, October 30, 1910, NA, RG59:893.51/169, 205; Straight to J. P. Morgan and Company, January 31, 1910, and Straight to Davison, February 16 and March 12, 1910, Straight Papers.

15. J. P. Morgan and Company to Morgan, Grenfell and Company, November 7, and to Grenfell, November 4, 1910, NA, RG59:893.51/206, 182.

16. Straight to McKnight, November 10, 1910, Straight Papers.

17. Fletcher to Knox, March 5, 1910, NA, RG59:1518/369; Hubert

Baugh to the Assistant Secretary of State, April 18 and 22, 1910, and Navy Department to Knox, May 16, 1910, NA, RG59:1518/380, 391, 376; Menocal to J. P. Morgan and Company, June 8, 1910, NA, RG59: 893.77/1004.

18. Admiral John Hubbard, CC Asiatic Fleet, to the Navy Department, July 26, 1910, NA, RG59:893.00/432; Calhoun to Knox, September 7 and October 25, 1910, and Huntington Wilson to the Secretary of the Navy, September 15, 1910, NA, RG59:893.00/442, 449, 432; Straight to Huntington Wilson, December 19, 1910, Straight Papers.

19. Calhoun to Rockhill, November 26, 1910, Rockhill Papers; Calhoun to the Secretary of State, May 24, 1911, NA, RG59:893.51/481; Calhoun to Knox, December 19, 1910, NA, RG59:893.51/292; Menocal to J. P. Morgan and Company, November 9, 1910, NA, RG59:893.51/235; Calhoun to the Secretary of State, November 23, 1910, NA, RG59:893.51/209.

20. Fletcher to Knox, April 19, 1910, NA, RG59:893.51/108; Précis of a conversation between the Assistant Secretary of State and the Chinese Minister, June 14, 1910, NA, RG59:893.51/132; Huntington Wilson to Calhoun, July 22, 1910, NA, RG59:893.51/111A; Calhoun to Knox, August 17, 1910, NA, RG59:1518/429.

21. Knox to Calhoun, December 19, 1910, and Memorandum by E. T. Williams, December 27, 1910, NA, RG59:893.51/246, 280; Memorandum to Knox, December 28, 1910, unsigned, Knox Papers; Amended memorandum by Liang, January 2, 1911, NA, RG59:893.51/288; Knox to Liang, January 18, 1911, NA, RG59:893.51/288.

22. Memorandum by Willard Straight, November 9, 1910, and Knox to the American Legation at Peking, November 11, 1910, NA, RG59:893.51/187; Straight to McKnight, November 16, 1910, Straight Papers; Straight to Davison, November 22, 1910, NA, RG59:893.51/256.

23. Straight to Davison, January 2, 1911, Straight Diary, January 14 and 21, 1911, Straight to E. V. Morgan, January 29, 1911, and Straight to Huntington Wilson, February 12, 1911, Straight Papers.

24. Straight to Davison, February 13, 1911, Straight to McKnight, February 15, 1911, Straight to Fletcher, February 20 and 26, 1911, and Straight to Davison, February 21, 1911, Straight Papers.

25. Einstein to Knox, October 17, 1910, Knox Papers; Knox to the American Legation at Peking, January 13, 1911, NA, RG59:893.51/274; Straight to George Bronson Rea, March 13, 1911, Straight Papers.

26. Straight to Davison, December 6 and 19, 1910, Straight to Fletcher, December 11, 1910, and Straight to Davison, February 13, 1911, Straight Papers.

27. Memorandum, Division of Far Eastern Affairs, December 1, 1910, NA, RG59:893.51/248; Knox to the American Embassy at Tokyo, December 2 and 14, 1910, NA, RG59:893.51/222, 245a; Schuyler to the Secretary of State, December 7 and 12, 1910, NA, RG59:893.51/233, 270.

28. E. C. Grenfell and Paul Warburg to J. P. Morgan and Company, October 4, 1910, NA, RG59:893.77/1086; Straight to J. P. Morgan and Company, November 28, 1910, and J. P. Morgan and Company to Straight and to Morgan, Grenfell and Company, November 29 and 28, 1910, NA, RG59:893.51/221.

29. Straight to J. P. Morgan and Company, February 15, 1911, and to Herman Harjes, May 5, 1911, Straight Papers.

30. Straight to Davison, February 8, 1911, NA, RG59:893.51/298; "Memorandum on Procedure Negotiations Currency Loan," January 15, 1911, Straight Papers.
31. Straight Diary, January 18, 1911, Straight to Davison, February 21, 1911, and Straight Diary, February 24, 1911, Straight Papers.
32. J. P. Morgan and Company to Straight, February 24, 1911, NA, RG59:893.51/310.
33. Straight to J. P. Morgan and Company, April 16, 1911, Straight Papers.
34. Calhoun to Knox, April 27, 1911, NA, RG59:893.51/470.

CHAPTER NINE

Defeat in China

On the surface prospects looked good for the American bankers and their colleagues in the late spring of 1911. The Currency Loan was safely concluded and then, in May, the long drawn out negotiations for the Hukuang Loan successfully came to an end. The task had not been accomplished without some cost. A sour atmosphere surrounded the bankers' conference convened at Paris in May, 1910, to discuss the loan. Bitter at American intervention that had prevented a swift conclusion of the business, the European financiers felt that they were victims of a "big stick."

Neither did affairs in China help matters. Chang Chih-tung, the imperial official who was in charge of the Hukuang project, died just as the provincial gentry of the affected Hukuang provinces were openly displaying their hostility to foreign loans for the railroad. It was a situation that did not escape Washington's notice, and the State Department had the difficult task of persuading Peking to accept terms while it nimbly tried to avoid charges of contributing to the foreign domination of China.[1] Strong diplomacy exerted against Peking "in order to coerce the provinces might bring on a serious revolt," Straight warned.[2] After a series of fits and starts in which the now reconciled members of the International Banking Consortium clashed with each other and with the delaying tactics of the Peking government, the Hukuang

Loan agreement for thirty million dollars finally was signed in May, 1911.

Thus, almost two years after Washington had intervened in the Hukuang Loan, the American Group was able to offer its congratulations to the Secretary of State. Elated by their accomplishment in the Currency Loan, Schiff and Davison had regarded the Hukuang Loan not as a business venture, but as another means of assuring the "United States an equal standing in Chinese financial and commercial affairs." [3] A year later, China was shaken by revolution.

It was ironic that the signature of the Hukuang Loan helped precipitate the outbreak. Rebellion flared up in Szechuen in September, 1911, while China's gentry, its press, various Chinese provincial assemblies, and the Chinese Senate all attacked Peking for its loan policy and attempts at railway centralization. The next month, the "ill-conceived, intolerant, fanatical ferment" redirected the loan effort in China and weakened the entire structure of reluctant partners in the first Chinese Consortium. [4]

Confronted with a revolution that threatened to topple the régime from power, the Manchus requested a loan from the Consortium in order to finance its military operations against the rebels. The corruption and inefficiency of the imperial régime were conveniently ignored in the emergency as the new American chargé d'affaires in Peking, E. T. Williams, and Straight urged the necessity of a loan to preserve the government.

Both men were loath to drop the Currency and the Hukuang Loans, particularly after the expenditure of so much effort and the disappointment experienced in Manchuria. Straight riveted his attention on the financial issue, permitting nothing to divert him from retaining the gains already made. Bitter at the realization that the Chinese reformers needed a "sop" to throw to the "howling parliamentary horde," he kept clear of association with those Chinese officials who had taken the lead in advocating the centralization of China's railroads after the gentry had failed to raise funds to build the Hukuang lines. His distaste for what he had to do, however, was mitigated considerably by assurances that the frightened Manchus would recall Yuan Shih Kai to head the imperial government in order to put down the opposition. The fact that Yuan was Tang Shao-yi's political sponsor and protector encouraged Straight to envision close Sino-American ties because of Tang's pro-American attitude. With Yuan in control of the government, moreover, China was bound to undertake a reform that would place the empire's credit on a sound basis and permit the flotation of more loans.[5]

Straight's reasoning had no effect upon Washington. Despite Williams' contention that the United States had a "moral responsibility" to see the Manchus through the crisis, the State Department felt that the decision to lend funds was a business matter which it left up to the bankers. Of course, if the American Group did offer money to China, then it would have to do so in conjunction with the Consortium bankers in order to maintain international cooperation in Chinese finance. After glancing uneasily at the lagging State Department, the American Group took heed. Lacking overt support from Washington and wary of the unstable political situation in Peking, it refused to lend any funds to its friends in Peking "for business reasons which would surely be appreciated by the Chinese themselves." [6]

The Chinese, however, were in no position to "appreciate" the American Group's point of view. Desperate for funds, they spoke to Straight about a large loan for government reform, and when the Consortium refused to lend money for military purposes, the Chinese, in true business style, went elsewhere. On October 27, 1911, an Anglo-Belgian-French syndicate, headed by Baron Cottu, floated a loan of one and a half million francs, and the Consortium raised a cry of protest.

The American Group was particularly aggrieved, for the Cottu loan's high rate of interest would have a harmful effect on the projected Currency Loan issue and the remainder of the Hukuang Loan. New York complained to Washington and called a meeting of the Consortium in order to meet Cottu's competitive thrust and prevent the flotation of the rival loan.

Unlike their American associates, the English bankers refused to be stampeded. The revolution did not surprise them, for they believed that a weak and corrupt government was at its weakest point when it attempted to reform. As for Yuan Shih Kai, the English felt that he was not to be trusted because of his record of opportunism. Eventually he might be the one man to whom the bankers could look in an emergency, but the times were not yet propitious. Still, business caution indicated the need for care in lending money to China. The Consortium resisted China's appeal for funds; it refused to advance money on the Currency Loan, or remit Hukuang Loan funds until the internal situation had stabilized under the aegis of a responsible government at Peking. Thus, guided by British reserve, the Consortium extricated itself from a damaging position when the French government refused to support the Cottu loan.[7]

The crisis in China persisted. During November, 1911, while the bankers were running for cover, Straight and the other Consortium representatives explored ways and means of bolstering the imperial government. Disgusted with Peking's inability to control the revolutionists, dismayed at the effect that the upheaval had on the loan picture, and hostile to some of the rebels, Straight wanted to bring all possible support to Yuan Shih Kai. With the premier's approval, he suggested that the Consortium lend money to finance a constitutional monarchy in China headed by Yuan. Straight requested that Washington use its influence with the other powers in persuading the Manchus to fall in with the plan, but nothing came of the proposal.[8]

Undaunted by this disappointment, Straight worked closely with Minister Calhoun in attempting to persuade both Washington and New York of the importance of a loan to China. He continued to focus his attention on Yuan, particularly after the unrelenting determination of the rebels to unseat the Manchus forced the abdication of the Prince Regent. Yuan agreed to meet the rebels in Shanghai for discussions regarding the future government of China, while at the same time he negotiated with the Hongkong and Shanghai Bank for an advance on a future loan. Hoping that money would strengthen Yuan's hand at the Shanghai meetings, the Consortium representatives approved of the lead taken by the English. The Washington and the American Group held back support, the British effort failed, and Straight was left to reflect sadly that the powers would not save the imperial government in China.

Yuan managed to survive in spite of his lack of financial support, and after the Manchu abdication in February, 1912, he agreed to form a republic. The new régime, however, had inherited old problems. It turned to the Consortium, which now furnished advances to meet the government's immediate financial needs in return for China's promise to borrow three hundred million dollars to be used for the reorganization of its government.

This loan project had been broached earlier by Tang Shao-yi, who had fulfilled Straight's expectations by emerging as Yuan's right hand man and premier of the new government. Tang's proposal fell in the midst of uncertain and confused events. There were rumors of Chinese dealings with bankers who were not members of the Consortium; fresh outbreaks of violence by Yuan's unpaid troops required quick action

by the Consortium governments in approving advances; and
the bankers wrangled with China over their demand for an
exclusive option on further loan advances and on the Reorganization Loan.[9]

Driven by the threatening attitude of the troops and impatient at the delay caused by the haggling of the Consortium, Tang signed a loan agreement with an Anglo-
Russian-Belgian syndicate for five million dollars. Once
again China had wandered off the reservation, and again
the Consortium bankers expressed their surprise and outrage.
Had they consulted Straight, however, they might have
spared themselves needless aggravation. For the American
Group's representative knew of Tang's accusation that the
Consortium sought to monopolize China's finances. Obviously, the recently appointed premier had dealt with the
rival syndicate in order to gain better terms from the Consortium, and, as one American official ironically phrased it,
to maintain the "open door for financiers."

Together with the aid of its supporting governments, the
Consortium insisted that Peking halt the loan. Britain and
France refused to back the Belgian group in the rival syndicate, and the Russians withdrew. In the face of such strong
opposition China had to retreat. The Belgian loan was cancelled on April 27, 1912, and Peking resumed negotiations
with the Consortium. Although the breach between the Consortium and China was now closed, the bankers, particularly
those of the American Group, were confronted with difficulties of a slightly different nature.[10]

Russia and Japan were alarmed over the effect of the
earlier Currency Reform Loan on their position in Manchuria and Mongolia. Intent on protecting their interests,
both nations moved to enter the Consortium or block the
activities of the bankers. For its part, the American Group
exhibited little enthusiasm for admitting the two powers.
Although the State Department took the opposite view, it

drew the line at taking the responsibility for deciding on the measure of participation to be given by the bankers. Thus, the Belgian syndicate, with its strong Russian influence, made a flank attack on the Reorganization Loan by signing with Tang.

Straight had predicted the eventual success of the Russo-Japanese coalition. It became apparent to him that the powers were jealous of the American lead in this project and were also determined to weaken the Currency Loan by demanding removal of the Manchurian provisions from the agreement. The bankers in the American Group were placed in a difficult position. If they consented to remove the disputed sections, they felt they were recognizing Russo-Japanese claims for special privileges in Manchuria. Such a step threatened to destroy the whole American effort in the region. Moreover, insofar as Jacob Schiff was concerned, Kuhn, Loeb and Company refused to cooperate with Russia, a resolution that caused a split within the American Group.[11] As late as November, 1911, Straight was unhappy at the prospect of Russo-Japanese cooperation with the Consortium because of his conviction that it was impossible to work together with "these pirate powers." [12] But the revolutionary upheaval in China, the American Group's firm membership in the Consortium, as well as its expectation of joining in the Reorganization Loan, shook New York's resolution.

And when his superiors wavered, Straight wearily surrendered. He was no longer able to contrive makeshift plans to circumvent damaged hopes and aspirations. He interpreted the international situation with some accuracy now that he was unhampered by his customary driving optimism. It seemed certain to him that Russia and Japan had made good their claims to Manchuria. If both powers were made to feel secure in their areas north of the Great Wall, they would join the Consortium together with Belgium in "a sort of international administration of China proper." The United

States must give up the idea of being "regarded as champions of the 'Open Door,' " he informed Davison, and "admit to a participation in all Chinese business our Russian and Japanese friends."

"It is rather galling to me to admit being well-licked," Straight wrote, "but as far as Manchuria goes I think we'd better take our medicine, and with this general upset as a good excuse, come to some arrangement with Russia and Japan which will enable the four Groups to do business in their respective spheres of influence. . . . The Chinese themselves will not attempt to keep up the struggle for sovereignty in the home of their hated Manchu over-lords, and if they don't want to why should we." [13]

Gone were the arguments that opposed collaboration with Russia and Japan on moral or "ultimate business grounds." In his capacity as the American Group's representative, Straight had to admit that Russo-Japanese entrance to the Consortium would be "both a practical and profitable" course of action.[14]

This admission was a decisive defeat for Straight, one that led him to reverse completely his attitude toward Japan. "Our hats are off to the Bandarlog [Straight's code word for Japan]," he wrote Bland. He now had Japan in better perspective. Tokyo's administration of Korea gained his admiration, and what was good for Korea was equally good for China. "We might all be better off if these little devils had charge of China's destiny, after all," he added. What of his past opposition to Japan? That was water over the dam, for Japan's policy was less militant. No one would "be more pleased" than he if the Consortium could work together with its former rivals, particularly if it meant linking American financial strength with "the political influence of Japan." [15] The times had changed indeed.

Even the State Department experienced a change of heart, but in characteristic fashion, it arrived at its conclusions backwards. In company with Britain, France, and Germany, the United States heeded the objections of Russia and Japan to the Manchurian provisions in the Currency Loan and assented to a modification of the agreement in order to placate the two Manchurian powers. Yet the problem of the open door remained. Agreement with Russo-Japanese claims in Manchuria would be an admission of failure in view of the American effort to uphold the open door policy. Expediency and improvisation, however, provided a solution. Washington would strike out the Manchurian section of the Currency Loan and tie currency reform to the Reorganization Loan. Since everyone accepted the principle of the open door, it could be asserted at a "more non-contentious and proper occasion."

At least in this way, the open door as a doctrine would be salvaged. And the substance of the doctrine—what of Manchuria? Washington now reasoned that the creation of a six-power bankers' group would strengthen China proper through loan assistance. Indirectly this would help China "in working out its own salvation in such outlying districts as Manchuria." There was no other way if the six-power Consortium was to be preserved. This rationalization of defeat permitted the State Department to discard Manchuria as a legitimate open door sphere.[16]

Early in 1912, the four-power Consortium invited the Russians and Japanese to join it and participate in the Reorganization Loan. Vigilant in defense of their interests in Manchuria and Mongolia, St. Petersburg and Tokyo demanded that these areas be omitted from any agreement dealing with future banking activity. The Consortium refused these terms and rejected additional Russian and Japanese demands for the issuance of bonds through their own outlets rather than through the member banks of the Consortium.

Obviously China needed additional funds in order to

maintain a government in power. Unwilling to weaken its diplomatic program in China, Washington urged the American Group to continue the negotiations and make the loan advances. For its part, the State Department was prepared to recognize Russo-Japanese claims in Manchuria and Mongolia, provided that they were based on existing treaty rights.[17]

After considerable maneuvering by Russia and the United States, the six banking groups drew up an agreement in June, 1912. The Russians, who actually opposed the Consortium, insisted on having the right to withdraw from any future loan if they disapproved of its purpose—a convenient loophole to prevent the possible incursion by the powers into Manchuria and Mongolia. Relieved at the prospect of concluding the negotiations and happy to gratify the wishes of their allies, the British and French agreed and were followed by the Germans. The United States was left to make the fateful decision.

The State Department could have followed the advice of the American Minister in Peking. He was convinced that there was little hope for successful international cooperation in China, particularly with the admission of Russia and Japan to the Consortium. Calhoun expressed the desire that the United States withdraw from the Consortium rather than risk "spoliation" of China. Yet, the Minister missed the point, according to Huntington Wilson. "If you can't get what you want," he commented on the margins of Calhoun's dispatch, "you'll take nothing?" But the line-up of the powers in China merely reflected the international political tension in Europe, Calhoun stated. There was no guarantee that British and French support of Russia and Japan in the Far East would be a sufficient restraint on those two aggressive powers. "Oh, really!" Huntington Wilson exclaimed.[18]

It was clear that Washington had other plans. For one thing, the American Group refused to sign the six-power agreement with the other bankers unless the State Department gave its approval. At the same time, Russia's reservations about Manchuria and Mongolia were designed to force the United States into open opposition, thus forcing the breakup of the conference. There was nothing for the United States to do but go ahead, approve the signature of the agreement and hope that the Russian reservations would be transferred to the interested governments as a political matter. With President Taft's approval, the agreement was signed on June 20, 1912.[19]

Now China had to be brought to terms. The enlarged Consortium wanted control of funds lent to China in order to make certain that they were honestly and effectively used. It also desired a monopoly of China's loan business until the complete Reorganization Loan had been floated. The governments sympathized with the bankers' demands for the control provision but viewed the grant of a financial monopoly in a different light. The problem was to provide the control desired by the bankers and governments while giving the bankers the monopoly that they sought.

A proposal made earlier by Frank McKnight, Straight's replacement in Peking for the American Group, gained New York's support. McKnight developed the idea of a fiscal agency for China under Consortium direction which, by receiving the right to exclusive control of the Chinese loan market, could issue bonds without consulting Peking whenever conditions appeared favorable. Appalled at China's financial inefficiency, Calhoun supported the idea and justified the monopolistic features of the plan on the grounds that it would prevent the waste stemming from reckless competition between foreign bankers. Although Washington agreed with the idea, it did little more than offer its support in principle.[20] Despite continued discussions of the plan, it was dropped principally because of the objections of the Hongkong and Shanghai Bank, the British representative in the Consortium.

Straight attacked the Chinese for resisting the loan terms. A supporter of McKnight's fiscal agency, he argued for strict control of Peking's finances. He had warned that China's unwillingness to accept the bankers' terms might bring on chaos. In view of such a possibility, it would be best "for all concerned" to bring about a foreign dictatorship of China with the Consortium acting under the auspices of the interested powers. Straight preferred a breakup of China rather than have the bankers surrender by so modifying their control demands "as to make them palatable to the Chinese and practically valueless" to the financiers.[21] The extremism of Straight's views was matched by China's determined refusal to accept the Consortium's terms throughout most of the summer of 1912. But when British financial interests protested against London's continued support of the Hongkong and Shanghai Bank in the Consortium, the Chinese were presented with an opportunity.

Late in August, 1912, Peking signed a large loan with an English banking syndicate headed by Charles Birch Crisp, a London stockbroker. Indignant at China's perfidy and the unpleasant prospect of competition, the members of the Consortium refused to negotiate with China unless the Crisp loan was dropped. The six-power governments protested to China, and, when it became apparent to Peking that the Crisp forces were having difficulty in floating the loan, the agreement was cancelled in December, 1912.

Negotiations with the Consortium were begun once more, but additional difficulties complicated the talks. France demanded repayment from Reorganization Loan funds of damages suffered by its nationals during the looting and pillaging that accompanied the outbreak of the Revolution. The Russians insisted upon a varied issue price of the loan bonds, while the powers became involved in an exhausting argument over the choice of auditors and financial supervisors who were to oversee the loan expenditure.

France and Russia, both eager to break the Consortium, advocated naming these officials on the basis of nationality, a proposal that stimulated the jealousy and antagonism of the other powers. When China threatened to break off negotiations, the British and Germans appeared ready to bolt the Consortium in order to float the loan themselves.

The difficulty of cooperation within the Consortium and the endless chaffering with China finally prompted the American Group to take stock of its own position. The Chinese kept asking for the specific date of the loan's flotation if they agreed to terms. Not until there was "a very substantial improvement before April, 1913, in China's credit," replied McKnight, the American Group's representative.[22] It was a significant remark, for in the last few months of 1912 and early in 1913, three factors became operative and affected the Group's attitude toward its participation in Chinese financial affairs.

In November, 1912, the progressive ferment in the United States split the Republican party and brought the Democrats to control in Washington with Woodrow Wilson as President. This turn in events forced the Group to reconsider its position. The Republicans under Taft had given the official invitation to the Group to enter China's loan scramble. Depending heavily on their anti-big business crusade, the Democrats did not appear likely to provide a receptive atmosphere for the continuance of the Group's operations in China. By February, 1913, the Group regarded Wilson's assumption of the Presidency in the coming month "with apprehension." [23]

Secondly, Kuhn, Loeb and Company were strongly opposed to Russia's participation in the Consortium. Schiff's firm had withdrawn from the American Group on June 30, 1912, in protest against the Russian inclusion but had rejoined the next day. In December, the firm withdrew again as a protest against giving China further advances. By February, 1913, Kuhn, Loeb and Company demanded that the American Group leave the Consortium.[24]

The third and most important factor was the continued instability of the general financial situation. Both Calhoun and McKnight reported on the critical nature of the situation in China late in October, 1912. Two months later, the American Group's European agents sent word that the international market could not handle a large amount of Chinese bonds. New York agreed with this dour estimate of market conditions, although it remained in the negotiations with China in spite of its intention not to float the loan until conditions improved.[25] More evidence of financial trouble appeared in February, 1913. The deterioration of American relations with Mexico "badly chilled" the investment market, and the underwriters syndicate formed to take Chinese loan bonds refused to be committed beyond the middle of the month. If the situation continued to worsen, the American Group warned, it would be forced to withdraw.[26]

Uncertain of financial conditions, doubting that the new administration would lend its support, and discouraged by the intricate political maneuvering in Peking, the Group sought either to conclude the loan by the first of March, 1913, or give it up entirely.[27]

The bankers' decision was merely another blow to Knox's China policy, for on the political level he was engaged in a losing battle for the recognition of China. From the time of the Manchu abdication in February, 1912, and Yuan's election as President, the Secretary of State had advocated a policy of international cooperation for recognition of the new republic. But American public opinion, distrusting the powers and overstimulated by China's turn in the direction of a republican form of government, made the State Department uneasy.

On February 29, the House of Representatives passed a resolution applauding China's adoption of a republican form of government and pressed the White House for early recognition. Washington quickly explained the resolution to Calhoun in Peking. It was not a recognition act by the United States, Huntington Wilson stated, and after suggesting that it might be of some use in solidifying Sino-American relations, he repeated that the United States was pledged to recognize the new republic only "in harmony with the other powers." [28] But it was difficult to maintain this course of action.

The Consortium's clashes with Russia and Japan on the one hand and with China on the other placed the United States in the position of following the policies of the other powers whose activities in China had long been criticized in the United States. In April, 1912, the House resolution was passed as a Congressional concurrent resolution, calling on the administration to recognize China. Since the powers refused to move ahead, the State Department found itself lagging behind the pressure of Congress and public opinion. Although Knox's attempts to prod the powers into recognition were unavailing, he was proud of his policy. When Calhoun, in January of 1913, urged on Knox a similar recognition procedure because the Consortium had failed in putting through the Reorganization Loan, the Secretary of State testily replied that the Consortium was not breaking up.

The Secretary argued that Congress had no power to recognize another country; that the new government of China was not as stable as American public opinion imagined; and that recognition depended on whether immediate individual action by the United States was better for the national interest than the cooperative policy that had been followed to date. Harassed by Congress, Knox was now confronted with the American Group's determination to drop out of the Reorganization Loan.

Knox warned Peking of the American bankers' restlessness and thanked them for the "patriotic motives" that had induced them to join the Consortium and experience the disappointments stemming from the political matters in which they were not involved.[29] Facing the dreary prospect of capping his diplomatic failures in China with the Group's abrupt departure, the Secretary called Davison long distance. Davison assured the harried Secretary of State that no change would be made to embarrass the Taft administration. But the negotiations were difficult, and the "time must come" when they had to be concluded "one way or another." [30]

Having laid down a smoke screen to cover his retreat, with Davison's aid, the Secretary informed chargé Williams in Peking that a poor financial market and the political issues connected with the Reorganization Loan had hardened the American Group's intentions to withdraw. Sympathizing as he did with the Group's feeling, yet reluctant to coerce the Chinese into accepting a loan on repugnant terms,[31] Knox met the dilemma by doing nothing. Once the decision was made, he sat back and watched the clock.

Woodrow Wilson was inaugurated as President on March 4, 1913, and he appointed William Jennings Bryan, his chief rival for the Democratic nomination of 1912, Secretary of State. The President's ideas did not deviate much from the main stream of popular dogma prevalent in the early years of twentieth century America. He was an expansionist, though after the fact, a believer in the superiority of Western culture, a good Christian moralist who recommended altruism to aid the weak and self-help to discipline the strong. He advocated the view that culture followed trade and that morality was linked to the market. All this he believed when he assumed office after a campaign in which his party castigated big business and documented, through the Democrat-controlled Pujo Committee, the existence of a money trust with a strong influence on American business. Among those firms investigated by the Pujo Committee in 1912 were J. P. Morgan and Company, Kuhn, Loeb and Company, the First National Bank, and the National City Bank—the members of the American Group.[32]

And Bryan? The new Secretary of State knew little about foreign affairs, but he had opposed the expansionists of 1898. Like his chief, he was a good Christian, interested in spreading the gospel in China, which long had been a field of endeavor for American mission activity. This combination of religious idealism in the two men caused tremors of apprehension in Taft's confidant in China, Thomas F. Millard. "It makes me shiver to think of some missionary like Bryan as Secretary of State," he wrote. "Well, it's up to Wilson, and if he isn't careful his administration will be another Taft affair." [33]

Wilson, however, was no Taft in his attitude toward Wall Street, as the bankers soon learned. On March 10, 1913, Davison, Paul Warburg, and Straight marched on Washington. They found Bryan "courteous and open-minded," but they were blunt with the Secretary. "The administration was asked almost brutally to declare its position," Straight reported, for the Group insisted that Washington request it to continue its loan operations. As Bryan understood the conditions, New York wanted assurance that no other American financiers would be admitted to the loan and that the American Group would control future loans. Furthermore, Chinese government revenues were to serve as loan security, and the American government had to be ready to use force, in conjunction with the other five powers, to compel China to live up to the contract.[34] Attorney General McReynolds, who attended the conference with Bryan, summed up the Group's position with the lawyer's care: "As I understand the situation, unless the Administration requests you to continue in these negotiations you will withdraw. If we do

DEFEAT IN CHINA 209

request you to continue, you will consider the matter." Well, not exactly, Davison replied. It was difficult to make an advance commitment for unsound business. The Group would try to help the present administration, as it had aided Taft, and would assist a future administration. "I rather gather we will not be requested to go on," Straight predicted, four days after the meeting.[35]

Bryan introduced the matter at a cabinet meeting on March 14, and President Wilson discussed a policy statement regarding Chinese loans with the cabinet on March 18.[36] "There appears to be no likelihood," wrote one observer, referring to the American Group's approach to the administration, "that this rather peremptory assumption of a philanthropic attitude in their chafferings will be humored by the administration." [37] On the same day, without consulting the State Department, Wilson released a policy statement on American participation in the Reorganization Loan.

The President divided his declaration into two sections. He refused to request the American Group to continue its efforts in the Reorganization Loan on the ground that "forcible interference" in the financial and political affairs of China might be necessary, an eventuality for which he wished to bear no responsibility. Moreover, because the loan conditions included the pledging of "antiquated and burdensome" taxes, as well as the supervision of the taxes by foreign agents, it affected China's "administrative independence" and was "obnoxious" to the principles that underlay American government.

On the surface Wilson's statement appeared to be a repudiation of Taft's policy, but the President indirectly repaid the bankers in the same coin for the manner in which they boldly approached his Secretary of State. By linking them with a move to prevent the newly risen Chinese government from realizing its power and "its obligations to its people," he attributed dark motives of antidemocratic activity in China to Wall Street. Since the United States sympathized with China's emergence as a free government, Wilson continued, Americans wanted to "participate and participate very generously" in opening China's resources. Trade relations between both countries, therefore, were most important, and the President pledged his administration to urge legislation giving American commercial, manufacturing, and technical interests the "banking and other financial facilities" that they lacked in order to compete successfully with their rivals. It was the government's duty to do that much "in the development of China." And the open door? That was "a door of friendship and mutual advantage." [38]

It was a brilliant declaration, one that received approbation from anti-imperialists and anti-Republicans. It also gave Huntington Wilson a chance to make a martyr of himself. Having turned in the customary resignation, when the administration changed hands, he stayed on to run the Department while Bryan's attention was diverted by political patronage matters. Huntington Wilson argued for continuance of support of the American Group, but the President's statement and the manner of its release forced him to offer his resignation again. The President, he charged in the press, had ignored the State Department's officials in announcing his change in policy; the policy ignored facts, preferred theories, and obscured the motives and purposes of the previous policy; and it was formulated too hastily and in too unusual a manner.[39]

Wilson met the blast calmly. Warnings were already on the way to the White House urging Huntington Wilson's removal, but the President accepted the Assistant Secretary's resignation and informed Bryan "that things will go on perfectly well without him." There was a touch of melodrama about the affair, but "for better or worse, the moving spirit of the old order" had departed from the scene.[40]

One more step was necessary. Once Wilson's administration took power, demands for the American recognition of China mounted. Wilson was eager to recognize the republic, but no adequate government body was available in Peking to be recognized! Finally, after several false starts, the United States recognized the Chinese Republic on May 2, 1913,[41] almost four years from the first days of American excitement over the Hukuang Loan. With the notice given by the American Group of its withdrawal from the Reorganization Loan and the four-power Consortium of 1910 and the six-power agreement of 1912,[42] the United States, for a short time at least, ended its effort in China.

NOTES

1. Knox to Fletcher, January 19, 1910, NA, RG84: Peking Legation Archives; Memorandum by R. S. Miller, February 1, 1910, NA, RG59: 893.77/963.
2. Straight to J. P. Morgan and Company, April 22, 1910, NA, RG59: 893.77/924.
3. Davison to Knox, May 25, 1910, and Schiff to Knox, May 24, 1910, NA, RG59:893.77/939, 942.
4. Williams to Knox, October 19, 1911, NA, RG59:893.51/610; Straight to Davison, October 28, 1911, Straight Papers.
5. Straight to Davison, October 28, 1911, Straight Papers; Straight to J. P. Morgan and Company, October 21 and November 9, 1911, NA, RG59:893.51/620, 631.
6. Miller to Knox, October 17, 1911, Knox Papers; Memorandum by Miller, October 21, 1911, NA, RG59:893.51/621; J. P. Morgan and Company to Morgan, Grenfell and Company, and to Straight, October 21 and 25, 1911, NA, RG59:893.51/622, 620, 631.
7. S. Simon to Charles Addis, December 5, 1911, NA, RG59: 893.51/698; Morgan, Grenfell and Company to J. P. Morgan and Company, January 3, 1912, NA, RG59:893.51/731.
8. Straight to J. P. Morgan and Company, November 2, 1911, NA, RG59:893.51/645; Straight to J. P. Morgan and Company, November 12, 1911, McKnight to Straight, January 16, 1912, and Straight Diary, November 1–29 and December 4, 1911, Straight Papers.
9. Calhoun to Knox, February 23, 1912, NA, RG59:893.51/771; Straight Diary, March 4, 6, and 7, 1912, Straight Papers.
10. Straight to Calhoun, March 15, 1912, and J. P. Morgan and Company to Knox, March 16, 1912, NA, RG59:893.51/843, 804; Straight Diary, March 7–18, 1912, Straight Papers; Admiral Murdock to the Secretary of the Navy, March 25 and 28, 1912, NA, RG59:893.00/1284, 1216; Wilbur T. Gracey to the American Legation at Peking and Knox, March

26 and 27, 1912, NA, RG59:893.51/856; Calhoun to Knox, April 27 and 29, 1912, NA, RG59:893.51/859, 860.

11. Davison to J. P. Morgan and Company, September 22, 1911, and Minutes of the Berlin Conference, October 23, 1911, NA, RG59: 893.51/566, 584.

12. Straight to J. P. Morgan and Company, November 14, 1911, NA, RG59:893.51/685.

13. Straight Diary, December 12, 1911, Straight to Davison, December 18, 1911, and January 16, 1912, Straight to ffrench, January 16, 1912, Straight to Whigham, January 16, 1912, and Straight to J. P. Morgan and Company, January 20, 1912, Straight Papers.

14. Straight to J. P. Morgan and Company, January 28, 1912, Straight Papers.

15. Straight to Bland, February 24, 1912, Straight to Bonar, March 13, 1912, and Straight to McKnight, January 21, 1913, Straight Papers.

16. Memorandum, Status of the Currency Reform Loan, unsigned and n.d., but written after October, 1911, Knox Papers.

17. Knox to J. P. Morgan and Company, May 20, 1912, and Knox to Herrick, June 7, 1912, NA, RG59:893.51/898F, 928.

18. Calhoun to Knox, June 11 and 14, 1912, NA, RG59:893.51/981, 942.

19. Herrick to Knox, June 19, 1912, NA, RG59:893.51/956; Davison and Mortimer L. Schiff to J. P. Morgan and Company, June 20, 1912, and Herrick to Knox, June 21, 1912, NA, RG59:893.51/960, 964; Taft to Herrick, June 20, 1912, and Herrick to Taft, June 23, 1912, Taft Papers.

20. Calhoun to Knox, March 30, 1912, NA, RG59:893.51/825; Huntington Wilson to J. P. Morgan and Company, April 1, 1912, NA, RG59:893.51/822.

21. Straight to Casenave, May 22, 1912, Straight Papers.

22. McKnight to J. P. Morgan and Company, October 4, 1912, NA, RG59:893.51/1125.

23. J. P. Morgan and Company to Morgan, Grenfell and Company, February 7 and 13, 1913, NA, RG59:893.51/1283, 1285.

24. Straight to McKnight, February 24, 1913, Straight Papers.

25. Calhoun to Knox, October 22, 1912, and McKnight to J. P. Morgan and Company, October 24, 1912, NA, RG59:893.51/1156, 1121.

26. J. P. Morgan and Company to Morgan, Grenfell and Company, February 14, 1913, NA, RG59:893.51/1305.

27. Memorandum by Miller, February 20, 1913, NA, RG59:893.51/1342.

28. Huntington Wilson to the American Legation at Peking, March 2, 1912, and to Taft, February 26, 1912, NA, RG59:893.00/1146a, 1105.

29. Knox to Davison, February 20, and to the American Legation at Peking, February 21, 1913, NA, RG59:893.51/1342.

30. Memorandum, Division of Far Eastern Affairs, February 21, 1913, NA, RG59:893.51/1341.

31. Knox to E. T. Williams, February 27, 1913, NA, RG59:893.51/1309.

32. Tien-yi Li, *Woodrow Wilson's China Policy, 1913–1917* (New York, 1952), 11–19; Harley Notter, *The Origins of the Foreign Policy of Woodrow Wilson* (Baltimore, 1937), 216.

33. Millard to Crane, January 21, 1913, Crane Papers; Wilson to Bryan, February 21, 1913, Bryan Papers.

34. Straight to Fletcher, March 18, 1913, Straight Papers; Thomas W. Lamont, *Henry P. Davison: The Record of a Useful Life* (New York, 1933), 198; Straight to Whigham, March 13, 1913, Straight Papers; William Jennings Bryan, *The Memoirs of William Jennings Bryan* (Chicago, 1925), 362.

35. Straight to McKnight, March 14, 1913, Straight Papers.

36. David F. Houston, *Eight Years with Wilson's Cabinet, 1913–1920* (2 vols., New York, 1926), I, 44–49; Li, *Wilson's China Policy*, 33–40.

37. John V. A. MacMurray to Rockhill, March 18, 1913, Rockhill Papers; Straight to Paul Reinsch, June 30, 1914, Straight Papers.

38. *Papers Relating to the Foreign Relations of the United States, 1906–1913* (Washington, 1909–1920), *1912*, 170.

39. Huntington Wilson to Bryan, March 16, and to Wilson, March 19, 1913, Bryan to Huntington Wilson and Bryan to Woodrow Wilson, March 16, 1913, Woodrow Wilson Papers; Francis M. Huntington Wilson, *Memoirs of an Ex-Diplomat* (Boston, 1945), 244.

40. James Brown Scott to Charles R. Crane, March 13, 1913, Crane Papers; Wilson to Bryan, March 20, 1913, Wilson Papers; MacMurray to Rockhill, March 20, 1913, Rockhill Papers.

41. Li, *Wilson's China Policy*, 57–84.

42. J. P. Morgan and Company to Morgan, Grenfell and Company, and to McKnight, March 19, 1913, and Straight to Bryan, March 19, 1913, NA, RG59:893.51/1360.

In Sum

He based his foreign policy on realities, Taft informed the Congress, in December, 1912. His China policy encouraged financial investment in order to give "new life and practical application" to the open door by encouraging Chinese reforms and promoting international cooperation. The United States had matured, and it was time that older diplomatic principles were refitted to new situations. He took a "broad and modern view," the President declared. He had discarded the "outworn dogmas of the past."

And these "outworn dogmas," what were they? Huntington Wilson, out of office and out of Washington by 1916, knew that one of them, John Hay's open door, was "rather illusory." Only a practical policy, the "dollar diplomacy" of the Taft administration, he insisted, could offset the "national foible for grandiloquent sentimentality" that some interpreted to be the meaning of the open door formula. According to Huntington Wilson, the government had gained a foothold in China for its economic interests; in the same manner, these interests secured a stronger political position in the empire for the United States.

Without its verbiage and pretensions of political realism, the China policy of the Taft administration was a shopkeeper diplomacy. Its proponents were aware of swelling inventories at home and mindful of commercial competition in China. They viewed China as a potential customer for American-made goods and demanded that policy be shaped to further this end. It was not a new conception of the function of diplomacy, and it was quite harmonious with the times. If it

214

appeared to be a simple matter for Washington to accept
responsibility for protecting and extending American business in China, it was more difficult to implement it on the
diplomatic level. Indeed, this "practical" policy did not have
so complete a mastery of the situation as it pretended.

The Manchurian issue is a case in point. Harriman's railroad plans and Straight's desire to extend American economic influence in the region helped to direct the attention
of the United States to Manchuria after the Russo-Japanese
War. Although he was the American Consul General in
Mukden, Straight acted as Harriman's political secretary,
pointing out the economic virtues of Manchuria and linking
Harriman's projects with the plans of Manchuria's officials
who sought to check Russia and Japan.

Harriman, however, was impatient. He was, as he said,
a businessman devoted to business and not to politics or
diplomacy. Once he ventured into Manchuria, Harriman set
a fast pace. His railroad projects were the sole end of his
activity, and he soon left the diplomats lagging behind him.
He rejected the first Manchurian offer because business was
bad in 1907. On the other hand, the Root-Takahira agreement, whose political implications disturbed the lower eche-
lons of the State Department, only postponed the economic
projects for Manchuria discussed by Straight, Harriman, and
Tang Shao-yi.

There was a dualism in American policy in the last months
of the Roosevelt administration which was a tactical overlap.
Roosevelt was concerned about the immigration dispute with
Japan and was cautious. The State Department, however,
was converted to the view that Manchuria was important for
commercial reasons and that a strong economic stake there
would justify American political claims on behalf of its interests. Secretary Root unofficially supported Tang's loan
negotiations in the United States. Bacon, complaining that
there were no strong American interests in Manchuria, did

what he could to help Harriman install some in the area. Straight cooperated on one hand with Tang and on the other with the Harriman-Kuhn, Loeb forces. Huntington Wilson hoped to soften the effect of the Root-Takahira agreement on China and was "delighted" with Straight's successful contacts with Manchurian officialdom. Even Phillips, who hedged at first, shifted in the direction of the pro-Manchurian wing in the State Department late in 1908 and early 1909.

Taft's assumption of the Presidency at this juncture proved to be a key development. He and Secretary of State Knox were partial to the business view of diplomacy, an attitude that enhanced the power of the Manchuria clique in the State Department. Temporarily blocked by Tang's recall and the Root-Takahira agreement, the Hukuang Loan controversy afforded an opportunity to reassert American claims for railroad loans in China proper.

Private American interests already had been engaged in China proper, and the occasion for American protest was not fortuitous. The International Banking Corporation and the National City Bank, as well as J. P. Morgan and Company, had been active in one way or the other in the Hukuang lines. Although the House of Morgan had long since left the Hankow-Canton Railroad project, the developments in the spring of 1909 prompted the firm to consider sending a man to China. With the Kuhn, Loeb-Harriman faction already interested in Manchuria and with Straight in a crucial position in Washington, the two private enterprises were forged into an instrument of diplomacy.

It was a mere formality then for Washington to invite the four important banking houses, led by Kuhn, Loeb and Company and J. P. Morgan and Company, to create the American Banking Group. All concerned were in agreement that the American Group was the State Department's means of politically asserting American claims in China. In this way, they believed, diplomacy and finance would work together for the benefit of the American national interest. There is no need to quarrel with the oft-asserted view that it was Washington's initiative that created the American Group; but the events that occurred in Manchuria and China proper before the formation of the Group should revise the superficial observation regarding the primacy of the State Department in the negotiations.

This is not to say that Washington's role was not crucial. On the contrary, it was very important, since the State Department's successful representations to China and the powers in the summer of 1909 permitted American capital to venture into a field from which it might have been excluded. But the stated policy of employing the American Banking Group as an instrument in China for political ends became something else in practice. It became a covering plan for Harriman's activity in Manchuria.

Not much of a talker, Harriman cared more for his own Manchurian projects than for the American Group's supposed activity in the Hukuang lines. He identified the entire American enterprise with his own negotiations for the Chinchow-Aigun Railroad. The marvel is that Straight converted the American Group to take up the Harriman plan after the railroad magnate died. For despite its initial hesitation, the American Group's acceptance of the Chinchow-Aigun line proposal carried the Harriman-initiated schemes forward, increased the American concentration on Manchuria, and brought American diplomatic support along with it.

Now, in 1909–1910, Washington stepped forward with its neutralization proposals that were ostensibly designed to promote international cooperation in Manchuria by removing economic sources of discontent. In diplomatic terms, the United States thought that it had a very good case. England was friendly, and Russia was weak. With the exception of Japan, who among the interested nations would step forward in opposition?

The Russians did. For the American approach to Russia had a "big stick" quality about it which antagonized St. Petersburg and made its alliance with Japan all the more certain. It is true that American overtures were inept, but not solely because Rockhill withheld information from Iswolsky. The answer is more likely to be found in the nature of the American proposals. Made aware of Harriman's past plans, the State Department adopted them, and assumed that the American Group had the rights to the Chinchow-Aigun Railroad. This, according to Washington, was a substantial American economic stake and justified a political pronouncement for Manchuria. It also concealed a bid for American economic supremacy in the region if the powers had accepted the Knox proposal. And largely because the Chinchow-Aigun rights were *not* in American hands, the State Department's overture was an international failure.

Although Washington took the lead in neutralization, its diplomatic initiative was not so strong as the economic motives that were part of it. The powers found it comparatively easy to reject the American political approach in political terms, thus defeating the predominantly economic purposes of the whole plan. One cannot help but sense the urgency that agitated the State Department. Washington seemed fearful that its chosen instrument might forge on ahead and make the government an adjunct of the American Group. Despite its frantic effort to acquire control of Manchurian affairs, Washington's policy met disaster.

With the defeat of neutralization and the consequent stifling of the Chinchow-Aigun Railroad, the American drive in Manchuria and, as it turned out, in China proper, was defeated as early as 1910. Ironically enough, only the Hukuang Loan was issued in its entirety, while the Currency Reform Loan and the Reorganization Loan were frustrated in part because of American political and economic entanglement in Manchuria.

This involvement led not only to close relations between Russia and Japan, but because it met the political needs of Paris and London in Europe, it resulted in the entrance of Russia and Japan into the International Banking Consortium. In spite of protestations to the contrary, American participation in the Consortium that now included Russia and Japan associated the United States with the two powers most feared by Peking.

It was one thing to use political means to further China's march to progress and another to employ a financial instrument which had responsibilities of its own to meet. Once understood, then, the whole Harriman episode and the differences between members of the American Group and between the Group and the State Department become clear. Knox's plea to Davison to postpone withdrawal from the China field until the Taft administration had departed was fitting testimony that a policy praised for its sophistication and realism was, in the final analysis, captured by its own propaganda, unable to discern clearly where to draw the line between private and national interest, and the victim of the financial tool that it had employed with such optimism in 1909.

And the bankers? For them it had been a trial: they made little money, they could not expect to make any in a troubled Chinese future; and when general financial conditions took a turn for the worse, they maneuvered an already hostile President into releasing them of their obligation. Within the terms of their understanding, they had attempted to cooperate with the administration. Although they were a willing diplomatic instrument in a policy they hoped would be successful, they were unwilling to be made a financial sacrifice to an unsuccessful policy.

SELECTED BIBLIOGRAPHY

MANUSCRIPT COLLECTIONS

PRIVATE COLLECTONS
Charles R. Crane Papers
George Marvin Papers
Whitelaw Reid Papers
Willard Straight Papers

LIBRARY OF CONGRESS
Chandler P. Anderson Papers
William Jennings Bryan Papers
George Kennan Papers
Philander C. Knox Papers
Theodore Roosevelt Papers
Elihu Root Papers
William Howard Taft Papers
Woodrow Wilson Papers

HARVARD UNIVERSITY LIBRARY
William W. Rockhill Papers

YALE UNIVERSITY LIBRARY
Colonel Edward M. House Papers

URSINUS COLLEGE LIBRARY
Francis M. Huntington Wilson Papers

RECORDS IN THE NATIONAL ARCHIVES

Record Group 59: General Records of the Department of State
Record Group 84: Records of the Foreign Service Posts of the Department of State
Record Group 38: Records of the Office of the Chief of Naval Operations

GOVERNMENT DOCUMENTS AND PRINTED RECORDS

Dispatches from United States Ministers to Japan, September 5, 1905–February 28, 1906. (Microfilm copy.)

Gooch, G. P., and Temperley, H. W. V. (ed.). *British Documents on the Origins of the World War, 1898–1914*. Vol. 8. London, 1929.

Interstate Commerce Commission Reports. *Decisions of the Interstate Commerce Commission of the United States, November, 1906 to December, 1907.*

MacMurray, John V. A. (comp. and ed.). *Treaties and Agreements with and Concerning China, 1894–1919*. 2 vols. New York, 1921.

Monthly Consular and Trade Reports. Department of Commerce and Labor, Bureau of Manufacturers. Washington.

Papers Relating to the Foreign Relations of the United States, 1906–1913. Washington, 1909–1920.

NEWSPAPERS AND MAGAZINES

Far Eastern Review. scattered references.
Journal of the American Asiatic Association. 1905–1911.
London Times. 1906–1913.
New York Herald. scattered references.
New York Times. scattered references.

AUTOBIOGRAPHIES, BIOGRAPHIES, AND MEMOIRS

Adler, Cyrus. *Jacob H. Schiff, His Life and Letters*. 2 vols. New York, 1928.

Baker, Ray Stannard. *Woodrow Wilson; Life and Letters*. 8 vols. New York, 1927–1939.

Bishop, Joseph B. *Theodore Roosevelt and His Time Shown in His Own Letters*. 2 vols. New York, 1920.

Bryan, William J. *The Memoirs of William Jennings Bryan*. Chicago, 1925.

Burr, Anna R. *The Portrait of a Banker: James Stillman*. New York, 1927.

Butt, Archibald W. *Taft and Roosevelt, The Intimate Letters of Archie Butt*. 2 vols. New York, 1930.

Croly, Herbert. *Willard Straight*. New York, 1924.

Dennett, Tyler. *John Hay*. New York, 1934.

Dennis, Alfred L. P. *Adventures in American Diplomacy, 1896–1906*. New York, 1928.

Griscom, Lloyd C. *Diplomatically Speaking*. Boston, 1940.

Houston, David F. *Eight Years with Wilson's Cabinet, 1913 to 1920*. 2 vols. New York, 1926.

Howe, M. A. De Wolfe. *George von Lengerke Meyer; His Life and Public Services*. New York, 1920.

Huntington Wilson, Francis M. *Memoirs of an Ex-Diplomat.* Boston, 1945.

Iswolsky, Alexander. *Recollections of a Foreign Minister,* trans. by Charles Seeger. New York, 1921.

Jessup, Philip C. *Elihu Root.* 2 vols. New York, 1935.

Jusserand, Jean J. *What Me Befell.* New York, 1934.

Kahn, Otto H. *Edward Henry Harriman.* New York, 1911.

Kennan, George F. *E. H. Harriman.* 2 vols. New York, 1922.

———. *E. H. Harriman's Far Eastern Plans.* New York, 1917.

Korostovetz, Ivan I. *Pre-War Diplomacy.* London, 1920.

Lamont, Thomas W. *Henry P. Davison: The Record of a Useful Life.* New York, 1933.

Lodge, Henry C. (ed.). *Selections from the Correspondence of Theodore Roosevelt and Henry Cabot Lodge, 1884–1918.* 2 vols. New York, 1925.

Longworth, Alice Roosevelt. *Crowded Hours.* New York, 1933.

Morison, Elting E. (ed.). *The Letters of Theodore Roosevelt.* 6 vols. Cambridge, 1951.

Powell, John B. *My Twenty-Five Years in China.* New York, 1945.

Pringle, Henry F. *The Life and Times of William Howard Taft.* 2 vols. New York, 1939.

———. *Theodore Roosevelt.* New York, 1931.

Pyle, Joseph G. *The Life of James J. Hill.* 2 vols. New York, 1917.

Rosen, Baron Roman R. *Forty Years of Diplomacy.* 2 vols. New York, 1939.

Seymour, Charles (ed.). *The Intimate Papers of Colonel House.* 4 vols. Boston, 1926–1928.

Varg, Paul A. *Open Door Diplomat—The Life of W. W. Rockhill.* Urbana, 1952.

Yarmolinsky, Abraham (ed. and trans.). *The Memoirs of Count Witte.* New York, 1921.

SECONDARY WORKS

Aaron, Daniel. *Men of Good Hope.* New York, 1951.

Adler, Cyrus, and Margolith, Aaron M. *American Intercession on Behalf of Jews in the Diplomatic Correspondence of the United States, 1840–1938.* New York, 1943.

Bailey, Thomas A. *Theodore Roosevelt and the Japanese-American Crisis.* Stanford, 1934.

Bau, Mingchien J. *The Foreign Relations of China.* New York, 1921.

———. *The Open Door Doctrine in Relation to China.* New York, 1934.

Bland, J. O. P. *Recent Developments in China.* New York, 1913.

————. *Recent Events and Present Policies in China*. Philadelphia, 1912.

Cameron, Meribeth E. *The Reform Movement in China, 1898–1912*. Stanford, 1931.

Campbell, Charles S., Jr. *Special Business Interests and the Open Door Policy*. New Haven, 1951.

Clark, Grover. *Economic Rivalries in China*. New Haven, 1932.

Clinard, Outten J. *Japan's Influence on American Naval Power, 1897–1917*. Berkeley, 1947.

Clyde, Paul H. *International Rivalries in Manchuria*. Columbus, 1928.

Dennett, Tyler. *Roosevelt and the Russo-Japanese War*. New York, 1925.

Dennis, Alfred L. P. *The Anglo-Japanese Alliance*. Berkeley, 1923.

Feis, Herbert. *Europe: The World's Banker, 1870–1914*. New Haven, 1930.

Field, Frederick V. *American Participation in the China Consortiums*. Chicago, 1931.

————. *Economic Handbook of the Pacific Area*. New York, 1934.

Griswold, A. Whitney. *The Far Eastern Policy of the United States*. New York, 1938.

Harrington, Fred Harvey. *God, Mammon, and the Japanese: Dr. Horace N. Allen and Korean-American Relations, 1884–1905*. Madison, 1944.

Hofstadter, Richard. *Social Darwinism in American Thought (1860–1915)*. Philadelphia, 1945.

Hsu, Mongton Chih. *Railway Problems in China*. New York, 1915.

Kahn, Otto H. *Of Many Things*. New York, 1926.

Kantarovich, Anatole. *Amerika v Borbe za Kitai*. Moscow, Satsegiz, 1935.

Kawakami, Kiyoshi K. *American-Japanese Relations*. New York, 1912.

Kent, Percy H. B. *The Passing of the Manchus*. London, 1912.

————. *Railway Enterprise in China*. London, 1907.

Langer, William L. *The Diplomacy of Imperialism, 1890–1902*. 2 vols. New York, 1935.

Levi, Werner. *Modern China's Foreign Policy*. Minneapolis, 1953.

Lewis, Cleona. *America's Stake in International Investments*. Washington, 1938.

Li, Tien-yi. *Woodrow Wilson's China Policy, 1913–1917*. New York, 1952.

Livezy, William E. *Mahan on Sea Power*. Norman, 1947.

McCormick, Frederick. *The Menace of Japan*. New York, 1917.

Millard, Thomas F. *America and the Far Eastern Question*. New York, 1909.

Millard, Thomas F. *Our Eastern Question*. New York, 1916.
Notter, Harley. *The Origins of the Foreign Policy of Woodrow Wilson*. Baltimore, 1937.
Overlach, Theodore W. *Foreign Financial Control in China*. New York, 1919.
Price, Ernest B. *The Russo-Japanese Treaties of 1907–1916 Concerning Manchuria and Mongolia*. Baltimore, 1933.
Reid, John G. *Manchu Abdication and the Powers, 1908–1912*. Berkeley, 1935.
Reinsch, Paul S. *International and Political Currents in the Far East*. New York, 1911.
Remer, Charles F. *Foreign Investments in China*. New York, 1933.
———. *The Foreign Trade of China*. Shanghai, 1926.
Romanov, Boris A. *Rossia u Manchzurii, 1892–1906*. Leningrad, 1928.
Straight, Willard. "The Present Situation in Manchuria," *China and the Far East*. Clark University Lectures, ed. by George H. Blakeslee. New York, 1910.
Treat, Payson J. *Japan and the United States, 1853–1921*. Boston and New York, 1921.
Tupper, Eleanor, and McReynolds, George R. *Japan in American Public Opinion*. New York, 1937.
Vagts, Alfred. *Deutschland und die Vereinigten Staaten in der Weltpolitik*. 2 vols. New York, 1935.
Viallate, Achille. *Economic Imperialism and International Relations During the Last Fifty Years*. New York, 1923.
Williams, William A. *American Russian Relations, 1781–1947*. New York, 1952.
Willoughby, Westel W. *Foreign Rights and Interests in China*. Baltimore, 1927.
Young, C. Walter. *The International Relations of Manchuria*. Chicago, 1929.
———. *Japan's Special Position in Manchuria*. Baltimore, 1931.
Zabriskie, Edward H. *American-Russian Rivalry in the Far East, 1895–1914*. Philadelphia, 1946.

SPECIAL ARTICLES

Barrett, John. "America's Duty in China." *North American Review*, 171 (August, 1900):146.
Boulger, Demetrious C. "America's Share in the Partition of China." *North American Review*, 171 (August, 1900):173.
Buell, R. L. "The Development of the Anti-Japanese Agitation in the United States." *Political Science Quarterly*, 37 (June, 1922):605–639.
Cameron, Meribeth E. "American Recognition Policy Toward the

Republic of China, 1912–1913." *Pacific Historical Review,* 2 (June, 1933):214–230.

Conant, Charles A. "The Economic Basis of Imperialism." *North American Review,* 167 (September, 1898):326.

Dennett, Tyler. "The Open Door Policy as Intervention." *The Annals,* American Academy of Political and Social Science, 168 (July, 1933):78–83.

Hall, Luella T. "The Abortive German-American-Chinese Entente of 1907–1908." *Journal of Modern History,* 1 (June, 1929); 219–233.

Hill, James J. "The Future of Our Oriental Trade." *World's Work,* 10 (August, 1905):6465.

Huntington Wilson, Francis M. "The American Foreign Service." *Outlook,* 82 (March 3, 1906):499–504.

———. "The Relation of Government to Foreign Investment." *The Annals,* American Academy of Political and Social Science, 68 (November, 1916):298–311.

Iyenaga, T. "Manchuria's Strategic Railroad." *World's Work,* 20 (June, 1910):13019–13028.

Kaneko, Baron Kentaro K. "American Millions for Japan's War." *World's Work,* 10 (May, 1905):6124–6126.

Kemble, John H. "The Transpacific Railroads." *Pacific Historical Review,* 18 (August, 1949):336.

Knox, Philander C. "The Achievements of Dollar Diplomacy." *Saturday Evening Post,* 184 (March 9, 1912):3–4.

———. "International Unity." *International Conciliation,* 28 (March, 1910):3–13.

———. "The Spirit of American Diplomacy." *Speech at the Commencement Exercises of the University of Pennsylvania,* June 15, 1910.

Marvin, George. "Willard Straight." *Japan,* 13 (November–December, 1924):67–89.

Millard, Thomas F. "America in China." *The Forum,* 44 (July, 1910):67–89.

———. "Our Blundering Diplomacy in the Far East." *American Magazine,* 70 (July, 1910):417–425.

Rea, George Bronson. "The Fakumen Railway Question." *Far Eastern Review,* 5 (May, 1909):419.

Schiff, Jacob H. "Japan After the War." *North American Review,* 597 (August, 1906):161–168.

Straight, Willard. "American and Chinese Railroads." *Journal of the American Asiatic Association,* 16 (January, 1917):373–375.

———. "China's Loan Negotiations." *Journal of Race Development,* 3 (April, 1913):369–411.

Straight, Willard. "Foreign Relations and Oversea Trade." *Address at the Southern Commercial Congress,* Muskogee, Oklahoma, April 30, 1915.

————. "Foreign Trade and Foreign Loans." *Address at the National Foreign Trade Convention,* Washington, May 27–28, 1914.

————. "The Foreign Trade Aspect of the Tariff." *Speech at the Fourth National Trade Convention,* Pittsburgh, January 25, 1917.

————. "Governmental Policy and Trade Relations with the Far East." *Proceedings,* Academy of Political Science, 6 (October, 1915):147–153.

————. "The Politics of Chinese Finance." *Address at a Dinner of the East Asiatic Society of Boston,* May 2, 1913.

————. "The Relation of Public Finance to Private Credit." *American Economic Review,* 6 (March, 1916):210–215.

————. "The Tariff in Its Relation to Foreign Trade." *Address at the National Implement and Vehicle Manufacturers Association Convention,* October 20, 1916.

Young, C. Walter. "Economic Factors in Manchurian Diplomacy." *The Annals,* American Academy of Political and Social Science, 152 (November, 1930):293–307.

INDEX

D.. & Due